.

Metaphor: Implications and Applications

Metaphor: Implications and Applications

Edited by

Jeffery Scott Mio
California State Polytechnic University, Pomona

Albert N. Katz
University of Western Ontario

LEA LAWRENCE ERLBAUM ASSOCIATES, PUBLISHERS
1996 Mahwah, New Jersey

Lawrence Erlbaum Associates, Inc., Publishers
10 Industrial Avenue
Mahwah, New Jersey 07430

Cover design by Semadar Megged

Library of Congress Cataloging-in-Publication Data

Metaphor : implications and applications / edited by Jeffery Scott
   Mio, Albert N. Katz
          p.   cm.
      Includes bibliographical references and index.
      ISBN 0–8058–1650–X (alk. paper)
      1. Metaphor.   I. Mio, Jeffery Scott.   II. Katz, Albert N.
   PN228.M4M46   1996
   401'.43—dc20   95–52842
                                                          CIP

Printed in the United States of America
10 9 8 7 6 5 4 3 2 1

To my parents, George and Ruby Mio, who were my emotional support, and to Roger L. Dominowski, who was my intellectual support.

JSM

To my wife, Rhonda Peterson, and my children, Meredith Katz and Jeremy Peterson-Katz, without whom life would be impoverished.

ANK

Contents

Preface

With language, as with much of cognitive psychology, one can contrast an Aristotelian and Platonic approach to the understanding of the world. The Aristotelian approach emphasizes how one represents and presents external reality. The goal of the cognitive system is to perform these functions with efficiency, and accuracy (i.e., match of the internal world with the external world) is the mark of the fully functioning efficient system. The Platonic approach, on the other hand, argues that our understanding of reality is at best a faint reflection of a more enduring truth. In effect, analysis of how we understand the world does not give us an indication of accuracy, but rather gives us insight into how our mind organizes the world. From the perspective of language, the Platonic approach places the workload in the organization of our conceptual world, and not in the processing modules that deal with linguistic input alone.

Until very recently, the study of metaphor and other instances of figurative language was very much localized within the Aristotelian tradition. The guise taken was that of modern concerns with computational questions: Namely, how do people recognize that a given statement is intended as a figurative expression (and not, as is often the case, the literal expression that is being asserted) and, once recognized, how does one actually compute the intended figurative sense? For instance, if one heard the statement, *"Juliet is the sun,"* the modern question of interest was in understanding how one recovered the intended meaning. Assuming that the cognitive system evolved to accurately represent the world, statements of this sort pose a problem, because it is unlikely that the speaker of such a statement intended us to recover the literal sense of the utterance: namely that Juliet is a huge ball of flaming gas. How then can we compute the meaning when the literal sense is not true? Much of the last 20 years of research in figurative language has been devoted to answering this question.

But figurative language is especially interesting. Not only does it pose the Aristotelian challenge just described, but it also suggests a Platonic challenge: Figurative language might be best viewed as a means of understanding conceptual knowledge, rather than as a linguistic problem dealing with recovering or expressing reality. The modern expression of the Platonic tradition can be traced to Lakoff and Johnson (1980) who argued that natural language presumes and expresses conceptual meanings represented in some basic root metaphors. As an example, consider the following statements: *"he swallowed the whole argument," "it took her a long time to digest the new concept," "they regurgitated the professor's pet theory."* These statements, although quite different, can be tied together by a common underlying—or root—metaphor, namely, *"IDEAS ARE FOOD."* Presumably, our ability to comprehend statements involves making contact with the metaphoric and conceptual structuring of the world. And our ability to comprehend or generate new metaphors can be understood by an extension of the root metaphor. In Lakoff and Johnson (1980), language is dominated by metaphor and not, as in the Aristotelian tradition, by literal language.

The chapters in this volume meet at the intersection of the Aristotelian and Platonic traditions. The common theme is that our understanding of how we represent and understand figurative language is best approached from a pragmatic perspective, that is, in understanding how figures of speech are used in a variety of real-life contexts. Why, and when, would a person prefer to use a figurative statement when the same point can be made by use of a literal statement? What is the effect that use of a metaphor has on subsequent cognitive functioning and, alternatively, what is the effect that metaphors might have on how we structure and conceptualize our understanding of the world? How are metaphors and other tropes used in everyday social situations? It is to these social and pragmatic questions that the authors of the chapters presented here have turned.

Across the chapters in this book, one will find many contrasts: The poet and the comic, the good and poor reader, the child and the adult, the ironist and metaphorist, the blind and the sighted, the patient's and the professional's metaphor, the political novice and the political expert, and even the woman and the man. These are not random contrasts, these are the arenas in which we live and act. It is in these arenas that figurative language is expressed and understood. And, from a pragmatic perspective, it is in understanding the use of figurative language in these arenas that, we argue, new insights arise into the nature of metaphoric speech and thought.

THE LAYOUT OF THIS BOOK

The target audience for this book is reflected in the four sections of the book. Part I closely discusses issues at the interface of the Aristotelian and Platonic approaches using data gathered on the adult and child populations most often studied in the cognitive and developmental literatures. These three chapters light the way for future resaerchers interested in how pragmatics play a part in determining metaphor usage and understanding. Again, most of the past metaphor research was basic in nature, not designed to answer questions in pragmatics nor application. Katz examines the effects of context in determining the interpretation given to statements ambiguous with respect to speaker's intentions. Social factors, such as the type of audience and beliefs about the speaker are shown to be important. Moreover, Katz demonstrates that the interpretation given to a statement (as either irony or metaphor) determines how we both organize in memory and subsequently remember the statement. In a related chapter, Kreuz carefully analyzes the cues displayed in a statement that act as heuristics in driving the interpretation of a statement toward an ironic reading. He too shows that there are constraints in the use of irony that reflect deeply held cultural norms and beliefs. Finally, Reyna presents both child and adult data to show that participants store in memory both the verbatim (literal) statement and its gist. Moreover, these two representations are independent of one another. The role played by either representation is driven by pragmatic factors and social knowledge. She argues that figurative language is similar to literal language, but that important differences can nonetheless be seen and she speculates on the ways that the two representations interact.

Part II generally deals with how patients and professionals conceptualize symptoms differently, depending on what metaphors they use to describe their situations. All of these chapters are generally in the Aristotelian tradition, as they are primarily concerned with the process of metaphor understanding and how these metaphors can effect change. However, from a Platonic standpoint, therapeutic change may not occur unless the metaphors used reflected some basic truth about the individual. Therapists use more metaphors than they would otherwise surmise. Many authors in the past have extolled the virtues of metaphors in clinical settings (e.g., Barker, 1985; Edelson, 1983; Rosenblatt, 1994), but relatively few have actually collected data to support these notions. The first two chapters in this section were written by two researchers who have attempted to support the clinical usage of metaphor via empirical evidence. Along with Conway, McMullen reviewed much of her past research in this area. They found that metaphors associated with self-change seemed to have resonance with clients. Moreover, metaphors dealing with the self being intact or whole resulted in positive therapeutic change, whereas those metaphors dealing with fragmentation were not. They conclude that metaphors may serve as self-fulfilling prophecies for both positive and negative change. This has implications for how therapists may effect change by identifying metaphors to more positive ones. Next, Angus reviews some of her past findings, one being that successful therapy has been associated with a relatively limited number of metaphors arising from client–therapist interaction. Unsuccessful therapeutic outcome was associated with clients seemingly floundering for a dominant core set of metaphors that could best describe their conditions. She then applied her findings to a case study, where a client engaged in a collaborative process with her therapist to shift from one dominant metaphorical theme to another. Rose next shifted therapy to a different format—divorce mediation. Here, the therapist is seeing two people already having made a decision that their marriage has failed. The challenge for the therapist is to transform this tense separation into an amicable one. She identifies common metaphoric themes that arise in the divorce mediation process for both positive and negative outcomes. Finally, Banks and Thomspon step out of the psychotherapy domain and into the medical domain. They examine how laypersons view the circulatory system. Their metaphors of this system can lead them to a degree of understanding, but these metaphors can also lead to problems in understanding. This has implications for following treatment regimes or, more negatively, *not* following treatment regimes due to inappropriately simplistic metaphors.

Part III deals with metaphors in the political domain. Again, these chapters are generally within the Aristotelian tradition of examining processing issues with respect to metaphor. However, once again, metaphor effectiveness in politics is dependent on the underlying truth—the Platonic tradition—to which the metaphors resonate. Political scientists who may desire a more empirically based understanding of how metaphors are used in politics may be particularly interested in this section. Politics, being essentially an abstract entity, rely heavily on metaphors to make concepts more tangible. Mio begins this section by reviewing the literature on metaphors in politics in both the political science and psychology arenas. Political scientists tend to use the term "symbol" as the most general of terms. Symbol encompasses objects such as the Lincoln Memorial, themes such as the Pledge of Allegiance, activities such as flag burning, and issues such as gun control, as well as metaphors. Psychologists use "metaphor" as the most general of terms because it is the use of political *language* that is of primary interest. He finishes with a discussion of his empirical work in metaphor sequencing in the context of political debates. Next, Gramm examines economic metaphors vis-á-vis public policy. As he sees it, economics have tended to be dominated by mechanistic metaphors, such as *"physics," "equilibrium,"* and *"elasticity."* He sees advantages in a shift to more organic metaphors, such as *"photosynthesis," "life cycles,"* and *"evolution."* Such metaphors will lead to the integration of humanism back into economic theory. Chantrill and Mio next examine distinctions between metaphor and metonomy. Researchers in the area tend to use metaphor as a metaphor for all figurative language. However, Chantrill and Mio point out that metaphor invites individuals to compare one set of circumstances with another, whereas metonymy invites individuals to be a part of a larger entity. This has implications for gender differences. Women are socialized to be more communal, whereas men are socialized to be more independent. Communality resonates more with metonymy's part-to-whole essence, whereas independence resonates more with metaphor's implicit comparison of one thing with another. The authors present some preliminary data supporting these general gender differences. Finally, Thompson examines the use of metaphors by political elites versus novices (masses). A major orienting difference between elites and the masses is that elites are charged with making and implementing public policy, whereas the masses are primarily spectators of the political process. From a more cynical perspective, a goal of many in the political elite class is to construct metaphors that have policy implications while at the same time placate the masses into passive acquiescence of these policies. Thus, metaphors may be used to further widen the gulf between the political elite and the general public.

The last section of the book examines the use and functions of metaphor in a set of diverse domains and situations. In each case, the goal of using metaphor in a specific domain is to increase and challenge our theoretical understanding of metaphor. And each domain or situation challenges distinctions based on separating literal from nonliteral meaning. Whitney, Budd, and Mio examine the role played by metaphor in aiding the comprehension of expository text, especially as related to individual differences in reading ability. The research is largely within the Aristotelian tradition: The aim of their participants is to recover the intended meaning being presented. Good readers (as indexed by working memory span) recalled expository text equally well if presented with metaphoric or literal summaries of the text; however, poor readers performed as well as the good readers only when provided metaphoric summaries. Because metaphoric summaries are less directly tied to the text, these data pose a challenge, especially if one argues that metaphoric interpretation only follows attmepts at literal interpretation. Moreover, the results suggest that individual differences in how one approaches the relations in text determines the efficiency with which the text is processed. Kennedy provides data that directly challenges the Aristotelian approach to metaphor. He describes a program of study with blind participants that indicated not only that blind participants, who have no experience with the patterned visual world, can recognize raised-line pictures, but can do so, even when the picture is used in a "nonliteral" way! As he points out: "The key lesson from tactile pictures is that the principles of metaphor operate in novel media, because the principles are not the grammar of any particular medium of communication. Rather they are based in cognition, which can be expressed in any medium" (p. 225). Finally, Pollio presents a wide ranging discussion of the properties of humor and of metaphor that is set at the intersection of literal and nonliteral language. His approach is in the Platonic tradition of understanding the conceptual underpinnings of how language is used.   He argues that both humor and metaphor focus on split-reference and alternatives. In a tour de force, Pollio rephrases the distinction of humor and metaphor in terms of cognitive acts that play with conceptual boundaries in different ways. In humor, the boundary is made salient but cannot be crossed or obliterated; in metaphor, the boundaries are not only crossed, but the concepts might even be fused. Metaphor, not humor, is revolutionary and challenging to social reality.

Over the years, we have sponsored many symposia at APA conventions to discuss our work in metaphor. Although most of the authors in this book were a part of these symposia, many other contributors to these symposia do not appear on these pages. We would be remiss if we did not acknowledge them here, for many have contributed to our understanding of this domain. Past contributors are Raymond W. Gibb, Sam Glucksberg, Arthur C. Graesser, Earl R. McCormac, Karen J. O'Donell, David S. Palermo, Michael K. Smith, and Nigel Turner. We thank all of you for your contributions, support, and interest over the years.

Albert N. Katz
Jeffery Scott Mio

REFERENCES

Barker, P. (1985). *Using metaphors in psychotherapy.* New York: Brunner/Mazel.
Edelson, J. T. (1983). Freud's use of metaphor. In A. J. Solnitz, R. S. Eissler, & P. B. Neubaur (Eds.), *The psychoanalytic study of the child* (Vol. 38, pp. 17–59). New Haven, CT: Yale University Press.
Lakoff, G., & Johnson, M. (1980). *Metaphors we live by.* Chicago: University of Chicago Press.
Rosenblatt, P. C. (1994). *Metaphors of family systems theory.* New York: Guilford.

I

Pragmatics of Metaphor

1

On Interpreting Statements as Metaphor or Irony: Contextual Heuristics and Cognitive Consequences

Albert N. Katz
University of Western Ontario

INTRODUCTION

In this chapter I will be discussing sentences such as:

(1) "The Siamese cat is the prince of beasts."
(2) "Albert Katz is the Barry Bonds of his hockey team."

Because a cat is not a prince, and I am not Barry Bonds, these sentences can be considered as proportional or analogical metaphor. To date, the major problem of study for cognitive scientists has been in determining how the meaning of a vehicle concept, "prince" for instance, can be stretched so as to apply to an unconventional topic, in this case the concept "Siamese cat" (see Katz, 1992; Martin, 1992).

I would like to address two additional problems for cognitive scientists. First, how does the recipient of a figurative sentence recognize that it is a metaphor (or irony, hyperbole, or any other trope)? The answer that I propose is that recognition is based on inferring speaker intent, and that this process is mediated by a set of heuristics.

The second problem has to do with the cognitive consequences of deciding that the utterance was intended to be taken as metaphor (or irony, or hyperbole, etc.). By cognitive consequence I emphasize the role of comprehension for the structure of conceptual knowledge about the terms in the sentence and subsequent memory of that sentence. For instance, one prevalent argument is that the act of metaphorizing identifies or creates a similarity relation between two concepts. That is, once we recognize that the sentence is a metaphor we perform operations that will permit us to understand how a

1

prince is similar to a cat (see for instance Glucksberg & Keysar, 1990; Katz, 1992). It has long been recognized in the cognition literature that similarity acts to enhance recall for unrelated items, such as obtains with the topic and vehicle of metaphor, (e.g. Begg, 1978). Consequently one might expect that recognition of the sentence as a metaphor should lead to facilitated memory. However a given sentence often can be understood in different ways. Sentences (1) and (2) for instance could be understood as irony. I argue that the mnemonic consequences of deriving an ironic interpretation should differ from those obtained from deriving metaphoric intent from the exact same sentence.

ON THE RECOGNITION OF METAPHOR AND IRONY

In much of experimental psycholinguistics, our ability to comprehend sentences is studied in a decontextualized manner. That is, the participant is presented a sentence, and asked to make a judgment on it. In essence, the participant is provided none of the contextual background about the conditions under which the sentence is uttered. Studies of this type have been used to give hints about some of the sentential characteristics that may predispose a comprehender to treat a sentence as a metaphor. For instance, Katz, Paivio, Marschark, and Clark (1988) found that people will treat sentences of the form *"An A is a B"* as metaphor when the vehicle (but not the topic) is concrete and easy to image, the sentence is rated as comprehensible and not anomalous, and the topic and vehicle are semantically related. One could argue that participants will attempt a metaphoric reading of a sentence when it does not have an obvious interpretation and also meets the conditions just outlined (see Pollio, this volume).

Analyses based on decontextualized sentences are limited, however, and ignore the ecology in which we encounter and produce figurative language. In everyday life, a speaker will utter figurative language in a conversational or environmental context and will employ such language in order to meet some communication goal. Consider again sentences (1) and (2). The default interpretation may be as a metaphor, and the cognitive consequence is to emphasize the similarity of a "Siamese cat" to salient characteristics of "princes," or of "Katz" to a category exemplified by "Barry Bonds." However, with little effort, one can envision contexts in which the intended meaning and cognitive consequences are quite different, for instance when (2) is uttered after Katz falls down while on a breakaway. In effect, under these conditions, the speaker uttering (2) may be making the sarcastic argument that Katz is like Bonds—NOT. That is, recognition of the ironic intent should have the cognitive consequence of *undercutting* the similarity "Katz" and "Bonds."

So how do we know if sentence (1) or (2) is intended as metaphor or as irony? In the ecology in which metaphor or irony is uttered, the context will provide cues as to the speaker's intent. I discuss this in more detail later. When a given sentence is presented out-of-context, such as (1) or (2), contextual cues are not readily available, yet people have little difficulty in rating such items along a set of dimensions, including degree of metaphoricity and metaphor goodness (see Katz et al., 1988). Kreuz (this volume) argues that the same is true for ironic sentences and outlines some of the characteristics of a sentence that invite ironic interpretation, for instance exaggeration (e.g., "Joe sure is the best friend a person can have").

I assume that the out-of-context sentences presented in experiments are, at least in part, understood by participants as the result of an active process so that they attempt to *construct* contexts in which the sentences would meet Gricean principles of communication, such as being relevant and informative. (In effect the recipient would be asking himself or herself: When does someone use exaggeration like this?).

I would argue further that some utterances are conventionally understood in their figurative sense, rather than their literal sense. This certainly is true of familiar metaphor (*"My car is a lemon"*), proverbs (*"The grass is greener on the other side of the fence"*), and idioms (*"kick the bucket"*). I argue that something akin also is found with ironic usage. Presumably, for a familiar trope, the context in which it would be employed is automatically engaged or easier to construct than would be the case for a less familiar trope. In essence, I would argue that out-of-context sentences are not really contextually free; rather, the context is internal and based on our experiences with linguistic usages and conventions. Thus for familiar items presented out-of-context, one may easily mentally construct a metaphoric or ironic context and ratings of metaphoricity or the like will depend in part on these constructed contexts.

The Role Played by Context

In everyday life, sentences are not presented out of context but rather emerge in an ongoing discourse, and are based on knowledge shared by speaker and listener, writer and reader. In this section I discuss some of the functions played by context in inviting ironic or metaphoric interpretation.

Discourse and Communication Goals. One can argue that the communication goals of metaphor and of irony are quite different from one another and that the context may provide sufficient information about the reasons that a speaker or writer used the linguistic form that he or she did. Winner (1988), for instance, argued that although both irony and metaphor are devices for signaling the presence of new information, they function to serve different goals. With metaphor the aim is to "illuminate" new content, that is, metaphor is employed to convey information about the topic under discussion. With irony the aim is evaluative, that is, it is employed to convey the speaker's beliefs or feelings about the topic.

A simple variant of this position could hold that the communication goals of metaphor and irony are so distinct that sufficient context as to the "informative" or "evaluative" nature of the communication would make the metaphoric or ironic intent of the speaker obvious. That is, the context might set up something akin to a schema (either content or evaluative-based) that serves to limit the interpretation given an ambiguous sentence. I argue that there might be instances that work in the simple manner suggested previously. However, in many instances, the evaluative–informative distinction does not act as a clear discriminator of ironic from metaphoric speech, and context based on this distinction could not be used unambiguously in determining speaker intent.

In Table 1.1, I list what are arguably eight separable communication functions served by metaphors. Some of these functions or goals are discussed explicitly in the works of others and some were culled from the suggestions in the literature. Examination of this list suggests a relation between metaphors and literal language. Generally, the function can be separated into three general categories. Metaphors sometimes act as literal language (Goal 1), sometimes are used to describe phenomena that cannot be explained by literal language (Goal 8) and sometimes are used even though literal language counterparts are available (Goals 2–7). Presumably the role played by context is to enhance or support the various communication goals outlined here.

The last category is of most immediate interest because the use of metaphor here is preferred and not obligatory (in the sense that Goals 1 and 8 are), and presumably metaphor is chosen in these cases to make a special communication point. I argue that if a distinction between evaluative-based and content-based context plays an important role it should do so here precisely because figurative language is not obligatory and the possibility of interpretive ambiguity should be correspondingly high: Context should serve to reduce such ambiguity. However, one might also note that the simple distinction between evaluative and informative goals, outlined by Winner, are muddied in this category. In many cases in this category, when using metaphor the speaker is making a communication point that does not necessarily add to our knowledge of a topic, but rather it serves as a commentary on the speakers' or writers' attitude toward the topic. When people write letters to the editor stating that *"Israeli's were the Nazi's of the 1980s"* or about a well-known Canadian abortionist that *"Henry Morgentaler is a cancer on society,"* they are telling us about their attitudes toward Israel or about Henry Morgentaler. People who use a metaphor that only those listeners with the requisite knowledge in mythology or history could understand are making statements about the education and social class of the hearer, and by extension about their own education or social class. People who compare vomiting in public to pet owners who refuse to clean up the after their charges are making statements that aim to generate affect. In short, a speaker might use metaphor to serve the evaluative communication goals that Winner attributes to irony.

TABLE 1.1
Why Do We Use Metaphors?

Goal 1. Metaphors are a part of our lexicon and act as "words," or reflect the underlying conceptual system (Lakoff & Johnson, 1980). Some examples would be: *"My car is a lemon"* and *"Their marriage was a continual battle."*

Goal 2. Metaphors are a means of expressing concept in an elegant and beautiful way. As such, they are primarily stylistic and ornamental (Aristotle, cited in Ross, 1952). An example might be, taken from the poet Shelley: *"Tranquillity is a woodland river winding through hills in solitude"* (see Katz et al., 1988, p. 208).

Goal 3. Metaphor can be used to increase the memorability of concepts since the participant is forced to elaborate the topic and thus produce a stronger memory trace (see Whitney, Budd, & Mio, this volume).

Goal 4. Metaphor can be used to create a bond between the speaker (author) and hearer (reader). If one assumes the mutual knowledge hypothesis (see Gibbs, 1987) the use of a metaphor presupposes that a target audience will share, and be aware that he or she shares, "privileged" knowledge with the source. For example the metaphor *"Premier Bourassa of Quebec is a Quisling"* may be understandable if one is familiar with the Canadian political scene, and with the allusion to the Norwegian collaboration with the Nazis of Vidkun Quisling.

Goal 5. Metaphors are compact and efficient ways to state the intended message (e.g., the use of the term *"black hole"* in science; see Ortony, 1975).

Goal 6. Metaphors are vivid and as such, reduce ambiguity and increase the likelihood that the intent of the message is understood (see Ortony, 1975).

Goal 7. Metaphors are messages stated in such a way that some essential dissimilarities are obscured; a means of conveying a persuasive falsehood. For example, *"Saddam Hussein is the Hitler of our era"* obscures the differences that exist between modern Iraq and Germany of the 1930s.

Goal 8. The function of a metaphor is to illuminate, clarify or explain a concept in a way that cannot be done with literal language (see Ortony, 1975; Winner, 1988).

Winners' (1988) characterization of irony is not without historical precedence and, in fact, many of the distinctions outlined in Table 1.2 are also made in the scholarly literature on irony. Ironic counterparts to Goals 4 and 7 in Table 1.1, for instance, can be traced back to the Roman rhetorician Quintilian (35–100 A.D.), and its development by the Danish philosopher Kierkegaard (1841/1966), who argued that ironic utterances are designed to exclude some listeners from understanding the intended meaning, "just as kings and rulers speak French so as not to be understood by the commoners" (p. 26). Muecke (1969), Clark and Carlson (1982), Gibbs (1987) and others argued that speakers are generally at liberty to formulate their utterances so that the intended meaning is available to only a subset of listeners, creating a bond with a "privileged" audience and obscuring intentions to the "nonpriviledged" Muecke (1969) argued that this differentiation of audience is necessary in irony. The presence of a privileged audience and an obscured meaning in metaphor, and not just irony, would suggest that these characteristics are not sufficient in themselves in discriminating between ironic and metaphoric speech.

Many of the other functions of metaphor outlined in Table 1.1 can be shown to function similarly for irony and other tropes. For instance, the argument that metaphor serves to increase memorability (function 3 in Table 1.1) is generally supported in the empirical literature (see Marschark & Hunt, 1985; Whitney et al., this volume). However, increased memorability is not unique to metaphor and can be found with other linguistic forms. Keenan, MacWhinney, and Mayhew (1977) found greater memory for naturally occurring conversational statements that involved sarcasm, humor, or personal criticism. Kreuz, Long, and Church (1991) reported facilitated memory for ironic statements and, as I report, some of our research also indicates mnemonic advantages for irony, at least in some conditions. Finally, Table 1.1 lists three other conditions in which literal language could be used but metaphor is preferred: for stylistic reasons (2), for compactness (5), and for vividness (6). The exact same arguments advanced for these as properties of metaphor are also true of irony. Ironic utterances are stylistic, compact, and vivid means of conveying attitude. In short, metaphor need not, but can, convey information about speaker attitude in much the same way that irony does.

Not only can metaphor be used to convey attitude, one can argue that irony can be used to convey content. Once again, the seminal arguments can be traced back to Quintilian: an ironist utters an incongruent statement in order to convey the *opposite* meaning to that presented by the words. Grice (1975; also see Cutler, 1974) developed this theme. He argued that, in understanding an ironist, "the most obviously related proposition is the contradictory of the one that he purports to be putting forward" (p. 53). Taken together, the communication goals of irony and metaphor are often very similar to one another and often more a matter of emphasis than of type.

The point that I am trying to make here is that the goals of metaphoric and ironic communication often overlap. Consequently a *simple* algorithmic rule based on functional differences (such as context setting up an attitudinal versus content-based schema) often would be ineffective in discriminating ironic from metaphoric use of a sentence. I argue first, that participants have to be very sensitive to contextual cues, and second, that the rules for distinguishing speaker intent should be based on heuristic and not algorithmic procedures. By heuristics I mean "rules of thumb" available to the recipient that can be applied flexibly to linguistic input, and that, depending on the rule invoked, invite classification as irony, metaphor, or other figures of speech. Heuristics by their nature will have a reasonably high (but not 100%) a priori likelihood of success (i.e., the intended meaning will be correctly classified).

Kreuz (this volume) describes some such heuristics based on characteristics of the out-of-context sentence. I argue that context-based heuristics are also likely and based on experience with typical uses of an utterance. For instance, the presence of a privileged audience, although not unique to irony, is arguably more common in ironic than in metaphoric usage and contexts that suggest a privileged audience might tend to invite an ironic interpretation, even though a metaphoric one is logically possible. Katz and Lee (1993) found that the degree of irony perceived in a sentence was dependent on the presence of a privileged audience whereas degree of metaphoricity was not. Research is required to examine each of the communication goals outlined in Table 1.1 to determine the associated degree of ironic (or metaphoric) intent.

The previous arguments are based on sentences that could be stated in a literal form but were presented as metaphor. As outlined in Table 1.1, there are instances in which metaphor is used as literal language (Goal 1) and cases in which literal language is inadequate and metaphor has to be used (Goal 8). I argue that the evaluative or content distinction would have even less force in these two situations, though the contextual information might serve different ends for metaphor compared to irony. With respect to Goal 1, metaphor is used as literal language and thus the context provides little additional information. For instance, stating that *"my car is a lemon"* does not activate concepts of fruit, and the context in which it is used is well delineated to mechanical problems associated with one's vehicle. As such, context should play a relatively minor role in determining the meaning of the metaphor. To my knowledge there is not a literature that suggests that irony can be "literalized" in the same way that metaphor can, though I argue in a later section that familiarity with ironic use does play a functional role in determining the interpretation given to ambiguous sentences. In any event, it is unlikely that ironic usage is ever as conventionalized to the same extent as found with highly conventionalized metaphor and that, with ironic usage, some de-automatization is likely to occur. In fact, de-automatization might be an important component of irony. Muecke (1969), for instance, argued that the speaker, after having gone to the effort of crafting an utterance to have a meaning opposite to that being intended, wishes the audience to recognize and appreciate the juxtaposed meanings. As such, context should play a functional role in the interpretation of irony, even ironic uses that are fairly familiar, that is not found with metaphor. Tests of this possibility will be reported in a later section of this chapter.

I argue that the opposite occurs for items meeting Goal 8 (outlined in Table 1.1); that is, now context should have a greater effect on metaphor than on irony. Recall that the argument is that metaphor may serve an essential role in conceptualizing and communicating a concept that *cannot* be explained in literal terms. Examples of novel metaphoric use abound in both science and poetry. Presumably context serves to supplement and support the novel meaning, but cannot be used as a substitute for it. As such, context should play a special role in defining the domain in which the metaphor is relevant. I argue that irony cannot serve to communicate novel content and, as such, a domain-defining role for context would not be apparent in ironic use.

The Presence of a Human Referent. Consider a sentence such as the well known experimental metaphor:

(3) "Billboards are warts on the landscape."

Out-of-context, the "target" of this statement is presumably, billboards and the speaker is to a large extent providing information about his or her attitude about billboards. However consider a situation such as obtained in Katz and Lee (1993): the statement could be an indirect allusion to a specific person. In this case, the speaker's attitude is directed at a human target and not an inanimate object. Evidence suggests that metaphor and irony differ in the target toward which the utterance is made. Irony, especially sarcastic irony, often has a specific human target in mind (see Clark & Gerrig, 1984; Kreuz & Glucksberg, 1989). Indeed, Katz and Lee (1993) found that participants had little difficulty in inferring the ironic intent of a statement, even when the human target was alluded to indirectly. Although, the presence of an identifiable human target can be found in metaphor, such as in the Katz–Barry Bond example mentioned earlier, the modal picture for metaphor is one in which a general comparison is being made: For instance, virtually none of the more than 200 metaphors culled from works of poetry, and more than 250 experimental metaphors reported in Katz et al. (1988) had an identifiable, specific human topic. The opposite is often true of irony and is almost always true of sarcastic irony in which the communication is often about a specific person. Thus an important cue to ironic or metaphoric intent might be the ease with which an identifiable "victim" can be accessed from context (see Kreuz & Glucksberg, 1989, for experimental evidence).

Nature of the Speaker. This heuristic (and the one that follows) is based on a suggestion originally made by Quintilian about 2,000 years ago in his Institutio Oratorio. He stated:

[Irony] is made evident to understanding either by the delivery, character of the speaker, or nature of the topic. For if any one of these is out of keeping with the words, it at once becomes clear the intention of the speaker is other than what he actually says. (Institutio, VIII, vi, 54ff, cited in Quintilian, 1959)

To my knowledge the principle that irony is in part determined by knowledge of the speaker, has not been subjected to experimental test, though Gibbs, Kushner, and Mills (1991) did examine a related concept. They found that metaphors were understood as being more meaningful when the listener believed they were produced by a poet rather than by a computer program. Presumably the results of Gibbs et al. are a function of the listener's assumptions about authorial intent: a poet (but not a machine) is involved in the social act of trying to tell you something. Consequently, in the "poet" (but not the control "computer") condition, the listener was, in effect, asking himself or herself about the intended message being conveyed. Moreover, with a poet one might assume a figurative relation was intended, whereas the same statement made by a machine might be interpreted non-intentionally or as anomaly.

In a series of studies I conducted in collaboration with Penny Pexman, we examined whether a general characteristic of speakers, their occupations, could serve as a heuristic to speakers' intent (Katz & Pexman, 1995). In our studies participants were presented with a target sentence such as the following:

(4) "Children are precious gems."

We were interested if this sentence would be interpreted differently if uttered by people in different occupations (such as by priests or comedians). This sentence was presented either in a minimal context or in the context of a short passage meant to induce either an ironic interpretation (one in which the utterance is counterfactual with observational fact) or a metaphoric interpretation (utterance consistent with context). We have used these manipulations to invite ironic versus metaphoric interpretation successfully in the past (e.g., Katz & Lee, 1993).

The logic of the study involved two components. First, we had to demonstrate that people shared beliefs about the linguistic habits exhibited by members of different occupations, namely that members of some occupations tended to use irony frequently in speech whereas members of other occupations were more likely to speak metaphorically. Second, we had to demonstrate that these shared beliefs actually constrained the interpretations given to a somewhat ambiguous utterance.

The first aim was met in two norming studies. Participants were presented with a set of occupations and asked to rate the likelihood that a member of each occupation would use metaphor and irony in speech. The mean irony and metaphor ratings (and standard deviations) for the first norming study are presented in Table 1.2. As can be seen, considerable variability was observed across the occupations for both the irony, ranging from scientists (M = 1.5) to political critics (M = 6.47), and metaphor, ranging from truck drivers (M = 2.4) to artists (M = 7.0). Reliability ratings were respectably high. For the likelihood that a person of a given occupation would use metaphor, the non-corrected Spearman-Brown reliability coefficient was .61, which is equal to a reliability coefficient of .76 across all items. The reliability coefficient for irony ratings of occupations was higher, the non-corrected reliability being .95. Similar results were found in a second norming study that employed more subjects and a slightly different pool of occupations. Twenty-six of the occupations were the same in the two norming studies: Correlation among the two sets of ratings was r = .885, (p < .001), for metaphor ratings, and r = .785, (p < .001), for irony ratings, indicating that consensus exists within and across samples about the likelihood that people in different occupations make ironic and metaphoric statements.

The second aim was to see if these shared beliefs constrained the interpretation given to sentences such as (4). Though the studies differed in detail, this aim was met by placing sentences, such as (4), in a short passage. Each passage ended with a participant in the story making a comment. In each of the studies, we manipulated the occupation of the speaker: in half the cases the speaker, based on the norming data, came from an occupation perceived to use metaphor frequently, and in the other half the speaker came from an irony-high occupation. Across all stimuli, each statement would thus be uttered by either a member of a metaphor-high or irony-high occupation. An example of one questionnaire item (involving a member of a "metaphoric" occupation as the speaker, with the target utterance being placed in a consistent, metaphoric context) is as follows:

> Bob and Karen were watching a TV talk show. On the show a scientist was discussing his sister's numerous relationships with men. The scientist said: *"She is a magnet to men."*

Following presentation of each passage, the participant was asked questions regarding the reason that the speaker made the utterance. The specific dependent measures differed in the various studies: Participants were asked to judge how much the speaker knew about the topic, to rate the target for the degree to which it was ironic or metaphoric, or, in what turned out to be the most sensitive case, to answer a set of questions directed towards speaker intent. For the previous example, the questions were:

1. Is the scientist mocking his sister?
2. Does the scientist's tone of voice reflect what he means?
3. Did the scientist phrase the statement as he did in order to show that he is not being truthful?
4. Was the scientist trying to tell the audience something new about his sister?
5. To what extent is the scientist being sarcastic?
6. How appropriate is the scientist's statement to the situation?

Finally, following a set of such passages, participants were involved in a short distracter task and were then, unexpectedly, asked to recall as many of the target sentences as they could. Discussion of the recall data is postponed until a later section on the cognitive consequences of making ironic and metaphoric interpretation.

TABLE 1.2
Mean Irony, Metaphor Ratings, and Standard Deviations for Occupation

| Occupation | Mean Rating | | | |
	Irony	SD	Metaphor	SD
Political critic	6.47	1.60	5.80	1.52
Student	6.27	0.88	4.47	1.96
Cab driver	6.13	0.52	3.00	1.36
Literary critic	5.93	2.05	5.87	1.51
Actor	5.80	1.90	6.07	1.49
Movie critic	5.67	1.84	5.07	1.75
Comedian	5.60	2.35	4.53	2.59
Truck driver	5.60	1.40	2.40	1.06
Writer	5.53	1.77	6.87	0.35
Steel worker	5.50	1.65	2.57	1.45
Journalist	5.47	1.73	5.93	1.44
Poet	5.40	2.29	6.60	1.55
Policeman	5.33	1.63	3.60	2.32
Mechanic	5.13	2.00	3.00	1.93
Housewife	4.80	1.47	3.60	1.24
Professor	4.73	2.69	6.93	0.26
Bus driver	4.60	1.45	3.27	1.53
Lawyer	4.40	2.32	5.93	1.16
Senator	4.20	2.14	4.87	1.81
Politician	4.13	2.00	5.67	1.80
Principal	3.80	1.21	4.60	1.40
Artist	3.80	2.21	7.00	0.00
Mayor	3.33	1.59	5.53	1.30
Cook	3.27	2.34	5.20	1.74
Mortician	3.20	1.70	3.73	1.87
Clergyman	2.73	1.71	7.00	0.00
Accountant	2.73	1.10	3.27	1.53
Judge	2.60	1.72	3.87	2.56
Salesman	2.44	1.63	5.88	1.31
Doctor	2.33	0.90	4.67	2.06
Physician	2.27	0.70	5.20	2.24
Scientist	1.53	0.64	5.47	1.68

The data of most relevance here is the evidence that the interpretation of a given statement varies as a function of the person making the statement. Recall that in one of our studies, after reading each scenario, our participants were asked to rate how much knowledge they believed the speaker possessed about the topic under discussion. Note as well that the topic was presented in a sentence in the form of a metaphor, namely *"A is a B."* We correlated the knowledge ratings with the metaphoricity or irony ratings given to the target utterance. Significant relations emerged for both measures. The correlation of perceived knowledge with degree of metaphoricity was $r = .35$, and with degree of irony was $r = -.24$, both $ps < .01$. That is, it appears that the more we believe that a person knows about a topic the more likely that the utterance is seen as being metaphoric; the less known about a topic the greater the irony. Metaphor is most used for explanation (cf. Winner, 1988) and, as such, one might expect that the greater knowledge that a speaker has about a topic, the more likely they are seen as explaining, that is, using metaphor. Conversely, irony tends to be used to express authorial attitude about a topic or person. Our data are consistent with the speculation that we are more likely to see a comment as a statement of authorial attitude (such as irony) when uttered by a person whom we perceive as less knowledgable about the topic at hand. In any event, these data indicate that some knowledge of the speaker of a statement, based here on stereotypes about occupational membership, is related to perceptions of an utterance as irony.

The most persuasive evidence we use the nature of the speaker to invite ironic versus metaphoric interpretation is based on responses to the questions about speaker intent just described. A given statement was perceived as more sarcastic and more likely to be mocking someone when uttered by a person from an "irony-high" occupation than when the exact same sentence was uttered by a person from a "metaphor-high" occupation. Thus, overall, there is growing evidence that recognition of ironic (or metaphoric) intent is based in part on who makes the comment. This effect was modified by the type of statement made, as described in the next section.

The nature of the statement. The second heuristic cue based on Quintilian was that irony should vary as a function of the "nature of the topic." Consistent with this claim, Kreuz (this volume) describes characteristics of sentences that invite ironic interpretation and, as detailed earlier, Penny Pexman and I found that speakers perceived knowledge about a topic (presented in the form, *"A is a B"*) was related positively to the metaphoric, and negatively to the ironic, intent of the speaker.

Katz and Pexman (1995) also examined the role played by the nature of the topic more directly. We were interested to see if an analogue to conventionality was present with ironic statements, and if such conventionality was used to constrain interpretation of a statement. By conventionality I am referring to the canonical uses of a statement. For instance, when someone states the idiom, *"kick the bucket"* the canonical use is as a reference to death and does not relate to buckets or kicking. As discussed earlier in this chapter, I doubt that a statement is associated with ironic use to the same extent as is found with familiar idioms or metaphor. We were interested in the more modest possibility that some statements might be associated with ironic use and that this association might be a heuristic cue to ironic intent.

Katz and Pexman (1995) examined this question by, first, obtaining norming data to see if statements differ with respect to ironic and conventional uses and second, by experimentally placing high ironic (or conventional) statements in passages and determining the interpretation given these statements.

Across studies, and based on different samples, the norming data indicated that participants could reliably rate sentences (presented out of context) as to irony "goodness" (i.e., how *good* an example of irony a sentence was perceived to be) and to overall conventionality (familiarity with the sentence). Examples of high and low irony good statements, and more conventional and less conventional sentences are exhibited in Table 1.3.

TABLE 1.3
Mean Irony Goodness and Conventionality Ratings on Selected Statements

Irony Goodness Ratings Statements	Mean	SD
A mining town is a large tavern	5.73	1.75
Memory is a trashmasher	5.40	2.03
Artists are gods	5.33	1.95
A second marriage is a new car deal on a used model	5.27	2.43
Teenage girls are Barbie dolls	5.20	2.11
Love is a flower	2.00	1.73
Children are sponges	1.88	1.65
A museum is a history book	1.87	1.64
An old man is a living history book	1.87	1.60
Respect is a precious gem	1.53	1.06
Adventure is a roller coaster	1.40	0.74

Conventionality Ratings Statements	Mean	SD
Handshakes are doorbells	1.39	0.78
Their love is a coniferous tree	1.57	1.12
Their friends are houseplants	1.61	0.94
This textbook is a winning lottery ticket	2.13	0.42
His smiles are can openers	2.13	1.42
Her wedding ring is a "Sorry, we're closed" sign	2.22	1.73
His standards are at the ceiling	4.78	1.28
That comment hit the bull's eye	4.87	1.98
She is a magnet to men	5.61	1.67
That experience was a crushing blow	5.83	1.11
Children are precious gems	6.22	0.79

In both instances, notable variability is evident again across items. With respect to irony goodness, ratings ranged from sentences conventionally understood as good instances of irony (high = 5.73; *"A mining town is a large tavern"*) to those not prototypically used as irony (low = 1.40; *"Adventure is a roller coaster"*). The ratings were internally reliable, Spearman-Brown reliability coefficient *r* = .82. Similar findings were evident when conventionality norms were gathered. Once again, considerable variability was observed in ratings, ranging from statements rated as extremely unconventional (*"handshakes are doorbells,"* *M* = 1.39) to those rated as more conventional (*"children are precious gems,"* *M* = 6.22). And, once again, these ratings were reliable, *r* = .82.

In summary, participants had little difficulty in determining either the ironic content or the overall familiarity with a set of statements. Moreover, there was substantial agreement across our samples about which items were ironic from those that were not and about which items were conventional from those that were not. I assume that since the sentences were presented out of context that at least some of this consistency is based on culturally shared experiences with these types of items in everyday usage.

We examined whether this shared knowledge about irony goodness and conventionality played a role in comprehension by placing the sentences in short passages. As previously reviewed, the contexts were either minimal or were constructed to invite ironic versus metaphoric interpretation. Also the sentences could be uttered by a person from an irony-high or a metaphor-high occupation. The dependent measures varied across study. Omnibus ratings of irony goodness were employed in Study 1 (in which irony goodness level was manipulated) and ratings on specific aspects of speaker intent were employed in Study 2 (in which conventionality level was manipulated). Incidental recall of the target sentence was requested after a distracter task was completed. Discussion of the memory data is delayed until a later section.

The experimental data indicate that both irony goodness and conventionality can serve as heuristic cues to speaker intent inasmuch as both variables were taken to suggest that the speaker intended the utterance to be ironic in nature. The more interesting findings emerged when conventionality was manipulated and aspects of speaker intent were directly measured. Conventionality interacted both with context condition and with speaker occupation.

Context served the role expected of it. That is, an utterance, of the form *"A is a B,"* placed in a context that contradicted the accepted meaning of the words was taken as irony whereas the same utterance placed in a consistent, noncontradictory context was taken as metaphor. That is, the utterance was rated as more being more sarcastic, more likely to be mocking someone, spoken in an unusual tone of voice and the like when in the irony-inducing condition than when placed in the metaphor-inducing condition. Ratings of the same sentence presented as a control, without context, fell between these two extremes, though the ratings in the metaphor-inducing and control conditions were not significantly different from one another. This context effect was significantly greater with conventional (relative to less conventional) sentences. For instance, the rating difference in sarcasm between the irony-inducing and metaphor-inducing discourse context conditions is 2.5 rating points for conventional statements, but only 1.1 rating points for unconventional statements. So although discourse context is effective in inviting a listener to interpret a sentence as irony, it is more likely to do so when the sentence is fairly conventional.

The interaction between conventionality and speaker occupation modified the speaker effect described earlier. As you may recall, when the speaker is a member of an irony-high occupation, an utterance is perceived as more sarcastic and mocking in tone than when the same sentence is made by a member of a metaphor-high occupation. The interaction indicates that the speaker occupation effects are only apparent when the statement is unconventional: speaker effects are not reliable for the more conventional utterances.

Both interactive effects with statement conventionality can be explained by recourse to pragmatic experience with a given utterance. Conventional statements (by definition) are those with which the listener is familiar. As such, canonical scenarios or situations appropriate for when and how to use the statement would have been established in memory. With respect to the interaction between context and conventionality, one can speculate that the canonically appropriate usages of conventional statements are in metaphoric discourse contexts, because the ratings under neutral, context conditions are similar to those produced by the metaphor-inducing context. Consequently, an irony-inducing context for these items would be quite incongruent, leading to a heightened sense of irony. In contrast, unconventional items would not have an established or canonical framework for use and the sense of incongruity might not be as marked.

In a similar way, one can explain the interaction between speaker occupation and conventionality. Assuming that a well-established or canonical meaning is not accessible for unconventional statements, but is easy to access for more conventional statements, our data suggest that speaker intent (based on categorical information such as occupation) becomes especially important when interpretive ambiguity is high. That is, given unconventional statements for which a familiar usage is not available, the listener will employ other sources of knowledge to aid the comprehension process, such as beliefs about the speaker.

SUMMARY

In the previous sections I have attempted to make the argument that context-driven factors can be used as heuristics to constrain the interpretation of statements that could be understood as metaphor or as irony. Four such heuristics were suggested: context that leads to evaluative versus content-based interpretations, the presence or absence of an identifiable human target, knowledge of the speaker (such as occupational status), and knowledge of the pragmatic uses of statements (as indexed by irony goodness and conventionality). Moreover, I speculated and, in places, presented data on the complexity involved in making use of these heuristics. For instance, speaker occupation and statement conventionality were shown to have interactive effects, and I speculate that the role played by evaluative (relative to content-based) context is most likely to emerge when a message could be presented in a literal form, but the speaker chooses to present it figuratively. These complexities speak to a very sensitive processing system that combines and makes decisions on information from multiple sources, presumably simultaneously.

ON THE COGNITIVE CONSEQUENCES OF RECOGNIZING IRONY AND METAPHOR

In the previous section, I addressed the role played by contextual heuristics in inviting an ironic or metaphoric interpretation of a sentence. In this section, I briefly address the question of some of the cognitive consequences that occur when one interprets a given statement as metaphor or as irony. Two cognitive consequences are discussed in turn: consequences for the organization of concepts in memory and consequences for the mnemonic availability of the sentence.

Similarity and Recognizing Irony and Metaphor

Consider a statement of the form *"A is a B."* All of the examples that I have presented previously are of this form. As mentioned earlier, the typical interpretation of this sentence, if it is not literally true and especially if the "B" term is concrete, is as a metaphor. It has long been recognized that metaphor appears to induce similarity between topic ("A" term) and vehicle ("B" term). Not surprisingly there is controversy about what this similarity reflects. Some argue that the act of metaphorizing is parasitic on pre-existing semantic relations, albeit those that are salient until presented as metaphor (see Katz, 1992). Others argue that semantic relatedness is not used to create metaphor but rather that relatedness emerges as a consequence of recognizing the metaphor (see Glucksberg, 1991). In any event, metaphor is consistently associated with rearrangement of concepts in semantic memory to emphasize similarity between topic and vehicle.

Kelly and Keil (1987) demonstrated the role played by metaphor in restructuring conceptual relations. The task they employed had three phases. In Phase 1 a set of nouns were rated on semantic differential bipolar adjective scales. For instance, one can envision rating a set of people and foods (e.g., President Clinton, President Saddam Hussein, Prime Minister Major, quiche, steak, chicken wings, and the like) along a set of dimensions (e.g., good–bad, large–small, weak–strong). In the second phase, the people and food would be paired to make a metaphor (e.g., *"President Clinton is the quiche of politicians"*). Participants were asked to rate the metaphor for aptness and the like. Finally the same set of nouns were rated on the same semantic differential scales. One could use the semantic differential ratings to compute how similar the target concepts (e.g., Clinton, quiche) were initially and how similar they were after being paired in a metaphor. Kelly and Keil demonstrated that the concepts explicitly mentioned in the metaphor were rated as more similar *after* they were processed as metaphor, relative to the baseline measures taken during Phase 1. Of greater interest was their finding that similarity also increased for concepts not presented as metaphor but coming from the same semantic domains (e.g., other politicians and other foods). From this, Kelly and Keil argue that metaphor not only restructures our knowledge of the items explicitly presented as metaphor but also restructures the larger conceptual domains that they implicitly engage.

But what about irony? To my knowledge there is no direct analogue to the Kelly and Keil study in the irony literature. However some predictions can be made. As noted earlier, irony often serves to undercut the similarity relation. As such one might expect that the terms explicitly paired in an ironic utterance would either show less growth in similarity from Phase 1 to 3 (relative to the metaphor condition) or even show a growth of dissimilarity. That is, the paired terms (Clinton, quiche) might be less similar after being placed in ironic juxtaposition. Moreover, just as noted, irony is often directed at a specific human target, unlike metaphor, which is often directed at an instance from a larger conceptual domain. As such, one can postulate that in the irony case, unlike the metaphor case, any effects on similarity restructuring should be limited to the concepts explicitly juxtaposed and should not extend to larger conceptual domains.

Maggie Toplak and I have started to examine this question using a different methodology than that employed by Kelly and Keil. Our study was similar in many ways to Katz and Pexman (1995) described earlier. Participants received a statement of the form *"A is a B"* in one of three context conditions. The statement was made by a speaker as an utterance in either an incongruent irony-inducing context or a congruent, metaphor-inducing context or a neutral no context control condition. As a manipulation check participants were asked to rate the utterance to the extent the speaker was being sarcastic or mocking. As expected the manipulations worked: the utterance was perceived as more mocking and sarcastic in the irony-inducing condition (Ms = 3.89 and 3.67) than in the control condition (M = 4.70 and 4.68) and the control was perceived as more sarcastic and mocking than in the metaphor-inducing condition (Ms = 5.44 and 5.18). This is, of course, the same findings that Katz and Pexman report.

The novel aspect was asking participants to rate the semantic relatedness and similarity of the topic ("A" term) and vehicle ("B" term). The findings were exactly as predicted. When the utterance was made as a metaphor the paired terms were rated as being similar (M = 3.13) and semantically related (M = 2.90) to one another relative to the control condition (Ms = 3.61 and 4.23, respectively). When the utterance was made as irony the paired terms were rated as being reliably dissimilar (M = 4.43) and unrelated (M = 4.43) to one another relative to the control (and, of course, the metaphor-inducing) conditions. Thus, at least with rating data there is some evidence that the specific interpretation given an utterance (as metaphor versus irony) has consequences for the conceptualization of the concepts involved. Additional evidence comes from incidental memory data.

The Episodic Recall of Utterances Perceived as Metaphor Versus Irony

The type of processing done when information is presented has implications for its later recall. In word list studies, facilitated recall is associated with elaborative processing; the counterpart is found in more naturally occurring stimuli with factors such as the amount of pragmatic involvement. Both metaphor and irony should involve substantial pragmatic involvement and so the mnemonic differences between metaphor and irony might be very dependent on the specific processes that obtain at encoding. *Differences* in memory for the same item processed as metaphor or as irony would be evidence that the processing itself differed in the two cases. Consider, for instance, the Katz and Pexman (1995) research discussed earlier. You may recall that in that study we obtained rating data consistent with the hypothesis that speaker occupation and sentence conventionality both played a role in producing ironic interpretation of ambiguous statements. Presumably when hearing that an utterance was made by an irony-high speaker the utterance was interpreted as irony (and not, as could have occurred, as metaphor). Incidental memory for the target items provided some converging evidence. Overall recall was higher when the speaker of a statement was a member of an ironic profession than when the speaker was a member of a metaphoric profession. Moreover we found significant positive correlations between ratings of mocking ($r = .31$, $p < .01$) and sarcasm ($r = .33$, $p < .01$) and level of recall, but only in the condition in which ironic intent is most obvious (i.e., when conventional statements were uttered in the irony-inducing context condition by a speaker who was a member of an "ironic" occupation). These data additionally indicated that speaker occupation, conventionality of the utterance, and context are multiple constraints acting in coordination during comprehension.

The type of memory test employed, when considered in combination with the encoding task, can also provide insight into the processes involved in metaphor and irony comprehension. Consider the following study. The aim of this study was to induce participants to employ cognitive processes that mimic those used in either metaphor or irony comprehension. Assuming that metaphor processing leads to enhanced similarity between topic and vehicle whereas irony processing undercuts the similarity, participants presented a set of metaphors (out of context) and were asked to list either ways that the topic and vehicle were similar or ways that they were dissimilar. The former instruction was meant to mimic metaphor processing and the latter was meant to mimic ironic undercutting of the similarity relations. The metaphors themselves were taken from the Katz et al. (1988) norms in which metaphors were rated on a set of 10 dimensions, such as ease of interpretation and metaphor goodness. Following a distractor task, half of the people in each group were cued by either the topic or vehicle.

To give a concrete example, participants presented with the metaphor *"peace is a wild wood dove"* would have their memory elicited by a vehicle cue (___ is a wild wood dove) or topic cue (peace is ___) following a task in which either similarities or dissimilarities were generated. Overall, the sentences were more highly recalled when cued by the vehicle (relative to the topic) and when the encoding condition was to generate similarities (rather than dissimilarities). Neither of these findings were unexpected. There is a literature to suggest that the vehicle plays a central role in the interpretation of the metaphor and should act as a superior aid to memory (e.g., Verbrugge & McCarrell, 1977), and a literature (e.g., Begg, 1978) that indicates a mnemonic advantage when one generates similarities between weakly related concepts (such as obtains in metaphor).

Of more specific interest is the rotated factor structure presented in Table 1.4. The structure was obtained by a principle components analysis, followed by Varimax rotation, conducted across the 40 metaphors on which data had been gathered. Entered into the analysis were the 10 sentential dimensions rated in Katz et al. (1988), the 4 memory scores (e.g., vehicle cue-similarity listing), and the average number of similarities and dissimilarities generated for each item.

The first two factors are of prime interest here. In Factor I there is an association between the sentential dimensions of metaphor and the probability that the sentence will be recalled when cued by the vehicle (regardless of encoding task). That is, as suggested earlier, the degree to which out-of-context statements of the form *"A is a B"* are treated as metaphor, the more likely the item will be recalled when cued by vehicle. Moreover, because all the sentences were of a metaphoric form, it appears that listing dissimilarities did not eliminate the recognition of the metaphoric nature of the items completely, a finding in concordance with one obtained on similar items by Katz and Lee (1993). Factor II is quite intriguing. Listing dissimilarities, my crude analogue to irony processing, was independent of the metaphoricity of the items and memory was cued by both topic and vehicle.

TABLE 1.4
Rotated Factor Matrix (Varimax)

Variables	Factors			
	I	II	III	IV
Number of Similarities	—	—	.83	—
Number of Dissimilarities	—	.62	—	—
Recall: Sim. Encoding Topic cue	—	.76	—	—
Recall: Sim. Vehicle Cue	.40	.68	—	—
Recall: Dis. Topic Cue	—	.81	—	—
Recall: Dis. Vehicle Cue	.47	.67	—	—
Comprehensibility	.88	—	—	—
Ease of Interpretation	.88	—	—	—
Metaphoricity	.79	—	—	—
Metaphor Goodness	.80	—	—	—
Imageability	.38	—	.75	.32
Topic Imagery	.45	.51	.52	—
Vehicle Imagery	.47	—	.72	—
Semantic Relatedness	.77	—	.36	—
Familiarity	.86	—	—	—
Number of Alternative Interpretations	—	—	—	.92
Eigenvalue	7.3	2.3	1.4	1.1
% Variance	45.7	14.2	8.9	7.0

Note. Only factor loadings + .30 or greater are reported.

The factor analysis on the analogue data reported leads to some predictions. If the factor data can be extended to more ecologically valid instances of metaphor and irony processing, then one can predict that metaphor processing (associated with enhanced similarity between topic and vehicle) would lead to better recall when cued by vehicle (relative to topic); irony processing of the exact same items (associated with increased dissimilarity between topic and vehicle) should eliminate the vehicle cue advantage such that memory should be equally strong whether cued by topic or vehicle. The Katz and Toplak study cited earlier provides a direct test of this prediction. Recall that Katz and Toplak found that a metaphor-inducing context led to enhanced similarity of topic and vehicle whereas irony-inducing context led to a decrement in similarity. Following a short distracter task, participants were given a memory task in which memory for each target item was cued by either topic or vehicle. The findings essentially were as predicted. A strong vehicle cue superiority was found when the sentences were processed as metaphor, but, when processed as irony, recall was equivalent whether cued by vehicle or topic.

SUMMARY

Although many of the causal links are yet to be shown, I use the data to show our interpretation of a sentence cannot be determined by merely stretching the meaning of the words in a sentence. Rather the author of an utterance makes a sentence to meet some communication goal and presumably frames the sentence to provide the listener with hints about what that goal is. As discussed here, several such hints may be made available in the discourse context. These hints act in a heuristic manner to drive the comprehension process, in the cases described here toward a metaphoric or ironic interpretation of the exact same utterance. Finally, the specific outcome of the comprehension process, as metaphor or as irony, will have cognitive implications for the representation of concepts, and our memory for events.

ACKNOWLEDGMENTS

The writing of this chapter and the research from my laboratory reported herein was supported by a grant from the Natural Science and Engineering Research Council of Canada (NSERC 0007040) to Dr. A. Katz.

REFERENCES

Begg, I. (1978). Similarity and contrast in memory for relations. *Memory and Cognition, 6,* 509–517.
Clark, H. H., & Carlson, T. B. (1982). Context for comprehension. In J. Long & A. D. Baddeley (Eds.), *Attention and performance IX* (pp. 313–330). Hillsdale, NJ: Lawrence Erlbaum Associates.

Clark, H. H., & Gerrig, R. J. (1984). On the pretence of irony. *Journal of Experimental Psychology: General, 113*, 121–126.

Cutler, A. (1974). On saying what you mean without meaning what you say. In *Papers from the tenth regional meeting of the Chicago Linguistic Society* (pp. 117–127). Chicago: University of Chicago Press.

Gibbs, R. (1987). Mutual knowledge and the psychology of conversational inference. *Journal of Pragmatics, 11*, 561–588.

Gibbs, R. W., Kushner, J. M., & Mills, W. R. (1991). Authorial intentions and metaphor comprehension. *Journal of Psycholinguistic Research, 20*, 11–30.

Glucksberg, S. (1991). Beyond literal meanings: The psychology of allusion. *Psychological Science, 2*, 146–152.

Glucksberg, S., & Keysar, B. (1990). Understanding metaphoric comparisons: Beyond similarity. *Psychological Review, 97*, 3–18.

Grice, H. P. (1975). Logic and conversation. In P. Cole & J. L. Morgan (Eds.), *Syntax and semantics: Vol. 3. Speech Acts* (pp. 41–58). New York: Academic Press.

Katz, A. N. (1992). Psychological studies in metaphor processing: Extension of the placement of terms in semantic space. *Poetics Today, 13*, 607–632.

Katz, A. N., & Lee, C. J. (1993). The role of authorial intent in determining verbal irony and metaphor. *Metaphor and Symbolic Activity, 8*, 257–279.

Katz, A. N., Paivio, A., Marschark, M., & Clark, J. M. (1988). Norms for 204 literary and non-literary metaphors on 10 psychological dimensions. *Metaphor and Symbolic Activity, 3*, 191–214.

Katz, A. N., & Pexman, P. (1995, November). *What is said, and who says it, as cues to ironic intent.* Paper presented at the 36th Annual Meeting of the Psychonomic Society, Los Angeles, CA.

Keenan, J., MacWhinney, B., & Mayhew, D. (1977). Pragmatics in memory: A study of natural conversation. *Journal of Verbal Learning and Verbal Behavior, 16*, 549–560.

Kelly, M., & Keil, F. (1987). Metaphor comprehension and knowledge of semantic domains. *Metaphor and Symbolic Activity, 2*, 33–51.

Kierkegaard, S. (1966). *The concept of irony, with constant reference to Socrates* (L. M. Capel, Trans.). London: Collins. Original work published 1841.

Kreuz, R. J., & Glucksberg, S. (1989). How to be sarcastic: The echoic reminder theory of verbal irony. *Journal of Experimental Psychology: General, 118*, 374–386.

Kreuz, R. J., Long, D. L., & Church, M. B. (1991). On being ironic: Pragmatic and mnemonic implications. *Metaphor and Symbolic Activity, 6*, 149–162.

Lakoff, G., & Johnson, M. (1980). *Metaphors we live by.* Chicago: The University of Chicago Press.

Marschark, M., & Hunt, R. (1985). On memory for metaphor. *Memory and Cognition, 13*, 193–201.

Martin, J. (1992). Computer understanding of conventional metaphoric language. *Cognitive Science, 16*, 233–270.

Muecke, D. C. (1969). *The compass of irons.* London: Methuen.

Ortony, A. (1975). Why metaphors are necessary and not just nice. *Educational Theory, 26*, 45–53.

Quintilian. (1959). *Institutio oratoria of Quintilian* (H. E. Butler, Trans.). Cambridge, MA: Harvard University Press.

Ross, W. D. (Ed.). (1952). *The works of Aristotle: Rhetorica De rhetorica ad Alexandrumq Poetica.* Oxford, England: Clarendon Press.

Verbrugge, R., & McCarrell, N. (1977). Metaphoric comprehension: Studies in reminding and resembling. *Cognitive Psychology, 9*, 494–533.

Winner, E. (1988). *The point of words: Children's understanding of metaphor and irony.* Cambridge, MA: Harvard University Press.

2

The Use of Verbal Irony: Cues and Constraints

Roger J. Kreuz
The University of Memphis

INTRODUCTION

The social and contextual factors that accompany the utterance of a statement play a major role in how that statement will be interpreted. Although these pragmatic factors can affect language interpretation in a variety of ways, perhaps their most important role is to disambiguate potentially ambiguous statements. Consider the following utterance:

(1) My mother is a mouse.

Without any contextual cues, it would be impossible for a listener to arrive at the speaker's intended meaning. There are, for example, several possible metaphorical interpretations for this statement; it could be uttered, for example, by a son at a costume party to explain his parent's appearance; it could also be used to invoke the attributes we stereotypically apply to mice—that is, the speaker's mother is timid, shy, or extremely quiet.

It is also possible, however, that the speaker of (1) intends to communicate that his mother is resolute, outgoing, and gregarious. In other words, the speaker intends that (1) be interpreted ironically. If the context supports this interpretation (for example, if the listener is observing the speaker's mother dancing on a table), then the statement will be understood in the way it was intended. If the context is ambiguous or impoverished (e.g., the listener has never met the speaker's mother), then interpretation becomes problematic.

It is not unusual to hear someone say "Are you being serious?" as they struggle to interpret an ambiguous utterance. Typically, this statement really means "Are you being literal or ironic?" Interestingly, this question about seriousness rarely seems to be made in regards to metaphorical statements, suggesting that ironic utterances may be more difficult to interpret. Although a number of proposals have been made to explain how this process of interpretation occurs (e.g., Grice, 1978; Leech, 1983), the particular mechanisms at work have not been specified in any detail.

In this chapter, I attempt to elucidate some of the mechanisms that underlie the production and comprehension of verbal irony. I propose that verbal irony is a constrained phenomenon; that is, there are contextual and interpersonal constraints that govern its use. I also suggest the speaker has at his[1] disposal a variety of cues that can be used to accompany an ironic utterance. These cues may then be used by the listener to assist in the determination of ironic intent by the speaker.

The procedures used to interpret these cues are referred to as *heuristics*. These procedures could be thought of as rules, since other researchers, like Sinclair and Coulthard (1975), have described rules for interpreting directives in their analysis of classroom discourse. However, the term "heuristic" captures two important principles that are apparent in the procedures that I describe. First, heuristics are typically quite simple (e.g., "moss grows on the north side of trees"), and second, they can lead to predictable biases, as has been shown in the realm of decision making (e.g., Tversky & Kahneman, 1974). Just as a decision maker may over-employ the representativeness heuristic, a listener may use the irony heuristics to arrive at an ironic interpretation when the speaker intended his statement literally. As shown later, the irony heuristics I am proposing are quite general, and may frequently lead a listener astray (or at least create some uncertainty about the speaker's intention). In the following section, I identify and discuss a number of these heuristics.

CUES THAT SIGNAL IRONIC INTENT

How is a listener to know that a speaker intends an ironic interpretation of his utterance? As I have proposed, it seems likely that the listener can avail herself of a large number of pragmatic cues provided by the context and by the speaker. The speaker may not even be aware that he is providing these cues, but they can function as fairly reliable indicators of ironic intent. Similarly, the listener may not be aware of the various heuristics that she is using to evaluate these cues. Despite their implicit nature, I attempt to show that these cues do, in fact, exert powerful effects on linguistic interpretation.

The Counterfactual Cue

Clearly, an ironic interpretation may be appropriate if the speaker's statement deviates from reality. Of course, there are many other possible interpretations for a counterfactual statement (e.g., perhaps the speaker is being deceptive, or is mistaken), but the use of counterfactuals is perhaps the most salient cue for ironic intent. The listener may employ the following heuristic when the speaker utters a counterfactual statement:

(A) The larger the deviation from reality, the greater the certainty of ironic intent.

As an example, consider the following utterance:

(2) "What lovely weather!"

If (2) is uttered on a warm, sunny day, there is no deviation from reality, and the statement may be interpreted literally. If (2) is uttered on an overcast day, the statement becomes a bit more ambiguous. For example, if torrential downpours had occurred every day during the preceding week, then a day without rain might indeed seem "lovely." In this case, the use of the heuristic specified in (A) is problematic; there is a deviation between the utterance and reality, but because it is not extreme, an ironic interpretation may not be warranted. Finally, if (2) is screamed at the hearer over the howling wind, as speaker and hearer crouch in a tornado shelter, the use of (A) allows an ironic interpretation to be made with some certainty.

The counterfactual cue can be helpful, but there are many utterances for which it cannot be employed. The heuristic in (A) presupposes that a discrepancy between the utterance and reality can be computed, but it often cannot be. If, for example, the utterance refers to attitudes or past events the listener has no knowledge of, then no deviation can be calculated. Consider the utterance in (3):

(3) "Of course, I voted for Perot in '92."

Without knowledge of the speaker's political beliefs, there is no way to evaluate whether the statement is counterfactual. However, if the utterance were (4) instead of (3), then the counterfactual cue becomes useful once again:

(4) "Of course, like most people, I voted for Perot in '92."

The speaker signals a deviation from reality in the first part of his utterance, and the hearer may infer that the second part is a deviation as well (i.e., the speaker did not vote for Perot). Once again, however, other interpretations are possible. By uttering (4), the speaker may mean that he really did vote for Perot, but is aware that many others did not. In this case, he is expressing an ironic attitude *about* his vote, and the conclusion that he did not vote for Perot would not be warranted.

There are many cases in which the counterfactual cue can be used to determine ironic intent, but as we have seen, it is not infallible. The counterfactual cue becomes more useful when it is combined with other, similar cues that are discussed in the following sections.

The Hyperbole Cue

Another simple heuristic for detecting ironic intent is to assess the degree to which a statement is exaggerated. This heuristic can be defined as (B):

(B) The more extreme the statement, the greater the certainty of ironic intent.

Typically, ironic statements are very extreme, as in (5) to (7):

(5) "What an absolutely gorgeous day!"
(6) "The service here is really outstanding!"
(7) "Henry asked me a positively brilliant question today!"

There seems to be a stock frame for such utterances in American English (see Kreuz & Roberts, in 1995), for other examples):

(8) [adverb] + [extreme, positive adjective] = irony

If such statements were meant literally, one would be more likely to say that the day was nice, that the service was good, or that the question was interesting.

The use of exaggeration, however, does not necessarily mean that an ironic interpretation is warranted. Consider (9) and (10), in which the exaggeration surpasses the limits of physical possibility:

(9) "The line to buy tickets was a million miles long!"
(10) "I had to wait forever to get my car fixed!"

The use of the hyperbole cue for irony would lead to interpretations (9a) and (10a):

(9a*) The line for tickets was not very long.
(10a*) I had a very short wait for my car to be fixed.

These interpretations are problematic, because (9) and (10) would then be negative evaluations of positive situations, which is less common in verbal irony (see the section on asymmetry later). It seems more likely that the proper interpretations of (9) and (10) would be (9b) and (10b):

(9b) The line to buy tickets was very long.
(10b) I had to wait a long time to get my car fixed.

In other words, (9) and (10) are examples of utterances in which hyperbole is used simply to exaggerate for effect, and not for irony. Hyperbole, like counterfactual statements, can be employed in discourse to fulfill a variety of speaker goals (see Roberts & Kreuz, 1994), so the hyperbole heuristic is not infallible, either.

Kreuz and Roberts (1995) conducted an experiment in which veridicality and hyperbole were factorially manipulated in the utterances of characters within written vignettes. By veridicality, I mean whether the target statement was true of the world, or whether it was counterfactual. Thus, "Thanks for helping me out!" is veridical when someone provides assistance, but is nonveridical when someone actively hinders your progress. Similarly, "I'll never be able to repay you for your help!" is hyperbolic when someone provides assistance, whereas "Thanks for helping me out!" is nonhyperbolic.

Subjects in the Kreuz and Roberts study were asked to read vignettes that ended with an utterance of the kind just described. They were asked to rate this utterance on a 7-point "irony" scale from 1 *(not at all ironic)* to 7 *(very ironic)*. We found that both veridicality and hyperbole were reliable indicators of ironic intent, and that they were additive; the two cues together produced the highest ratings of ironic intent. Interestingly, some of the veridical, hyperbolic statements were rated as ironic, even though this violates the traditional definition of irony (i.e., the statement must be contrary to fact). This suggests that the use of hyperbole, all by itself, can trigger an ironic interpretation in some cases.

The Tag Question Cue

The application of tag questions to statements can also serve as a cue that they are intended ironically. Once again, the heuristic is very simple:

(C) If an utterance ends with a tag question, it may be ironic.

Consider the tag question constructions in (11) through (13):

(11) "You really showed him, didn't you?"
(12) "It's a good thing you remembered the umbrella, isn't it?"
(13) "Rwanda would be a wonderful vacation spot, don't you think?"

By using a tag question, the speaker seems to be calling attention to the utterance. One reason for highlighting an utterance, of course, is to suggest that the remark is not intended literally. Even though (11) through (13) still seem ironic when read without their tags, they seem less pointed and perhaps more ambiguous.

Once again, tag questions can be used for other purposes. For example, it has been claimed that tag questions are typical of "women's speech," in which direct statements are softened, disagreement is avoided, and intimacy is sought (e.g., Lakoff, 1975). In addition, such statements can be seen as examples of positive politeness in Brown and Levinson's (1987) analysis of linguistic politeness. A statement like "It's a beautiful vase, isn't it?" can serve to indicate that the speaker is aware of the listener's needs, and that the speaker values the listener's opinion. Nevertheless, such statements can also serve to signal ironic intent.

Direct Cues

Of course, the speaker can come right out and explicitly deny that a literal interpretation is appropriate. In cases such as these, no heuristic is necessary. A contemporary example of this cue involves using the word "not!" to make clear one's ironic intent, as in the following:

(14) "You're really something—*not!*"

Of course, there is nothing very clever nor innovative in signaling ironic intent in this way. Since one of the major discourse goals of irony is to be perceived as witty or clever (Roberts & Kreuz, 1994), this may turn out to be a passing fad in American English.

Kinesic and Prosodic Cues

In face-to-face discourse, a speaker can utilize an extensive repertoire of cues for establishing his intention. These factors include proxemic cues, such as the distance that the speaker maintains from his listener (e.g., Hall, 1966); visual cues, like eye contact and gaze duration (e.g., Argyle & Cook, 1976); kinesic cues, like facial movements (e.g., Birdwhistell, 1970); prosodic cues, like intonation (e.g., Egan, 1980); and paralinguistic cues, like yawns and pauses (e.g., Butterworth, 1975). Two of these cues seem especially important in verbal irony: facial expressions and the ironic tone of voice.

Facial expression. While talking to the listener, a speaker can simultaneously express attitudes about his utterances through a variety of physical cues. For example, a speaker can involuntarily shake his head to indicate wonder, or wet his lips to indicate nervousness. Other movements of the head, eyes, and eyelids can be quite deliberate, and many can be used to indicate ironic intent. Winking, for example, can be used to suggest that the speaker does not intend his utterance to be taken seriously. The speaker may also elect to slowly nod his head, or to roll his eyes. Once again, the heuristic for assessing ironic intent can be stated simply:

(D) Unusual facial expressions or gestures may signal ironic intent.

As before, the listener can make an ironic interpretation with greater confidence when this cue co-occurs with other cues described previously.

The Ironic Tone of Voice. An interesting aspect of verbal irony is that it seems to make use of certain prosodic properties. Cutler (1974, 1976) has suggested that the "ironic tone of voice" (hereafter, ITOV) possesses several specific characteristics. These characteristics can be summarized as another heuristic for verbal irony:

(E) Heavy stress, nasalization, and slow speaking rate may signal ironic intent.

The existence of a special ITOV seems odd at first. As Sperber and Wilson (1981) pointed out, there is no special tone of voice for other forms of nonliteral language. Indeed, it seems quite strange to consider a metaphorical tone of voice, or an idiomatic tone of voice. From the perspective of this chapter, however, the existence of the ITOV is not surprising at all. Because the likelihood of miscommunication is higher with the use of irony than it is for other types of nonliteral language, there is a tone of voice cue to assist in correctly determining ironic intent.

Many developmental studies have been conducted to evaluate whether children use this cue to determine ironic intent, but the evidence is mixed (for reviews, see Kreuz & Roberts, 1995; Winner, 1988). Although adults find it easy to detect and use the ITOV, it may be beyond the cognitive abilities of young children to understand that prosodic cues signal a special attitude by the speaker about what he is saying.

Even among adult speakers, evidence for the importance of the ITOV is equivocal. Although the ITOV is used frequently by adults, it is, of course, possible to be ironic by producing utterances in a totally deadpan way. In fact, this form of irony can seem especially clever (see Kreuz & Roberts, 1995). In addition, as we see later, many forms of communication do not allow prosodic features to be transmitted. In other words, the ITOV is not a necessary attribute of ironic statements, and it also may not be sufficient, because someone may be speaking in an exaggerated, nasal, or lethargic way for some other reason. After all, speakers who are excited, or who are suffering from head colds or a lack of sleep do not necessarily mean to be ironic. Once again, the heuristic is useful, but fallible.

Other Physical Cues. There may be other cues that speakers use to signal ironic intent, such as the practice of using one's fingers to form visual "quotation marks" in the air as an ironic attitude is expressed. Such cues may be less common, however, and it is possible that linguistic subgroups or even particular dyads may employ other cues besides those mentioned here. Given the wide range of possible kinesic and prosodic cues, and the linguistic inventiveness of individuals, it seems likely that many other physical cues may be employed to accompany ironic remarks.

Non-Visual Verbal Cues

Not all verbal interactions are face-to-face, and such situations pose additional constraints on the cues that speakers can employ and that listeners can detect. In telephone conversations, for example, speakers can employ prosodic and paralinguistic cues, but not proxemic, visual, or kinesic ones. This would suggest that speakers should rely heavily on the counterfactual cue and the ITOV in order to signal their ironic intentions. Because this range of cues is relatively restricted, however, it seems likely that misunderstandings of ironic statements are more common when speakers and listeners cannot see each other.

WRITTEN LANGUAGE CUES FOR IRONY

Much of our daily consumption of language comes from the printed, as opposed to the spoken, word. Ironic intentions, of course, are a part this medium as well (see Kreuz, Roberts, Johnson, & Bertus, 1996, for frequency estimates of ironic statements in short stories). We have expectations about ironic intentions based, in part, on genre: We might expect ironic statements in a story by Kafka, but not on the front page of the newspaper.

Are the cues for irony in the written medium the same as we have seen for conversation? The prosodic cues mentioned earlier can no longer be used, but there seem to be typographical surrogates that can stand in the place of spoken irony cues. In fact, the written medium seems to have spawned relatively novel ways of signaling ironic intent.

Typographic Devices

Consider the following versions of the same statement:

> (15) "We just *loved* the party," Martha cooed to her friends.
> (16) "We just **loved** the party," Martha cooed to her friends.
> (17) "We just <u>loved</u> the party," Martha cooed to her friends.
> (18) "We just 'loved' the party," Martha cooed to her friends.
> (19) "We just LOVED the party," Martha cooed to her friends.

The use of italics, boldface, underlining, quotation marks, and capitalization can stand in for the absent ironic tone of voice.

Use of "Smileys"

An unfortunate consequence of electronic communication is that it has further reduced the cues available to the potential ironist. In order to transmit messages to computers of different types and capabilities, most electronic mail systems, bulletin boards, and networks restrict users to the 128 ASCII characters available to users at the dawn of the computer age. As many users have discovered to their dismay, italics, boldface, and underlining cannot be used in electronic messages. There are some work-arounds, of course; two common ways of expressing emphasis are shown in the following examples:

(20) "We just _loved_ the party," Martha cooed to her friends.
(21) "We just *loved* the party," Martha cooed to her friends.

The bracketing of the emphasized word with the underscore character or asterisks provides a simple, if inelegant solution.

Why is it so important to have a way of expressing nonserious or ironic intentions in electronic messages? The answer is that the potential for misunderstanding on the "net" is extremely high. Users with very different levels of knowledge, beliefs, and opinions broadcast their thoughts not just to one other person, but typically to dozens or even hundreds of people. All too often, one of these users will take offense at a statement that may have been meant originally as a joke, such as "Everybody knows that Macintoshes are toy computers." The aggrieved party may send an inflammatory message back to the first person, and typically this response, called a "flame," is broadcast to the larger group of users as well. At this point, a "flame war" may erupt as many users rush to state their opinions on the issue.

Moderators of electronic mail systems, bulletin boards, and news groups, who correctly perceive these debates as a waste of time and bandwidth, frequently admonish users to make clear any nonserious or ironic intentions. For example, the use of "<g>" (for "grin") is frequently appended to ironic remarks so that they may be understood in the intended spirit.

A more creative approach can be seen in the following example:

(22) I'M JUST DELIGHTED WITH THE HIKE IN USAGE CHARGES! ;-)

The punctuation at the end of (22) can be interpreted by rotating the symbols (or one's head) 90 degrees: the punctuation becomes a winking, grinning face. These so-called "smileys[2]," therefore, embody the paralinguistic cues that are available in face-to-face communication. A very large number of variations exist, and entire dictionaries of these symbols have been published (e.g., Godin, 1993). Some examples from Godin include the following:

(23) :-/
(24) :-(
(25) :->

Godin labels (23) through (25) as "skeptical," "unhappy," and "sarcastic," respectively.

The use of "smileys" is a good example of how a constrained medium has enriched itself so that the nuances of face-to-face communication can be captured. Although these symbols can be used to reflect a wide variety of affective states, they are perhaps most commonly used in cases where the possibility of miscommunication is high—such as with irony.

CONSTRAINTS IN THE USE OF IRONY

As we have seen, ironists have many cues, and hearers many heuristics, that can be employed in the service of ironic communication. Does this mean that ironic statements can be produced and interpreted correctly in any context? Interestingly, the answer seems to be no. Two important constraints in the use of verbal irony are considered next.

The Asymmetry Constraint

Typically, ironic statements are *positive* evaluations of *negative* situations, as opposed to the reverse (Clark & Gerrig, 1984; Jorgensen, Miller, & Sperber, 1984). That is, a statement like (26), uttered during a downpour, is understood unambiguously as an ironic statement:

> (26) "What gorgeous weather!"

Several researchers (Kreuz & Glucksberg, 1989; Sperber & Wilson, 1981) have suggested that statements like (26) are really echoes of positive cultural norms; we declare that the weather is gorgeous because the weather *should* be gorgeous. When real life does not reflect our expectations, we can ironically invoke these norms, as in (27) and (28):

> (27) "That's just great!" (upon hearing some bad news).
> (28) "Thanks for all your help!" (to someone who has not been helpful).

Matlin and Stang (1978) have proposed a broader thesis they call the *Pollyanna Principle*; they argue that the mind processes positive information better than negative information, and that our thought processes and our languages reflect a bias for the positive that is culturally universal. The asymmetry constraint may be viewed as a special case of the Pollyanna Principle.

Let us consider the reverse; that is, *negative* evaluations of *positive* situations. Such statements are not necessarily perceived as ironic (and hence, the asymmetry just mentioned). The interpretation of a statement like (29), uttered on a warm, sunny day, is somewhat problematic:

> (29) "What hideous weather!"

In an empirical study, Kreuz (1987) found that statements like (29) are often perceived as anomalous or idiosyncratic, and not necessarily as ironic. When asked to provide the reasons for why a speaker would utter statements like (29), subjects made a variety of attributions (e.g., "The speaker was in a bad mood"). We can therefore propose an asymmetry constraint:

(F) Ironic statements are positive evaluations of negative situations; they can be negative evaluations of positive situations only under special circumstances.

What are these special circumstances? Some of the subjects in the Kreuz and Glucksberg study suggested that the speaker could be mocking an earlier, incorrect prediction. In other words, if one party had predicted bad weather the night before, and the next day was warm and sunny, the other party could utter (29) as an ironic echo of the failed prediction.

In this case, the first party can be described as the *victim* of the ironic remark; by echoing the incorrect statement the second party, in a feat of verbal judo, has used the other party's words against him. Kreuz and Glucksberg (1989) showed that the presence of a victim can cause statements like (29) to be interpreted unambiguously as irony once again. In other words, the presence of a victim can lead to interpretations of ironic intent when the statement is negative, and the situation is positive.

Are there other special circumstances? There seems to be at least one more, and it centers once again on the Pollyanna Principle. It can also be summarized as a simple heuristic:

(G) Is the "default" assumption positive?

If this "positive norm" test is passed, then everything is as before: positive evaluations of negative situations are perceived as ironic, and negative evaluations of positive situations are typically not, unless there is a clear victim of the remark.

What about situations in which the default assumption is negative? In such cases, everything seems to be reversed. Consider, for example, the expectations we have during times of war; many people are killed or wounded, and many others suffer great hardship. Clearly, the default assumption should be negative. If this is the case, then *negative* evaluations of *positive* situations should seem ironic, and indeed, they do. Consider (30):

(30) During their patrol of the occupied territory, the GIs discovered an abandoned chateau with a fully stocked wine cellar. As they sampled the select vintages stored there, one of the soldiers turned to the others and said, "War is hell!"

Here we have a negative comment, and no clearly defined victim. The only reason the statement succeeds as irony is because the default assumptions in this situation are negative. In other words, a statement that is at odds with the current situation will be perceived as ironic, as long as it is also at odds with the default assumptions inherent in the situation.

The Common Ground Constraint

As mentioned earlier, the successful interpretation of irony requires a certain degree of knowledge about a speaker's past experiences and present beliefs. Clark has referred to this knowledge as the *common ground* between the speaker and listener (Clark & Carlson, 1981; Clark & Marshall, 1981).

When two people interact, their speech is regulated by the common ground that they share. I don't tell strangers at bus stops about my uncle's coin collection, because (among other reasons), I know that the stranger has no context for understanding and appreciating this information. Similarly, I don't tell my sister about my father's habitual lateness, because my sister and I share this information (i.e., it is already in the common ground), and I am violating another of Clark's principles by providing only given information without any new information (see Clark & Haviland, 1977).

The sharing of common ground exerts an important constraint on the use of verbal irony, because it places limits on the types of people with whom one can be ironic. If a speaker shares common ground with his listener, then he can *infer* that the listener can correctly detect ironic intent. I argue that speakers are aware, at some level, of this inferability, and that this has important consequences for the use of irony. Once again, this idea can be expressed in terms of simple heuristics used by the listener:

(H) If inferability is high, then the speaker may choose to employ irony.

(I) If inferability is low, then the speaker will probably play it safe, and not use irony.

Because common ground is largely determined by how well people know each other, then a testable prediction can be generated: people familiar with one another should be more likely to use irony than people who are not. This prediction has been supported by the study described in the following section.

Test of the Common Ground Constraint. Subjects from introductory psychology classes were asked to consider their relationship with a wide-ranging group of individuals. In each case they were asked to provide the degree of closeness that they felt toward the individual(s). A list of the 25 relationships that were assessed appears in Table 2.1. In each case, subjects responded on a six-point "closeness" scale, with endpoints labeled *not close* and *very close,* and the middle points labeled *somewhat close.*

A second group of subjects considered the same relationships as in Table 2.1 but were asked how often they used sarcasm[3] with these individuals. Subjects were provided with a simple definition of sarcasm (statements that typically mean the opposite of what is actually said), and were shown three examples, along the lines of (27) and (28). Ratings were made on a six-point "sarcasm frequency" scale, with endpoints labeled *very rarely* and *very often,* and the middle points labeled *sometimes.*

Three of the assessed relationships were dropped from analysis because the number of subjects responding was very small. Few of our subjects were married, so the "spouse," "in-laws," and "children" categories will not be considered further. As expected, there was a positive correlation between the ratings from the two groups of subjects, $R^2 = .41$.

Table 2.1

Relationships Assessed in the Common Ground Constraint Study

distant relatives	your coworker(s)
store clerks	your father
strangers	your friends
waiters/waitresses	your grandparents
your aunts and uncles	your in-laws
your best friend	your mother
your boss	your neighbors
your boyfriend/girlfriend	your nieces and nephews
your brother's and	your parent's friends
sister's friends	
your brother(s)	your sister(s)
your children	your spouse
your classmates	your teacher(s)
your cousins	

All the points fall within an upward-moving band, except for one. The results for the "grandparent(s)" relationship were atypical; although the subjects felt close to their grandparents ($M = 4.54$), they were not likely to use sarcasm with them ($M = 1.67$). A couple of explanations can be advanced to explain this discrepancy. There may be a dimension of deference or respect that affects the use of irony, and because irony can be perceived negatively, this consideration may override the considerations of common ground. However, grandparent(s) also represent the oldest people among the relationships that were assessed, and it may be the case that grandparents and grandchildren tend to use language differently. Because this consideration would also affect inferability, it would also affect the use of irony.

Although inferability is important in interpreting irony, its effects can be seen for other forms of figurative language. In a referential communication task, Fussell and Krauss (1989) asked subjects to describe abstract figures for themselves or for other subjects. Although subjects frequently used metaphors and similes in this task (e.g., one figure was described as "a spider with many arms and legs"), subjects were more likely to use these figurative expressions for themselves than as descriptions for other subjects. Just as with irony, these subjects were "playing it safe": When inferability is in doubt, speakers avoid possible misunderstanding by speaking more literally.

CONCLUSIONS

As we have seen, irony is a complex phenomenon that can be easily misinterpreted by a listener. The listener may employ a number of heuristics to determine ironic intent, but by definition, these heuristics are fallible. In general, the listener can be more confident that irony is intended when several irony cues (e.g., hyperbole and the ironic tone of voice) are present at the same time.

Technological advances have provided us with forms of communication that lack the cues that are available in face-to-face communication. As we have seen, however, communication is very malleable, and new cues have arisen to signal ironic intent in new media. The typographic devices seen in print, and the affective symbols seen in computer messages, provide new ways of communicating ironic intent.

It is also the case, however, that irony cannot be employed in all situations; there are constraints in the use of irony that seem to reflect deeply held cultural norms and beliefs. Although these constraints may be circumvented in special situations (as with the ironic victim), ironic interpretations are strongly associated with certain statements (i.e., positive evaluations) and certain situations (i.e., negative outcomes).

Undoubtedly, there are other cues and constraints that play a role in verbal and written irony, but the examples provided here make clear the general shape of my argument. Ironic communication should not be thought of as anomalous or obscure; rather, its use allows us to glimpse important pragmatic principles which lie at the very heart of successful communication.

ACKNOWLEDGMENTS

An earlier account of the ideas appearing in this chapter was presented as a colloquium at Mississippi State University (1993, November). I am grateful to Susan Fussell for her invitation. Support for the preparation of this chapter was provided in part by a Center of Excellence grant from the State of Tennessee to the Department of Psychology at The University of Memphis.

ENDNOTES

[1] In order to avoid awkward constructions like "he or she," I have adopted the convention of referring to the speaker of an utterance as a male and the hearer of that utterance as a female.

[2]"Smileys" are also referred to as "emoticons" (e.g., Eisenberg, 1994). This term is less common but more accurate, since these symbols can be used to express many different affective states.

[3]Although verbal irony and sarcasm are not identical phenomena, pilot research has shown that college subjects tend to equate these two terms, and are more likely to use the latter (see Kreuz & Roberts, 1993, for a description of this distinction).

REFERENCES

Argyle, M., & Cook, M. (1976). *Gaze and mutual gaze.* Cambridge, England: Cambridge University Press.

Birdwhistell, R. L. (1970). *Kinesics and context.* Philadelphia: University of Pennsylvania Press.

Brown, P., & Levinson, S. C. (1987). *Politeness: Some universals in language use.* Cambridge, England: Cambridge University Press.

Butterworth, B. (1975). Hesitation and semantic planning in speech. *Journal of Psycholinguistic Research, 4,* 75–81.

Clark, H. H., & Carlson, T. B. (1981). Context for comprehension. In J. Long & A. D. Baddeley (Eds.), *Attention and performance IX* (pp. 313–330). Hillsdale, NJ: Lawrence Erlbaum Associates.

Clark, H. H., & Gerrig, R. J. (1984). On the pretense theory of irony. *Journal of Experimental Psychology: General, 113,* 121–126.

Clark, H. H., & Haviland, S. E. (1977). Comprehension and the given–new contract. In R. O. Freedle (Ed.), *Discourse production and comprehension* (pp. 1–40). Norwood, NJ: Ablex.

Clark, H. H., & Marshall, C. R. (1981). Definite reference and mutual knowledge. In A. K. Joshi, B. L. Webber, & I. A. Sag (Eds.), *Elements of discourse understanding* (pp. 10–63). Cambridge, England: Cambridge University Press.

Cutler, A. (1974). On saying what you mean without meaning what you say. In *Papers from the Tenth Regional Meeting, Chicago Linguistics Society* (pp. 117–127). Chicago: Department of Linguistics, University of Chicago.

Cutler, A. (1976). Beyond parsing and lexical look-up: An enriched description of auditory sentence comprehension. In R. J. Wales & E. Walker (Eds.), *New approaches to language mechanisms: A collection of psycholinguistic studies* (pp. 133–149). Amsterdam: North-Holland.

Egan, O. (1980). Intonation and meaning. *Journal of Psycholinguistic Research, 9,* 23–39.

Eisenberg, A. (1994, April). E-mail and the new epistolary age. *Scientific American, 270,* 128.

Fussell, S. R., & Krauss, R. M. (1989). The effects of intended audience on message production and comprehension: Reference in a common ground framework. *Journal of Experimental Social Psychology, 25,* 203–219.

Godin, S. (1993). *The smiley dictionary.* Berkeley, CA: Peachpit Press.

Grice, H. P. (1978). Further notes on logic and conversation. In P. Cole & J. Morgan (Eds.) *Syntax and semantics, Vol. 9: Pragmatics* (pp. 113–127). New York: Academic Press.

Hall, E. T. (1966). *The hidden dimension.* London: Bodley Head.

Jorgensen, J., Miller, G. A., & Sperber, D. (1984). Test of the mention theory of irony. *Journal of Experimental Psychology: General, 113,* 112–120.

Kreuz, R. J. (1987). *An investigation into some factors influencing the perception of sarcasm: The role of echoic mention, victims, and implicit norms.* Unpublished doctoral dissertation, Princeton University, Princeton, NJ.

Kreuz, R. J., & Glucksberg, S. (1989). How to be sarcastic: The echoic reminder theory of verbal irony. *Journal of Experimental Psychology: General, 118,* 374–386.

Kreuz, R. J., & Roberts, R. M. (1993). On satire and parody: The importance of being ironic. *Metaphor and Symbolic Activity, 8,* 97–109.

Kreuz, R. J., & Roberts, R. M. (1995). Two cues for verbal irony: Hyperbole and the ironic tone of voice. *Metaphor and Symbolic Activity, 10,* 21–30.

Kreuz, R. J., Roberts, R. M., Johnson, B. K, & Bertus, E. L. (1996). Figurative language occurrence and co-occurrence in contemporary literature. In R. J. Kreuz & M. S. MacNealy (Eds.), *Empirical approaches to literature and aesthetics* (pp. 83–97). Norwood, NJ: Ablex.

Lakoff, R. (1975). *Language and woman's place.* New York: Harper and Row.

Leech, G. N. (1983). *Principles of pragmatics.* London: Longman.

Matlin, M., & Stang, D. (1978). *The Pollyanna principle: Selectivity in language, memory, and thought.* Cambridge, MA: Schenkman Publishing.

Roberts, R. M., & Kreuz, R. J. (1994). Why do people use figurative language? *Psychological Science, 5,* 159–163.

Sinclair, J. M., & Coulthard, R. M. (1975). *Towards an analysis of discourse: The English used by teachers and pupils.* Oxford, England: Oxford University Press.

Sperber, D., & Wilson, D. (1981). Irony and the use–mention distinction. In P. Cole (Ed.), *Radical pragmatics* (pp. 295–318). New York: Academic Press.

Tversky, A., & Kahneman, D. (1974). Judgment under uncertainty: Heuristics and biases. *Science, 185,* 1124–1131.

Winner, E. (1988). *The point of words: Children's understanding of metaphor and irony.* Cambridge, MA: Harvard University Press.

3

Meaning, Memory, and the Interpretation of Metaphors

Valerie F. Reyna
University of Arizona

Recent research on reasoning has indicated that it is necessary to distinguish among alternative representations of presented information. That is, in tasks involving words or numbers, reasoners appear to represent information along a continuum that varies from verbatim precision to vague gist (Ackerman, 1992; Kreindler & Lumsden, 1994; Reyna & Brainerd, 1991, 1993). This distinction between verbatim and gist representations has been useful in explaining surprising dissociations between memory for problem information, which draws on verbatim memories, and reasoning based on gist (e.g., Fisher & Chandler, 1991; Reyna, 1995; Swanson, Cooney, & Brock, 1993).

In this chapter, I apply the verbatim–gist distinction, which is incorporated in fuzzy-trace theory, to the interpretation of metaphors. In particular, I address the question of whether interpretations of metaphors are represented as gist and whether verbatim and gist representations of metaphors display the same properties as analogous representations of other stimuli, such as numbers. I then discuss the theoretical implications of this analysis for such issues as the relation between literal and metaphorical interpretations (e.g., Glucksberg, 1991); developmental differences in the interpretation of metaphors that describe psychological states (e.g., Reyna, 1985; Winner, Rosenstiel, & Gardner, 1976); and the indeterminacy of metaphorical meaning (e.g., Kittay, 1987).

BACKGROUND

Before proceeding, it is important to clarify the kind of phenomenon that my discussion is intended to address. Most theorists separate metaphors from other kinds of figurative language, such as irony or sarcasm, and divide them into three types: nominal, predicative, and sentential (Reyna, 1986). The three types differ depending on which part of speech is used metaphorically. For example, the entire sentence is used metaphorically when *"The troops are on parade"* refers to students proceeding down a hallway. Most of the research I discuss involves nominal metaphors, as in *"Juliet is the sun,"* although it should be noted that there are psychological differences between nominal metaphors and other types (Reyna, 1987).

There is also a psychological difference between so-called fresh (or novel) and frozen metaphors. Although the "arm" of a chair may initially have been a novel expression, this meaning is now listed in dictionaries, along with other conventional usages. Once such metaphorical resemblances become conventional, it is unlikely that they are processed in the same way as novel metaphors. For instance, frozen interpretations are more likely to be retrieved than constructed (Reyna, 1986; see also Blasko & Connine, 1993; Martin, 1992).

Of course, metaphors are fresh or frozen by degrees, as in *"She is carved out of ice"* when used to refer to an emotionally unresponsive person. Although the interpretation of this sentence is not given explicitly in dictionaries, little construction of meaning is involved because the interpreter can rely on conventional interpretations of "icy" and "cold." In this chapter, however, I restrict my attention to metaphors at the fresh end of the continuum. This is because I focus on similarities between reasoning generally and metaphorical interpretation, and these are more likely to be observed for metaphors that require active processing. Thus, interpreting metaphors is compared to reasoning involving literal sentences, stories, or numbers. In both instances, correct responses cannot be generated simply by retrieving stored information.

CONSTRUCTIVISM, REALISM, AND FUZZY-TRACE THEORY

The first question, then, is whether memory for metaphors behaves in the same way as does memory for the gist of literal sentences (Kintsch, Welsch, Schmalhofer, & Zimny, 1990; Reyna & Kiernan, 1994), of stories (Kreindler & Lumsden, 1994) or of numbers (Reyna & Brainerd, 1993, 1994). In order to answer that question, it is necessary to review findings with conventional materials.

In the 1970s, the now classic experiments by Bransford and colleagues seemed to demonstrate that human memory is constructive (e.g., Bransford, Barclay, & Franks, 1972; Bransford & Franks, 1971). In those experiments, subjects were presented with ordinary sentences, such as "Three turtles sat on a floating log, and a fish swam beneath it." After a delay, a recognition test was given containing both originally presented sentences and sentences that had not been presented but were consistent with the gist of presented sentences, such as "Three turtles sat on a floating log, and a fish swam beneath them," as well as false sentences. Subjects often could not discriminate between presented sentences and unpresented sentences that preserved the gist of presented sentences. Under some conditions, memory confidence was higher for unpresented sentences than for those that had actually been presented. Thus, researchers concluded that memory was constructed based on subjects' understanding of the meaning of presented material.

Although the roots of constructivism in memory extend back to Piaget (e.g., Piaget & Inhelder, 1973), Bartlett (1932), and beyond, the false recognition experiments of the 1970s seemed to provide an empirical foundation for earlier proposals. Some investigators, however, questioned the interpretation of these experiments (reviewed in Alba & Hasher, 1983; see also Fletcher, 1992). For example, Flagg (1976) demonstrated that misrecognition of true inferences, which had been taken to be evidence for constructive memory, could be predicted by a model involving memory for superficial aspects of presented sentences. In fact, such false recognition effects were demonstrated using nonsense syllables, suggesting that subjects' understanding of the meaning of the material had little to do with these phenomena (Reitman & Bower, 1973; Small & Butterworth, 1981).

Two views of memory emerged from this research. There was the constructivist view, which held that actual experience was integrated in memory with an individual's understanding of that experience (Glucksberg & Danks, 1975; Jarvella, 1971; Prawatt & Cancelli, 1976; Schwartz & Reisberg, 1991; Turvey, 1974). As Reyna and Kiernan (1994) discussed, if understanding shapes memory in this way, then memory for semantic content must be positively dependent on memory for presented material. In other words, although memory for presented material does not totally determine recognition of semantically consistent inferences, for example, there ought to be some dependency between them.

Other researchers, however, have suggested that memory errors are inversely related to the quality of memory for presented material—that is, that they are negatively dependent (Reyna & Kiernan, 1994). This idea is captured in, for example, Belli's (1989) notion of misinformation acceptance and Loftus, Levidow, and Duensing's (1992) principle of discrepancy detection, which states that the poorer one's memory for presented material, the more susceptible one is to suggestion (see also Reyna, 1995). Some investigators have argued that discrepancy detection applies to misrecognition of semantically consistent or schema-consistent information (see Ceci & Bruck, 1993). In this view, misrecognition of semantically consistent material, such as true inferences, depends on the degree to which memory for actual experience has faded. I refer to this as the realist view of memory (e.g., Turvey, 1974).

A third view of memory, fuzzy-trace theory, implies that memory performance will sometimes conform to the expectations of constructivism, of realism, and of neither of these, depending on whether judgments are based on gist or verbatim memories. Consider recognition judgments of presented sentences and true inferences. If subjects were to base recognition of both old and new sentences on their memory for gist, those judgments (i.e., of presented sentences and true inferences) would be positively dependent, as predicted by constructivism. If recognition in both cases were based on verbatim memory for the original material, judgments would be negatively dependent, as realism predicts. That is, subjects would erroneously accept inferences if they did not remember the exact wording of original sentences, but reject inferences if they did remember original wording. However, if judgments of presented sentences and inferences were based on separate memory representations, verbatim in one instance and gist in the other, those judgments would be independent, which is predicted neither by constructivism nor by realism.

Predictions from both the constructivist and realist perspectives were contrasted with those of fuzzy-trace theory in Reyna and Kiernan (1994). As noted, according to fuzzy-trace theory, two kinds of memory representations of actual experience are deposited—verbatim and gist—that are independent of one another. Verbatim memory is generally less robust than gist memory—i.e., verbatim representations are more susceptible to forgetting and are acquired less efficiently by younger children (e.g., Clark & Clark, 1977; Kintsch et al., 1990; Reyna, 1995; Reyna & Kiernan, 1994). Thus, delay and development affect the accessibility of verbatim and gist representations.

Under conditions such as those typically used in sentence recognition experiments, for example, verbatim memory remains accessible and governs recognition of presented sentences. However, systematic misrecognition of new semantically consistent sentences (e.g., true inferences) cannot be based on verbatim memory for the simple reason that these sentences were never presented. Subjects sometimes say "yes" to semantically consistent sentences, however, because they cue memory for the gist of what was presented (e.g., Ackerman, 1992). Thus, according to fuzzy-trace theory, under these conditions, recognition of old sentences and misrecognition of new semantically consistent sentences should be independent.

Reyna and Kiernan's (1994) results confirmed the prediction that recognition of old sentences and misrecognition of new semantically consistent sentences were independent. (For a review of similar findings of independence in problem solving, see Reyna, 1992.) They also showed that this relation could be manipulated experimentally by varying whether judgments were based on verbatim memory, as opposed to gist. For example, merely instructing subjects to base all judgments on gist converted the relation between the same presented sentences and true inferences to positive dependency. Delaying the memory test until verbatim memory was no longer accessible had a similar effect. In addition, younger children, who were less likely to acquire an accurate verbatim representation, were also more likely than older children to display positive dependency. Finally, regardless of age, delay, or instructions, certain stimuli seemed to invite gist-based (as opposed to verbatim) memory judgments. Although the nature of the stimulus effect is not clear, it could be speculated that materials that elicit integrative imagery (e.g., sentences describing spatial relations) would be more likely to elicit gist-based judgments, whereas materials whose impact depends on an exact turn of phrase (e.g., jokes that rely on puns) would be more likely to elicit verbatim-based judgments. If these findings for literal sentences regarding age, delay, and instructions were applied to judgments about stimuli such as metaphors, what might one expect to find?

MEMORY FOR METAPHORS

As noted, Reyna and Kiernan (1994) compared memory for presented literal sentences to memory for their gist. A similar approach was used by Lim (1993) and by Reyna and Kiernan (1995) to study memory for metaphors and their interpretations. [Lim (1993) studied adults and Reyna and Kiernan (1995) studied six- and nine-year-olds, but their materials and procedures were otherwise essentially identical.] In the metaphor studies, subjects received eight vignettes (see Table 3.1), such as:

The woman was shopping in the grocery store.
The woman saw the lost boy near the door.
The woman was an aspirin, kneeling by the lost boy.

Following presentation of each vignette, subjects were given a recognition test. On the recognition test, sentences were tested one at a time (in a different random order for each subject), including the three target sentences as well as various true and false lures. Subjects were given the same recognition test again after a delay (of seven days for the children and twelve days for the adults). As in Reyna and Kiernan (1994), one group of subjects was given verbatim memory tests; they were told to accept only presented sentences. The other group was instructed to accept all sentences that were consistent with the meaning of presented sentences. For both instruction groups, recognition tests contained the same sentences. Judgments of presented metaphors were compared to those of various metaphorical interpretations, and to false sentences.

Table 3.1
Presented Metaphors and Alternative Interpretations

Presented Metaphors

The woman was an aspirin, kneeling by the lost boy.
Tom was a vacuum cleaner, listening to the story.
Kathy was a camera, watching the children in the show.
Mr. Jones was a bulldozer, meeting with the workers.
The coach was a volcano, talking to the team.
John was a ping-pong ball, chatting with the guests.
The mother was a thunderstorm, speaking to the girl.
The babysitter was a cup of cocoa, staying with the kids.

Alternative Interpretations

Literal—Perceptual—Psychological [Gist]
was medicine—was round—made him feel better
  [eased discomfort]
was a machine that sucked things up—was noisy—paid
  attention [took in]
took pictures—was small—remembered everything
  [recorded]
was a dirtmover—had big muscles—was bossy [pushed]
was a fiery mountain—was hot and sweaty—was mad
  [was intense]
was a bouncing ball—moved around—was friendly
  [was in motion/made contact]
was a big rainshower—was yelling—was angry
  [let loose on]
was hot chocolate—was warm—was nice [comforted]

Note. Interpretations are abbreviated here; subjects were
tested using full sentences that were similar in form to
presented metaphors. The first four psychological
interpretations were classified as "Literal" (i.e., linked to
literal functions) and the second four were classified as
"Perceptual" (i.e., linked to perceptual features).

The main purpose of the verbatim memory test was to assess the degree to which subjects could discriminate between presented metaphors and various potential gists, namely different metaphorical interpretations. These included sentences incorporating literal synonyms, perceptual interpretations, and psychological interpretations of presented metaphors (e.g., Winner et al., 1976; see Table 3.1). For example, in the previous vignette, the woman kneeling by the lost boy is described metaphorically as *"an aspirin."* The literal synonym described the woman as *"medicine"*; the perceptual interpretation referred to her as "round"; and the psychological interpretation indicated that she made the boy feel better. Corresponding false stimuli were related either to the metaphorical term (e.g., *"cough syrup"*), or to the literal synonym (e.g., "nurse"), or they were erroneous perceptual features (e.g., "red cheeks"), or psychological interpretations of the same positive or negative valence as the appropriate psychological interpretation, though they were false (e.g., "proud"), respectively.

According to most accounts, only the true psychological interpretation represents an apt interpretation of the metaphor. All of the true interpretations, however, are semantically related to the metaphor. Therefore, the interesting empirical question regarding verbatim memory tests is whether subjects misrecognize any of these interpretations—literal or metaphorical—as having been presented, as they do for true inferences and other kinds of gist.

In particular, as discussed, theories of memory predict either positive dependency among all sentences that are consistent with gist (i.e., true sentences) or negative dependency between presented sentences and lures. It might be argued, however, that theories of metaphor predict specific relations among subsets of lures. For example, if children initially interpret psychological metaphors perceptually, but ultimately reject such interpretations in favor of psychological ones, one might expect a negative dependency between acceptance of true perceptual interpretations and acceptance of true psychological interpretations (see Reyna & Kiernan, 1995; Winner, 1988).

It might also be argued that metaphors have a special verbatim advantage over other kinds of verbal material. Exact wording or surface form may be especially vivid or it may play a special role in conveying the meaning of figurative expressions. For example, *"Juliet is a yellow star at the center of our solar system"* is metaphorical, and the reference to our sun is the same as in the well-known metaphor. The rhetorical effect of the yellow-star wording, however, is not the same as that of the original wording. For this reason, one might expect that there should be better verbatim memory for metaphors, as opposed to literal language.

In addition to examining the level of verbatim memory for metaphors, I consider how judgments of the various recognition stimuli are related to one another; and whether age, delay, and instructions affect results for these stimuli much like they affected results for other kinds of verbal materials (e.g., Reyna & Kiernan, 1994). I discuss results for children, followed by those for adults.

Level of verbatim memory can be assessed by comparing acceptance rates for presented sentences to those for semantically consistent, but unpresented, sentences. Such differences (or lack thereof) in acceptance rates between presented and true unpresented sentences led earlier investigators to argue that verbatim memory became inaccessible soon after presentation. More recently, investigators have found that clarifying instructions, for example, by including examples of the kinds of true sentences that should be rejected, produced much higher rates of verbatim discrimination for literal sentences (Reyna & Kiernan, 1994).

In order to assess verbatim discrimination for metaphorical sentences, Reyna and Kiernan (1995) compared children's acceptance rates for presented metaphors to acceptance rates for true interpretations. They found that children's verbatim memory for metaphors was excellent on the immediate test, although there was some elevation in recognition errors for literal synonyms. Note that literal synonyms cannot be rejected by a general rule that eliminates any nonfigurative sentence. Over the delay, however, misrecognition of true psychological interpretations increased significantly, as did misrecognition of true perceptual interpretations, although the increase was larger for the psychological interpretations. Although the level of discrimination between presented sentences and gist sentences was higher in this experiment with metaphors than in earlier experiments with literal sentences, there was, nevertheless, a tendency to misrecognize sentences that were semantically related to presented sentences (gist), especially after a delay.

Also consistent with earlier findings, recognition judgments for presented sentences were independent of judgments of semantically related sentences. As in Reyna and Kiernan (1994), however, judgments of sentences that expressed the gist of presented sentences were sometimes dependent on each other. For example, judgments of psychological interpretations were positively related to judgments of literal interpretations and to judgments of perceptual interpretations. Overall, positive dependencies were more likely to be observed among younger children than among older ones.

Results from the instruction condition that stressed meaning bolstered the conclusion that children's misrecognitions in the verbatim task were based on their representations of the gist of the metaphors. When asked to judge meaning, children affirmed true psychological interpretations more often than any other type, including true perceptual interpretations. Although the relative popularity of these two types of interpretations was the same for older and younger children, there was a smaller difference between true and false perceptual and psychological interpretations for the younger children. In other words, both age groups favored psychological and, to a lesser degree, perceptual interpretations, but younger children seemed less able to discriminate true from false interpretations.

Lim (1993) found that adults also have excellent memory for the surface form of metaphors. Indeed, verbatim discrimination was better among adults than among children, consistent with developmental differences for literal sentences (Reyna & Kiernan, 1994). On the immediate recognition test, adults were able to differentiate metaphors from all other sentences, true or false. After a delay, misrecognition of sentences with literal synonyms rose, and true sentences generally were affirmed more often than false ones (once the effects of acquisition were partialed out). These differences were quite small, however. Recognition performance for adults remained at a high level even after 12 days, resembling recognition performance for children tested immediately.

The pattern of dependencies with presented sentences differed from those found with children. Judgments of true interpretations tended to be negatively dependent on judgments of the presented metaphor (whereas these had been independent for children). On the other hand, the relations among judgments of unpresented true sentences were similar to those found for children. Judgments of different true interpretations were generally positively dependent on one another (for details, see Lim, 1993).

As in the experiments with children, adults in the meaning condition favored the true psychological interpretations over other types. True perceptual interpretations, however, were affirmed at a relatively high rate, 40%, roughly comparable to the rate for children, 47%. (False perceptual interpretations were accepted only 8% of the time). Consistent with previous results with children and previous results with literal sentences, dependencies among true sentences (including presented metaphors) were generally positive in the meaning condition.

In summary, responses to metaphors and their interpretations generally resembled responses to literal sentences and their semantically related sentences, with some interesting exceptions. Under verbatim recognition conditions, the "gist" of metaphors—their true interpretations—were misrecognized more often than false interpretations. However, adults were less prone than children to misrecognize metaphorical gist, and such gist was less subject to misrecognition by all age groups, compared to the gist of literal sentences. Also under verbatim conditions, children independently recognized presented metaphors and their interpretations, but this relation tended to be negative for adults. As in the case of literal gist, judgments of unpresented true interpretations were usually positively dependent.

Under meaning instructions, all judgments tended to be positively dependent. Children and adults favored the psychological interpretations of metaphors, but the ability to discriminate true from false interpretations steadily increased with age. Although perceptual interpretations were not the most widely accepted interpretations for any age group, they were affirmed at a surprisingly high rate, even among adults.

INTERPRETING MEMORY DATA FOR LITERAL VERSUS METAPHORICAL SENTENCES

The explanation offered by Reyna and Kiernan (1994) for their independence findings (i.e., that judgments of old sentences and new semantically consistent sentences were independent) can be applied straightforwardly to children's verbatim memory for metaphors. That is, metaphors themselves cue verbatim memory, but their interpretations cue memory for gist. This explanation is further supported by the finding that the independence relation could be manipulated by varying instructions to base judgments on gist, as opposed to verbatim memory. Instructing children to base all judgments on gist converted independence to positive dependency for the same presented sentences and true interpretations. For adults, negative dependency was converted to positive dependency. The result that judgments of different true interpretations were positively dependent, regardless of instructions, is also consistent with the claim that these interpretations cue memory for gist.

Delaying the recognition test until verbatim memory was no longer accessible increased misrecognition of true interpretations. Such misrecognition also varied with age. Younger children were less likely than older children, and older children were less likely than adults, to discriminate between verbatim metaphors and true interpretations. This developmental trend supports the conclusion from earlier research that younger children are less able to acquire accurate verbatim representations. Although younger children were slightly more likely than older children to display positive dependency, and delay was slightly more likely to elicit positive dependency, these effects were smaller than previously observed with literal sentences (Reyna & Kiernan, 1994).

As suggested by previous research, certain stimuli seem to influence whether memory judgments are based on verbatim or gist representations. In particular, metaphors appear to encourage verbatim verification, although this factor is modulated by age, delay, and instructions (verbatim or gist). As some commentators have speculated, the exact wording of metaphors remained accessible for longer periods of time, compared to literal sentences. Adults, and even children, were easily able to discriminate presented metaphors from equally metaphorical sentences containing literal synonyms, as in *"The woman was medicine, kneeling by the lost boy,"* or the false metaphorical sentence *"The woman was cough syrup, kneeling by the lost boy."* Discrimination in these cases may have been aided by subtle nuances of meaning, as well as by differences in surface form. The literal so-called synonym, *"medicine,"* does not, in fact, encompass exactly the same subtleties of meaning as the metaphor, *"The woman was an aspirin, kneeling by the lost boy."*

This effect of materials also explains the main deviation from previous research, namely the finding of negative dependencies between presented sentences and true interpretations for adults (under verbatim instructions). Such negative dependencies would be expected if verbatim memory were so accessible that it would be retrieved even with gist as a cue. Thus, the idea is that true interpretations were rejected at such a high level because those rejections were based on accessing verbatim memory, resulting in a "mismatch" judgment. If true interpretations were rejected based on verbatim memories, but the presented metaphors were accepted based on those same verbatim memories, this would lead to the observed relation of negative dependency.

Because the prediction of negative dependency turns on the accessibility of verbatim memory, it makes sense that negative dependency was not observed for children judging metaphors and related sentences, nor for children or adults judging literal sentences. The level of verbatim discrimination of metaphors was lower for children than for adults; for instance, children displayed some tendency to misrecognize true interpretations on immediate tests, whereas adults showed no such increase in misrecognitions on immediate tests. Children's *acceptance* of true interpretations could not be based on verbatim memory, contrary to the conditions stipulated for negative dependency. Similarly, for both children and adults, verbatim discrimination of literal sentences was lower than that for metaphors and related sentences. Again, acceptance of true unpresented sentences could not be based on verbatim memory, violating conditions for negative dependency.

Apparently, although adults were able to access verbatim memory for metaphors, and therefore could reject interpretations consistent with gist, access to verbatim memory for literal sentences depended on the nature of the cue. When verbatim discrimination was at a lower level, as it was for literal sentences, presented sentences were still able to cue verbatim memories, but unpresented true sentences cued gist memories. Thus, although negative dependency was associated with high levels of verbatim memory, independence was associated with lower levels of verbatim memory at which judgments depended on cues (Reyna, 1995).

IMPLICATIONS FOR THE RELATION BETWEEN LITERAL AND METAPHORICAL MEANING

Traditional theories of the interpretation of figurative language suggest that literal meaning is processed first, and then rejected in favor of a figurative interpretation (Clark & Clark, 1977). A number of studies have called this serial model into question (e.g., Glucksberg, 1991; Ortony, Schallert, Reynolds, & Antos, 1978). It seems as though interpreters can simultaneously process both literal and figurative meanings, especially given sufficient supporting context. (For problems regarding the role of context in supplying the meaning of metaphors, however, see Reyna, 1986). However, this leaves open the question of how interpreters construct novel metaphorical meaning, in particular, how elements of literal meaning are incorporated or integrated into metaphorical interpretations, and how theorists ought to distinguish literal from metaphorical meaning.

Lim's (1993) results suggest that alternative aspects of meaning, including literal, perceptual, and abstract psychological features, do not necessarily operate in opposition to one another, as traditional approaches imply. Forced-choice tasks—that is, pick the "correct" interpretation—assume the mutual exclusivity of alternative interpretations. On the other hand, if subjects are permitted to make separate yes–no judgments for each alternative, they can indicate acceptance of more than one interpretation. Using such yes–no judgments, Lim (1993) found that, although virtually all adults accepted the psychological interpretations of the metaphors, they also sometimes accepted other kinds of interpretations.

Moreover, when subjects were asked to judge meaning, judgments of different interpretations were not negatively dependent on one another. In other words, subjects who accepted a psychological interpretation of a metaphor were not less likely to accept a perceptual interpretation or a literal–synonym sentence. On the contrary, they were more likely to accept such sentences (i.e., they were positively dependent). Not surprisingly, under instructions to process meaning, subjects often interpreted literal-synonym sentences metaphorically. For example, the sentence *"The woman was medicine, kneeling by the lost boy"* could be interpreted as the woman making the boy feel better, that is, the psychological interpretation.

Lim (1993) noted further that for some metaphors, literal–synonym sentences and psychological interpretations seemed to be linked, as in the *"medicine"* example, but for other metaphors, the perceptual and psychological interpretations were linked, as when a man was described as a ping-pong ball at a party, which could be interpreted perceptually as movement and mingling or psychologically as gregariousness. Lim (1993) divided the metaphors into two such categories, based on ratings from an independent group of subjects blind to the hypothesis. (Subjects rated the degree to which perceptual and literal meanings overlapped.) She found that dependencies among interpretations within each category conformed to her expectations about links between either literal and psychological or perceptual and psychological interpretations (see Table 3.1).

Specifically, Lim analyzed dependencies separately for the two categories of metaphors, referred to as Literal and Perceptual (depending on whether the psychological interpretations were linked to literal or perceptual interpretations, respectively). She found that judgments of literal–synonym sentences and perceptual interpretations were independent of each other for both categories of metaphors. Also for both categories, judgments of the metaphor's meaning and of the psychological interpretation were positively dependent. For the Literal category, however, judgments of the metaphor's meaning were positively associated with judgments of the literal–synonym sentence, but were independent of the perceptual interpretation. (The opposite was true for the Perceptual metaphors.) Also for the Literal type, literal and psychological interpretations were positively dependent, but perceptual and psychological interpretations were independent. This category included the *"aspirin"* example.

For the Perceptual category, which included the *"ping-pong ball"* metaphor, judgments of the metaphor and of the perceptual interpretation were positively dependent, but the metaphor and the literal sentence were independent. Unlike the Literal category, perceptual and psychological interpretations were positively dependent. Partial correlational analyses further confirmed that literal and psychological interpretations were linked for Literal metaphors and perceptual and psychological interpretations were linked for Perceptual metaphors.

Clearly, Lim's (1993) data demonstrated that alternative metaphorical interpretations are not mutually exclusive. These data also indicated that perceptual interpretations are processed by adults, especially for certain metaphors. Developmental theories that posit strict stagelike progress from perceptual to psychological interpretations are not supported by these data. Perceptual interpretations, however, do not constitute the most preferred interpretations in any case. Even for Perceptual metaphors, true psychological interpretations were favored.

Although Lim's data do not suggest that subjects pass through an initial literal stage of interpretation, aspects of literal meaning, both functional and perceptual, appear to afford a bridge to novel metaphorical meaning. For the *"aspirin"* metaphor, the literal function of an aspirin, to ease physical discomfort, provides a link to the interpretation that the woman eased the boy's psychological discomfort. For the *"ping-pong ball"* metaphor, the perceptual feature of movement provides a link to social interaction. Although these links can be appreciated intuitively, they raise fundamental questions about the distinction between literal and metaphorical meaning. That is, is the literal feature, for example, "to ease discomfort," transferred to (and perhaps integrated with) the metaphorical topic, in this case, the woman? Or, is the meaning of "to ease discomfort" different for aspirins and women, the first meaning being to quell pain literally and the second to do so only metaphorically?

THE INDETERMINANCY OF
METAPHORICAL MEANING

As discussed in the preceding section, Lim's (1993) analysis of metaphor types pointed out certain connections between functional and perceptual aspects of literal meaning and the interpretation of metaphors. Rather than reject these aspects of literal meaning—for example, to ease discomfort or to move about—subjects often judged them to be consistent with metaphorical interpretations, and the degree to which they were accepted was positively associated with acceptance of metaphorical interpretations. As I suggested, the status of such intermediate functional and perceptual features is unclear.

There are, basically, two answers to the status question. First, these functional and perceptual properties could be classified as literal features. In that case, easing discomfort would be seen as literally alleviating physical pain and moving about would be seen as literally bouncing back and forth. The problem for this approach, however, is to explain the empirical and intuitive connections to the metaphorical interpretations. In short, if the features are indeed literal, then they do not explain the metaphorical interpretation; the woman is not alleviating the boy's physical pain (subjects rejected the literal interpretation that she is a nurse) and the party goer is not really bouncing back and forth. Thus, this approach does not address what Ortony (1979) has called the "attribute inequality" problem, which is that "shared" attributes (e.g., easing discomfort) do not mean the same thing when they are applied literally versus metaphorically.

Another approach to this problem, one that does explain metaphorical interpretation, is to assume that, at some point during interpretation, literal features are processed at a generic level (Reyna, 1981, 1987). The functional and perceptual aspects of literal meaning that are linked to metaphorical meaning are interpreted in a broader or more general sense. Depending on the level of communicative precision that is required, these generic senses are re-instantiated in the metaphorical context to arrive at a specific interpretation. Informally, I am claiming that the literal property of aspirins, to alleviate pain, is interpreted in a broader or more vague way, and then applied to the scenario of a woman kneeling by a lost boy. The ultimate metaphorical interpretation, then, is a product of the generic sense of "to alleviate pain" coupled with a plausible re-interpretation of that generic sense in light of the specific scenario (see also Kittay, 1987).

In particular, I argue that interpreters process the gist of literal meaning in order to arrive at metaphorical interpretations. That gist is then episodically re-instantiated so that it coheres with the context at hand (e.g., Reyna & Brainerd, 1990, 1991). This analysis is similar to that offered by fuzzy-trace theory for reasoning and problem solving. For example, in transitive inference, reasoners might be presented with rods that vary imperceptibly in length. As each pair of rods is introduced (e.g., "The orange rod is longer than the blue rod"; "The blue rod is longer than the red rod," etc.), reasoners recognize the gist of a linear ordering, that as the rods are placed down in order that they decrease in length from left to right. When reasoners are then asked an inference question, such as whether the orange rod is longer than the red rod, they episodically instantiate the question by searching for the orange and red rods in the array, and identifying which rod is to the left. The answer to the inference question is based on memory for the gist that the rods decrease in length, rather than detailed memory for the absolute positions of different rods.

The experimental evidence that I have reviewed regarding the representation of metaphorical meaning suggests that such constructs as gist and verbatim memory can be interpreted in similar ways across different tasks. This evidence indicates that gist and verbatim representations are stored in tasks involving metaphors, so that gist is available during processing to act as a bridge between literal and metaphorical meaning. However, this evidence does not confirm the specific account of metaphorical interpretation that I have discussed. The drawing of parallels between ordinary reasoning and metaphorical interpretation also raises additional questions.

For example, if gist acts as a bridge in metaphorical interpretation, how does this differ from its role in literal interpretation? I would suggest that the difference is one of degree. Indeterminacy characterizes both literal and metaphorical meaning (e.g., Lehrer, 1992). The literal interpretation of words, for example, can be narrowed or broadened in context (e.g., Reyna, 1987). Theorists have proposed a number of ways of representing this vagueness of meaning, including fuzzy logic (e.g., Oden, 1984), assigning weights to semantic components (Lehrer, 1970), prototype theories of core meaning, and so on. Generally, a number of theorists now argue that literal meaning is generic, but that pragmatic principles allow the specification of the meaning of a word in a particular context (Lehrer, 1992). For example, the verb "to peel" is specified somewhat differently depending on whether the object to be peeled is an apple or a banana, and the difference is based on knowledge of the properties of apples and bananas (Reyna, 1987).

Of course, this approach to literal meaning resembles the one I have taken to metaphorical interpretation. The difference, however, is that the gist of semantic features must be interpreted more broadly in metaphorical interpretation. Because metaphorical comparisons traverse different categories, in a specific sense, literal attributes are not the same when they are applied metaphorically (Glucksberg, 1991). Because the woman is really not an aspirin, the features of an aspirin must be viewed in a more abstract way in order to apply them to women. (In contrast, literal usage would exploit more specific aspects of conventional meaning.) Evidence for this view is provided by response-time data, which show that time to interpret novel metaphors increases as the literal and metaphorical categories become more disparate (Reyna, 1981, 1987).

This analysis implies that there is a continuum that varies from literal to metaphorical interpretation, depending on how much the interpreter must stretch the meaning of semantic features. Such an account explains the fact that it is sometimes difficult to judge whether an interpretation is an extended literal sense of a word, or a metaphorical interpretation. It also explains how literal and metaphorical interpretation could proceed in parallel so that their effects converge, rather than disrupt one another (Keysar, 1989). The rationale for this convergence would be that similar pragmatic principles support both literal and metaphorical interpretation.

These pragmatic principles might exploit conventional aspects of denotation, as well as connotation, relations with related words, and knowledge of the situation and the world. For instance, the metaphor *"Their eyes locked"* could be interpreted positively (e.g., they looked lovingly into each others eyes) or negatively (e.g., they stared each other down). Appropriate interpretation of the metaphor requires pragmatic knowledge about what kind of situations imply each type of interpretation. Similar indeterminacy would apply, however, to the literal sentence "They stared at each other," which could likewise be interpreted as either a positive or negative gesture, depending on the situation. Thus, the meaning of "peel" in a sentence such as *"She peeled off her clothes,"* though metaphorical, is not sharply different from its meaning in "He peeled a banana" (the literal meaning of "peel" being to remove an outer covering), and substantial variation in that core meaning is observed across its literal interpretations (Miller, 1979; Reyna, 1981).

SUMMARY

Children and adults were administered verbatim and gist recognition tests for metaphors and their interpretations (Lim, 1993; Reyna & Kiernan, 1995). In order to determine whether these special verbal materials exhibited properties like those observed for literal language, recognition performance and dependencies between judgments for different sentences were evaluated. Specifically, subjects judged presented metaphors as well as sentences incorporating literal synonyms, perceptual interpretations, and abstract psychological interpretations. Results indicated that subjects represented verbatim metaphors in memory and their gist, and these representations were independent of one another, contrary to constructive theories of memory. In this respect, and in many others, memory for metaphors resembled that for literal sentences (Reyna & Kiernan, 1994).

Memory for metaphors did exhibit certain unique properties, however. Adults were able to recognize the exact wording of metaphors, and to reject highly similar distractors, even after a delay of 12 days. This level of performance distinguishes memory for metaphors from memory for literal sentences. Children's performance was nearly as good. In adults, verbatim memory was sufficiently accessible that it appeared to be used both to accept presented targets and to reject semantically related distractors (i.e., gist), producing negative dependency between judgments of these stimuli. When another group of subjects judged the same sentences for their consistency with meaning, positive dependency was observed. Thus, alternative interpretations—literal, perceptual, and psychological—were not mutually exclusive. Instead, functional and perceptual aspects of literal meaning appeared to serve as a bridge to abstract metaphorical interpretations. An implication of these findings is that interpreters use the gist of literal meaning in order to interpret metaphors, a proposal that addresses the "attribute inequality" problem.

REFERENCES

Ackerman, B. P. (1992). The sources of children's source errors in judging causal inferences. *Journal of Experimental Child Psychology, 54*, 90–119.

Alba, J., & Hasher, L. (1983). Is memory schematic? *Psychological Bulletin, 93*, 203–231.

Bartlett, F. C. (1932). *Remembering: A study in experimental and social psychology.* Cambridge, England: Cambridge University Press.

Belli, R. F. (1989). Influences of misleading postevent information: Misinformation, interference and acceptance. *Journal of Experimental Psychology: General, 118*, 72–85.

Blasko, D. G., & Connine, C. M. (1993). Effects of familiarity and aptness on metaphor processing. *Journal of Experimental Psychology: Learning, Memory, and Cognition, 19*, 295–308.

Bransford, J. D., Barclay, J. R., & Franks, J. J. (1972). Sentence memory: A constructive versus interpretative approach. *Cognitive Psychology, 3*, 193–209.

Bransford, J. D., & Franks, J. J. (1971). The abstraction of linguistic ideas. *Cognitive Psychology, 2*, 331–380.

Ceci, S. J., & Bruck, M. (1993). Suggestibility of the child witness: A historical review and synthesis. *Psychological Bulletin, 113*, 403–439.

Clark, H. H., & Clark, E. V. (1977). *Psychology and language.* New York: Harcourt Brace Jovanovich.

Fisher, R. P., & Chandler, C. C. (1991). Independence between recalling interevent relations and specific events. *Journal of Experimental Psychology: Learning, Memory and Cognition, 17*, 722–733.

Flagg, P. W. (1976). Semantic integration in sentence memory? *Journal of Verbal Learning and Verbal Behavior, 15*, 491–504.

Fletcher, C. R. (1992). Assessing recognition memory for surface forms in discourse: A methodological note. *Journal of Experimental Psychology: Learning, Memory, and Cognition, 18*, 199–203.

Glucksberg, S. (1991). Beyond literal meanings: The psychology of allusions. *Psychological Science, 2*, 146–152.

Glucksberg, S., & Danks, J. (1975). *Experimental psycholinguistics: An introduction.* Hillsdale, NJ: Lawrence Erlbaum Associates.

Jarvella, R. J. (1971). Syntactic processing of connected speech. *Journal of Verbal Learning and Verbal Behavior, 10,* 409–416.

Keysar, B. (1989). On the functional equivalence of literal and metaphorical interpretations in discourse. *Journal of Memory and Language, 28,* 375–385.

Kintsch, W., Welsch, D., Schmalhofer, F., & Zimny, S. (1990). Sentence memory: A theoretical analysis. *Journal of Memory and Language, 29,* 133–159.

Kittay, E. F. (1987). *Metaphor: Its cognitive force and linguistic structure.* Oxford, England: Clarendon Press.

Kreindler, D., & Lumsden, C. (1994). Extracting a narrative's causal gist: A modeling study based on fuzzy-trace theory. *Journal of Experimental Child Psychology, 58,* 227–251.

Lehrer, A. (1970). Indeterminacy in semantic description. *Glossa, 4,* 87–110.

Lehrer, A. (1992). A theory of vocabulary structure: Retrospectives and prospectives. In M. Putz (Ed.), *Thirty years of linguistic evolution* (pp. 243–256). Philadelphia: John Benjamins Publishing.

Lim, P. (1993). *Meaning versus verbatim memory in language processing: Deriving inferential, morphological, and metaphorical gist.* Unpublished doctoral dissertation, University of Arizona.

Loftus, E. F., Levidow, B., Duensing, S. (1992). Who remembers best? Individual differences in memory for events that occurred in a science museum. *Applied Cognitive Psychology, 6,* 93–107.

Martin, J. H. (1992). Computer understanding of conventional metaphorical language. *Cognitive Science, 16,* 233–270.

Miller, G. A. (1979). *Language and speech.* San Francisco: Freeman.

Oden, G. C. (1984). Integration of fuzzy linguistic information in language comprehension. *Fuzzy Sets and Systems, 14,* 29–41.

Ortony, A. (1979). Beyond literal similarity. *Psychological Review, 86,* 161–180.

Ortony, A., Schallert, D. L., Reynolds, R. E., & Antos, S. J. (1978). Interpreting metaphors and idioms: Some effects of context on comprehension. *Journal of Verbal Learning and Verbal Behavior, 17,* 465–477.

Piaget, J., & Inhelder, B. (1973). *Memory and intelligence.* New York: Basic Books.

Prawatt, R. S., & Cancelli, A. (1976). Constructive memory in conserving and nonconserving first graders. *Developmental Psychology, 12,* 47–50.

Reitman, J. S., & Bower, G. H. (1973). Storage and later recognition of exemplars of concepts. *Cognitive Psychology, 4,* 194–206.

Reyna, V. F. (1981). The animated word: Modification of meaning by context. *Dissertation Abstracts International, 42,* 3852B [Ann Arbor, MI: 82-03153].

Reyna, V. F. (1985). Figure and fantasy in children's language. In M. Pressley & C. Brainerd (Eds.), *Cognitive learning and memory in children: Progress in cognitive development research* (pp. 143–179). New York: Springer-Verlag.

Reyna, V. F. (1986). Metaphor and associated phenomena: Specifying the boundaries of psychological inquiry. *Metaphor and Symbolic Activity, 4,* 271–290.

Reyna, V. F. (1987). Understanding verbs: Easy extension, hard comprehension. In A. Ellis (Ed.), *Progress in the psychology of language* (Vol. 3, pp. 301–315). London: Lawrence Erlbaum Associates, Ltd.

Reyna, V. F. (1992). Reasoning, remembering, and their relationship: Social, cognitive, and developmental issues. In M. L. Howe, C. J. Brainerd, & V. F. Reyna (Eds.), *Development of long-term retention* (pp. 103–127). New York: Springer-Verlag.

Reyna, V. F. (1995). Interference effects in memory and reasoning: A fuzzy-trace theory analysis. In F. N. Dempster & C. J. Brainerd (Eds.), *Interference and inhibition in cognition* (pp. 29–59). San Diego, CA: Academic Press.

Reyna, V. F., & Brainerd, C. J. (1990). Fuzzy processing in transitivity development. *Annals of Operations Research, 23,* 37–63.

Reyna, V. F., & Brainerd, C. J. (1991). Fuzzy-trace theory and children's acquisition of mathematical and scientific concepts. *Learning and Individual Differences, 3,* 27–59.

Reyna, V. F., & Brainerd, C. J. (1993). Fuzzy memory and mathematics in the classroom. In R. Logie & G. Davies (Eds.), *Everyday memory* (pp. 91–119). Amsterdam: North Holland.

Reyna, V. F., & Brainerd, C. J. (1994). The origins of probability judgment: A review of data and theories. In G. Wright & P. Ayton (Eds.), *Subjective probability* (pp. 239–272). New York: Wiley.

Reyna, V. F., & Kiernan, B. (1994). The development of gist versus verbatim memory in sentence recognition: Effects of lexical familiarity, semantic content, encoding instructions, and retention interval. *Developmental Psychology, 30,* 178–191.

Reyna, V. F., & Kiernan, B. (1995). Children's memory and metaphorical interpretation. *Metaphor and Symbolic Activity, 10,* 309–331.

Schwartz, B., & Reisberg, D. (1991). *Learning and memory.* New York: Norton.

Small, M. Y., & Butterworth, J. (1981). Semantic integration and the development of memory for logical inferences. *Child Development, 52,* 732–735.

Swanson, H. L., Cooney, J. B., & Brock, S. (1993). The influence of working memory and classification ability on children's word problem solution. *Journal of Experimental Child Psychology, 55,* 374–395.

Turvey, M. T. (1974). Constructive theory, perceptual systems, and tacit knowledge. In W. B. Weimer & D. S. Palermo (Eds.), *Cognition and the symbolic processes* (pp. 165–180). Hillsdale, NJ: Lawrence Erlbaum Associates.

Winner, E. (1988). *The point of words.* Cambridge, MA: Harvard University Press.

Winner, E., Rosenstiel, A., & Gardner, H. (1976). The development of metaphoric understanding. *Developmental Psychology, 12,* 289–297.

II

Metaphors in Clinical Settings

4

Conceptualizing the Figurative Expressions of Psychotherapy Clients

Linda M. McMullen and John B. Conway
University of Saskatchewan

When clients in psychotherapy describe themselves as *"falling apart,"* feeling *"hemmed in,"* or being at *"rock bottom,"* how do we understand or conceptualize their experiences? For the psychotherapist, the answer might be relatively straightforward. If one is attuned to hearing these common figures of speech, and believes that they can serve as points of entry into a client's subjective experiencing, then one might focus the client's attention on these condensed expressions of experience with the goal of enabling the client to flesh out their particularized and personal meanings.

However, for the researcher who is interested in what these common expressions tell us about culturally and historically constituted conceptions of human experience and about the vicissitudes of the therapy process, the answer is not so straightforward. With the exception of clinical case studies, there are surprisingly few empirical studies of the use of figurative language in psychotherapy, and even fewer in which a theoretical or conceptual framework for organizing or understanding the meaning of these expressions has been employed.

We became interested in the question of how to conceptualize clients' metaphors when it became clear from previous work (McMullen, 1985, 1989) that these figurative expressions revealed a great deal about clients' major concerns, interpersonal relationships, perceptions of self and others, and affective experiences. What was, at first, of most interest to us were clients' views of self and others. Being familiar with interpersonal theory and the interpersonal circumplex (Leary, 1957), we set out to determine the heuristic value of employing this framework to organize the meanings of clients' figurative expressions of the self's and others' interpersonal actions.

In this chapter, we first highlight some findings from our study of the *interpersonal* metaphors of psychotherapy clients—specifically, how clients who benefitted most from therapy differed from their less successful counterparts in terms of their use of metaphors about their own interpersonal actions. We then turn to a consideration of *intrapersonal* metaphors commonly used by psychotherapy clients. We devote the bulk of the chapter to a discussion of the two most common classes of intrapersonal metaphors: metaphors of the self, and metaphors of emotion or cognitive–affective–behavioral states.

METAPHORS OF INTERPERSONAL ACTIONS

All of the data we discuss in this chapter come from 21 cases of psychotherapy which were selected from Phase 1 (therapy-as-usual) of the Vanderbilt II Psychotherapy Research Project (Henry, Strupp, Butler, Schacht, & Binder, 1993). The sample consisted of 15 female and 6 male clients (all White), ranging in age from 24 to 64 years, with predominant diagnoses of Major Depression, Dysthymic Disorder, Generalized or Atypical Anxiety Disorder, and Other or Mixed Personality Disorder. Therapy was short-term (to a maximum of 25 sessions) and was conducted by experienced psychologists and psychiatrists. Outcome was assessed by a variety of standard measures and ranged from very positive to very negative. For our purposes, we classified clients as high-change ($n = 6$), average-change ($n = 8$), or low-change ($n = 7$) based on their overall outcome scores.

From all available and usable audiotapes of sessions (471 in total), we documented every client-generated, therapy-relevant instance of figurative language and its surrounding context ($N = 9,904$).

For our study of interpersonal metaphors (see McMullen & Conway, 1994), we selected only those that pertained to the self's or others' actions toward the self or other ($n = 3,854$) and coded these instances using Kiesler's Acts Version of the 1982 Interpersonal Circle (Kiesler, 1985). This version consists of act descriptors and adjective descriptors for both mild to moderate and extreme levels of each of 16 Interpersonal Circle segments formed by the intersection of the two orthogonal, bipolar dimensions of dominance–submission (the vertical axis) and friendliness–hostility (the horizontal axis). Examples of figurative expressions coded as dominant included *"We had a run-in last night, but I held my ground"* and *"She walked over me"*; expressions coded as submissive included *"He caved in"* and *"I backed down."* Expressions such as *"I'm soft-hearted"* and *"He was so warm toward me"* were coded as friendly, whereas expressions such as *"He's that cold-hearted guy I've always known"* and *"She cuts down other people"* were coded as hostile.

Our results revealed a fairly clear relation between therapy outcome and clients' metaphoric representations of the self's, but not others', actions. Specifically, the majority of clients classified as high-change made use of metaphoric self-representations that fell in the dominant half of the circumplex (primarily the friendly–dominant quadrant), whereas the majority of low-change clients represented themselves with metaphors that fell on the hostile half of the circle (primarily the hostile-submissive quadrant). In addition, we found that in cases of better outcome the clients' perceptions of self actions were more varied, less rigid, and were distributed more evenly around the segments of the interpersonal circle, compared to those of their less successful counterparts.

These findings are in keeping with the view that psychological adjustment and well-being consist of (in part) a flexible, balanced variety of social behaviors (Leary, 1957) including, in particular, those behaviors that are highly valued in our society: extraversion, sociability, assertiveness, and independence (friendly dominance). The results highlight the significance of metaphoric representations of *self* actions and hint at the possibility that, for depressed clients (who usually are preoccupied with the sufferings of the self), the nature of these representations may be a better prognostic indicator than metaphors of others' actions.

CLASSES OF INTRAPERSONAL METAPHORS

In the data set described earlier, the two most common classes of intrapersonal metaphors were metaphors of the self and metaphors of emotion or cognitive–affective–behavioral states. Because our work on metaphors of interpersonal actions revealed differences between only the high-change and the low-change cases, we limited our analysis of metaphors of the self to these 13 cases. Instances from all 21 cases were considered in our analysis of metaphors of emotion or cognitive–affective–behavioral states.

Metaphors of the Self

The most common way clients represented the self was as *"FRAGMENTED"* versus *"TOGETHER"* or *"WHOLE."* Regardless of outcome status (high-change or low-change), clients described themselves as being comprised of *"parts,"* as not feeling *"all together,"* as being *"at loose ends—apart."* This sense of the self as *"FRAGMENTED"* or as being *"apart"* was subjectively distressing and was often accompanied with a desire *"to be put together"* or to *"pull [the] self together."* For example, one client said:

> I feel like, uh, I've just about finished the process of breaking down. Um, it's sort of like going down to the bottom in terms of my feelings about myself and now I'm wondering how the hell I'm going to come back up. How can I take all those pieces and fragments that I have broken down and put them back together in a way that makes some kind of sense for who I am? 'Cause I don't want to be apart.

Another client expressed her desire for self-integration in the following way:

> There are times when I'm doing something and part of me is, you know, so angry that I'm doing that . . . It's like there's two—I mean I'm not totally split but it's—there are two very different parts of me and uh, if I can get the extremes off both of those and have them work together as a whole, that'd be great.

In the latter example, the *"parts"* or *"two sides"* of the self were sometimes presented as being in conflict with each other. One client stated that *"it's almost like there are just two sides of me and they struggle so much inside of me,"* and another one said:

> I feel a—a sort of ripping away kind of thing. Like, uh, like something inside me is holding onto something real tight and—and, um, one part of me is struggling to say, "Okay, let go of that" and the other part's saying, "No, hold onto that," and . . . there's a battleground in there.

At other times, there was a sense that some *"parts"* worked against the self. As one client said, *"that piece of me can do more to undermine everything that I feel I've built in my life than, than anything else. . . . [I] just wish the other part of me would leave me alone."*

Variations on the theme of self as *"FRAGMENTED"* were the self as *"incomplete,"* *"lost,"* *"decentered,"* *"injured,"* and *"broken."* It is in conjunction with these variations that some differentiation according to therapy outcome emerged. Specifically, clients with more positive outcomes (high-change) began from a foundation of an existing or possible self, however misplaced, nascent, or wounded. For example, clients described a sense of *"losing my center,"* *"feeling like I've lost [a] part of me,"* or, as one successful client put it, *"[Going into marital therapy] is like losing a little bit of me again."* Others seemed to go a little further and stated that they *"had lost [themselves]"* and that they were now going to *"find [themselves]."* One client described this sense, saying *"It's almost like . . . I just didn't exist for so long and the search is—is so difficult and—and the search for the 'I' is where the fear comes in."* During the course of therapy, this same client said *"And it's really like—I think of myself as—there's a shell and then there's something—it's like an Easter egg, you know, there's something inside the egg and I—I'm in there"* and *"[I'm] just beginning to emerge from that egg."* Another client expressed her dissatisfaction with not being an individuated self by saying *"It's like selling my soul to be a carbon copy of somebody else . . . . I don't want to be a carbon copy anymore."*

For other clients with good outcomes, there was a sense that the self, although still intact, was significantly *"injured."* One female client, in the early stage of therapy, described herself as having *"put a scab on something and it just wasn't healing"*; by the end of therapy, she remarked *"I think my scabs are in good order but my scars are still sensitive"* Another client reported *"I just withdraw. Just like, like I have to heal. Like there's a scar that, that is still inflamed and it needs to heal and it's not going to heal with anybody else around . . . . I've got some serious healing that has to be done alone."* In a similar vein, another client stated *"But I'm vulnerable right now. I'm a little raw right now. So I—I've got to do what you suggested, see—like that—until something heals inside here and then maybe I can talk to you about it."*

By contrast, unsuccessful clients (low-change) appeared to be much more at a loss. One woman stated *"I just really don't know . . . how to find myself,"* and another said *"I don't feel very much that I'm centered in myself, you know, that the things that I do and things that I feel are really coming from inside. I feel like, uh, I feel like I'm blowing with the wind."* This latter client also described herself as *"kind of walking around and not feeling like a whole, solid, together person"* and as having a feeling *"that I'm incomplete, you know, that parts of me that would contribute a wholeness are just blocked off."*

In what might be considered more extreme versions of the sense of self as *"FRAGMENTED"* or *"lost,"* clients with poor outcomes spoke of the *"multiple"* self and of the self as *"stranger."* One client stated:

> *I'm feeling real separated. Um, I'm feeling like there are—there are ways to be and I'm not—I'm not pulling it all together. I'm not just me . . . trying to decide which direction I want—I want to go in and I don't mean career-wise or—I'm talking about which person to be. Um, I've got a lot of people inside me.*

Another client referred to himself as *"like two different people"* and asked his therapist if she wanted him *"to bring him [the angry person] next time."* He went on to say *"I don't like that guy [the angry person] . . . . I'll leave him [but] . . . He'll appear. I guarantee it—always has."*

For other clients with poor outcomes, there was a distinct sense of being unfamiliar with the self. One client said *"I'm not really used to, you know, saying a whole lot about how I feel. And it's hard sometimes—it really is—even for me to get in touch with myself . . . . I don't know. Sometimes I wonder if I know myself."* Another remarked *"I've begun to see that I have tried to side-step the deeper me . . . . I'm not one to look down deep . . . just touch the surface,"* and one other client stated quite explicitly *"I just really don't know who I am right now."*

At a broad level, these metaphoric representations of the self are consistent with Safran and Segal's (1990) view that people who seek help "live in a state of alienation, both from themselves and from others" (p. 249). We saw evidence in our sample that all of the clients, regardless of outcome, communicated a sense of having disowned parts of the self. However, those clients who benefitted more from therapy seemed to have a firmer sense of self-existence, in which some parts of the self were accepted while other parts remained disowned or in need of rediscovery. Clients who benefitted least from therapy presented an image of not being anchored in the self and of having repudiated certain parts of the self to the point that these parts were unknown to or were deeply separate from their selves. Given the importance that self-knowing and self-acceptance play in our conceptions of the goals of psychotherapy, it may not be surprising that the short-term therapy that was available to the clients in our sample did not benefit those who were deeply alienated.

We think it is important at this juncture to step back a bit from our data and try to situate them in a broader context. Specifically, where can we place these self-representations in reference to the burgeoning literature on self, and what are the implications of constituting the self in this way?

Although, as Triandis (1989) noted, the study of the self has a long tradition in psychology, there has recently been a resurgence of interest in the concept of the self (e.g., Young-Eisendrath & Hall, 1987) and, in particular, in the self in differing cultural contexts (e.g., Markus & Kitayama, 1991; Marsella, DeVos, & Hsu, 1985; Shweder & LeVine, 1984). In these latter works, the self of individuals living in Western, industrialized cultures is usually broadly contrasted with that of individuals from non-Western, nonindustrialized cultures (e.g., Asian, African, and Latin-American cultures). Although most researchers recognize the diversity within a particular culture, the Western self is broadly characterized as independent, separate, self-contained (Markus & Kitayama, 1991), analytic (Johnson, 1985), unique, more or less integrated, and a distinctive whole (Geertz, 1975). That is, the self is construed as separate from other beings and from the social context, as tending to see reality as an aggregation of parts, and as being relatively unified. In contrast, the non-Western self is characterized as interdependent, connected, relational (Markus & Kitayama, 1991), unindividuated (Marsella, 1985), "dividual" or divisible, mutable, and as striving for oneness with the environment (Bharati, 1985).

The traditional Western sense of the self is captured well in psychological conceptions of identity. McAdams (1994, p. 745 ff), for example, construed identity as a process of integrating discordant parts of the self into a personalized configuration, one that provides us with a sense of unity and purpose in life and that also gives us a sense of inner sameness and continuity.

Postmodern and social constructionist challenges to the view of the Western self as presented here currently abound (e.g., Shotter & Gergen, 1989). The primary call of these challenges is to view the self as multidimensional, multiple, decentered, open-ended, indeterminate (Sampson, 1989); as socially and linguistically constituted; and as irrational and contradictory. As Smith (1985) aptly stated, "The very concept of integral selfhood . . . is coming to seem an illusion" (p. 80).

Gergen (1991) afforded a good illustration of postmodern thinking about the self. We are being "thrust into an ever widening array of relationships" (p. 17), Gergen suggested, and we find ourselves "caught in often contradictory or incoherent activities" (p. 17), in "a chaos of competing opportunities and necessities" (p. 73)—a postmodern condition that he called "multiphrenia." The traditional assumption of a true and knowable self, of a sense of personal identity, is being eroded. Ultimately, the postmodern individual "ceases to believe in a self independent of the relations in which he or she is embedded" (p. 17) and can begin to experience something of the "raptures of multiplicitous being" (p. 17).

So, what sense can we make of clients' metaphoric self-representations in light of the contrasting traditional and postmodern conceptions of the self? What emerges most clearly from these self-representations is that it is normative for clients engaged in psychotherapy in the Western world to symbolize the self as less than fully integrated, known, and intact, and to strive for greater unity, wholeness, and familiarity. That is, the self in distress is characterized in terms that are very similar to postmodern conceptions of the self, and the desired state of selfhood is similar to the traditional Western conception. Although it might be argued that clients in psychotherapy are desiring a state of selfhood that is an illusion and that they have simply adopted the dominant Western discourse in speaking of the desired self, we maintain that the sense of inner self-integrity for which they strive is still alive and well. We agree with Smith (1985) that "[i]t is one of the problems of modern life in contemporary western society that integral selfhood is relatively rare and difficult to attain" (p. 80); nonetheless, the perceived distance from this state might continue to serve as a marker for clients' progress in psychotherapy.

A closer look at the use of metaphors of the self over the course of psychotherapy in the high-change and low-change cases provides some support for this view. What is most noticeable in cases of unsuccessful outcome is the extent to which clients spoke of being not together, of being a stranger to, distanced from, separated from, separate from, themselves, and the degree to which this sense of fragmentation and alienation persisted over the course of therapy. The client who was *"out of touch"* with her feelings remained so; the woman who had *"never really looked deep down inside"* herself, who had let others direct her life, still felt separated, wanted some direction, wanted to know *"Where am I?"*; the woman whose identity had *"really been shaken up,"* who had not *"put all the pieces back together,"* still felt *"unhinged"* and not *"all together";* and a client who wanted to *"pull [her]self together"* felt, in the final session, that she was *"falling apart."*

In contrast, the metaphors used by clients with successful outcomes (high-change) imply that, *from the beginning of therapy,* these clients construed the self as having existed at one time, as possibly still existing, and as being injured but substantially intact. In addition, there were indications at various points over the course of therapy that the self had come alive, had been born or transformed, or had begun to heal. For example, these clients spoke of becoming a *"new"* person, of being *"a mannequin [brought] to life,"* about the *"child me, the real me . . . [who has] wobbly knees . . . [and has] just learned to walk,"* about *"going through [a] period of repair,"* and of the *"very thin veneer"* and *"open wounds"* that were being replaced with *"scar tissue."*

Given our culture's emphasis on the normative self as one that is individuated, self-contained, self-knowing, more or less integrated, and a unified whole, presenting the self almost exclusively as unintegrated and unknown has the consequence of conveying that one has failed to achieve the normative state of selfhood. Conveying such a message may have the effect of diminishing one's competence in both one's own and others' eyes. As Siegelman (1990) emphasized, because metaphors serve both a representational and a determinative function, "[t]hey not only reflect past experience but also become filters that regulate how we see our present experience and how we project our future" (p. 65). For clients with unsuccessful outcomes, then, their metaphors of self may have become disabling self-fulfilling prophecies. By contrast, the metaphors of revival, healing, repair, and renewal (of generation and regeneration) that were used by clients with successful outcomes may have both reflected and influenced the sense of the self as possible and viable. A possible or viable self, although perhaps being a long way from the ideal of the integral self, at least allows for the potentiality of this ideal (however illusory the ideal has come to be regarded by postmodernists).

Metaphors of Emotion and Cognitive–Affective–Behavioral States

Given that psychotherapy often involves attempts by clients to describe what they are experiencing, we considered it to be a fruitful context for the production of metaphors of emotion. To begin our work in this area, we listed the basic emotions that are identified in the literature and that we expected would be represented in clients' figurative expressions: happiness, surprise, anger, fear, sadness, disgust, and shame. We then selected metaphors *of* emotion and *about* emotion from our corpus of nearly 10,000 instances. What we discovered very early on was that only one pure emotion—anger—and two more complex cognitive–affective–behavioral states—depression and general distress—were represented frequently in our instances.

Because Lakoff (1987) did such a masterful job of unearthing the coherence in the metaphors of anger that prevail in our culture, we provide examples from our major groupings to confirm that our data are similar to the instances that he generated and to provide a contrast for the metaphors of depression and general distress (see Table 4.1).

What seems clear from these examples is that our conceptions of anger involve a relation between the body (or the person) and the external environment (or other people); that is, anger is something that is *in* the body that eventually comes *out* and has an impact on the external world.

Table 4.1
Metaphors of Anger

"ANGER IS HEAT"	"ANGER IS INSANITY"	"ANGER IS A DANGEROUS ANIMAL"
"I lost my cool"	"I fly off the handle"	"I have to keep guard on it"
"We didn't know if she had simmered down enough to hear us"	"I just get blind mad"	"I would have jumped on somebody real fast"
"I'm sitting here stewing"	"I absolutely go beserk"	"I just attacked her"
"My anger boiled up"	"I threw a fit"	"We're just kind of barking at each other"
"I just sat there and steamed about it"	"I flipped out"	"I can't criticize him or lash out at him"
"I had to get her out of that trouble and that burns me"	"I snapped"	"The man I called chewed me out"
"I can blow up"		"I wanted to tear his head off"
"He just had a temper tantrum, just erupted"		"My fangs were out and I was furious"
"I shouldn't have fired back"		"I just feel venomous"
"I felt like I was a stick of dynamite with a fuse about a quarter of an inch long"		
"There were sparks flying"		

Depression, on the other hand, is quite differently constituted (see Table 4.2). In comparison with anger, depression appears to be much less related to the interpersonal domain. In these examples, there are neither explicit references to other people nor implications of impact on the external world. This contrast is consistent with views of these two states in Western psychological literature. The arousal of anger is considered to be a response to perceived environmental demand (Novaco, 1975), whereas the self-critical ruminations and hopelessness that are cardinal features of depression are thought to result from a disconnection of response from situation (Bowlby, 1980) or of feeling from its interpersonal source (Greenberg & Safran, 1987).

Table 4.2
Metaphors of Depression

"DEPRESSION IS DARKNESS"	"DEPRESSION IS CAPTOR"	"DEPRESSION IS DESCENT"
"It's really like a black cloud"	"I want to be free from it"	"After I saw you last Monday, I hit a low"
"I feel the rainy day is right around the corner"	"When I get depressed, I just am immobilized"	"I can really be down in the pit"
"I feel so dark"	"I want to break out of this"	"I don't want to go back down and have to slowly work my way back up"
"I got blue on Sunday"		"I haven't had the real valley like I had before"
		"I was at rock bottom"
		"He was in a slump"
		"I went through a real nosedive"
		"I don't know why I should get so dragged down"
		"When I wasn't in the mood to get anything done, it just kind of deflated my balloon"
		"I was totally unreachable"
		"I'm down in the dumps"
		"I was at the bottom of the trough when I started [therapy]"

Whereas anger can be thought of as a reaction to perceived environmental demand, distress can be thought of as a response to a perceived threat (Greenberg & Safran, 1987). Again, this psychological understanding of distress can be seen in the metaphors that clients used to describe it (see Table 4.3).

From these examples, it is apparent that the responses to a perceived threat or to danger are physical arousal, discomfort, instability, agitation, and/or disequilibrium—each of which, at least in the short run, serves to alert the individual, possibly enabling him or her to avoid *actual* threat or danger. In the long run, however, unrelenting arousal, discomfort, and agitation can result in actual physical damage to the individual, as is evident in several of these metaphoric expressions.

As with the metaphors of the self, we think it is important to place the metaphors of anger, distress, and depression in a context and draw out some possible implications and consequences of constituting subjective life in these ways. Given that our data came from the talk of individuals in psychotherapy in the Western world, it is not surprising that anger was the most metaphorically well-developed emotion.   Markus and Kitayama (1991) maintained that ego-focused emotions, such as anger, are more frequently expressed (and perhaps experienced) by those with independent selves (typical of individuals in Western cultures) than by those with interdependent selves (typical of individuals in non-Western cultures) and that expressing such emotions serves to assert and affirm the status of the self as an independent entity.   In Western cultures, the experience and expression of anger is usually accompanied by a sense of having been wronged, of an injustice having been committed.   To move oneself from the undesirable position of victim to the desirable position of agent requires that one assert control over the external world.   Clearly, to speak of (and consequently to enact or live out) the self as *"boiling over," "exploding," "throwing a fit," "attacking,"* or *"blasting others"* is to have a significant impact on the environment.   Actions such as these cannot go unnoticed.

Table 4.3

Metaphors of Distress

"DISTRESS IS QUICK OR UNPLEASANT BODILY MOTION"	"DISTRESS IS BODILY HARM"
"I get so stirred up"	"I looked over at him and went to pieces"
"My head was spinning"	"It just tore me up"
"It's kind of a whirlwind of confusion"	"When he fired them [co-workers], I was so crushed"
"My head was really buzzing around"	"But I started seeing things realistically and that really shattered me"
"I don't want to have these things turning around inside me"	"When he tells me that, it just destroys me"
"I get all wound up"	"I'm really debilitated"
"It leaves me feeling insecure and unsettled"	"He was tortured by it most of his life"
	"This is killing me"
	"That really bent me out of shape"
	"I couldn't get started on that [dissertation] and that sort of ate away at me"
	"I'm in up over my head"

Whereas the metaphors of anger signify the possible destruction of the self and/or of others, the metaphorical representations of distress signify the destruction of the self only.   To describe oneself as being *"torn apart," "devastated,"* or *"undone"* is to give the message that the viability of the self is threatened.   However, in sharp contrast with the metaphors of anger, there is no indication of asserting one's control over the environment; rather, there is a strong sense of the self as having no control.   The use of such metaphors may convey to others a sense of urgency and need for assistance (e.g., *"I'm going off the deep end"*); if forthcoming, such assistance might produce the desired effect of lessening the environmental threat and/or enabling the self to re-establish control.

A similar sense of uncontrollability is present in the metaphors of depression. However, rather than the continuity of the self explicitly being at risk, there is the sense that one has ended up (or possibly is being held) in a low, dark, isolated *place.* Although the desire to be agentic is sometimes expressed (e.g., *"I want to find something that I can pull myself up out of it when I get depressed"*), there is a clear sense that one has arrived at this place without having exercised personal will. Considering the determinative power of metaphor, representing one's subjective experience as lacking in agency and interpersonal contact may serve to exacerbate and accentuate the existential despair that characterizes Western depressive experiences.

CONCLUSION

So, what is gained by trying to conceptualize clients' figurative expressions? First, if we are able to demonstrate theoretically consistent relations between the use of these expressions and other significant variables (as we did in our work on metaphors of interpersonal actions), then a case can be made for according metaphor a pre-eminent position as a form of verbal expression in psychotherapy. Second, conceptualizing clients' figurative expressions adds concreteness to our more abstract psychological conceptions, such as interpersonal dominance or depression, and may amplify and extend these conceptions. For example, considering the paucity of references to other people and to felt bodily experiences in the metaphors of depression, we might re-examine our theories of treatment for this disorder and assess the degree to which our theories coincide with how people actually talk about depression. Third, having knowledge of the conceptual coherence of common metaphors used by clients in therapy might enable therapists to consider these metaphors as cultural glasses through which clients view their experiences. For example, being aware of the norm of "the *'FRAGMENTED'* self striving for *'unity'*" might sensitize a therapist to work more with the expressions that constitute this central metaphor and, at the same time, to recognize the constraints that this cultural metaphor imposes.

REFERENCES

Bharati, A. (1985). The self in Hindu thought and action. In A. J. Marsella, G. DeVos, & F. L. K Hsu (Eds.), *Culture and self: Asian and Western perspectives* (pp. 185–230). New York: Tavistock.

Bowlby, J. (1980). *Attachment and loss: Vol 3. Loss: Sadness and depression.* London: Hogarth.

Geertz, C. (1975). On the nature of anthropological understanding. *American Scientist, 63,* 47–53.

Gergen, K. J. (1991). *The saturated self: Dilemmas of identity in contemporary life.* New York: Basic Books.

Greenberg, L. S., & Safran, J. D. (1987). *Emotion in psychotherapy: Affect, cognition, and the process of change.* New York: Guilford.

Henry, W. P., Strupp, H. H., Butler, S. F., Schacht, T. E., & Binder, J. L. (1993). Effects of training in time-limited dynamic psychotherapy: Changes in therapist behavior. *Journal of Consulting and Clinical Psychology, 61,* 434–440.

Johnson, F. (1985). The western concept of self. In A. J. Marsella, G. DeVos, & F. L. K. Hsu (Eds.), *Culture and self: Asian and Western perspectives* (pp. 91–138). New York: Tavistock.

Kiesler, D. J. (1985). *The 1982 interpersonal circle: Acts version.* Unpublished manuscript, Virginia Commonwealth University, Richmond.

Lakoff, G. (1987). *Women, fire, and dangerous things.* Chicago: University of Chicago Press.

Leary, T. (1957). *Interpersonal diagnosis of personality.* New York: Ronald Press.

Markus, H. R., & Kitayama, S. (1991). Culture and the self: Implications for cognition, emotion, and motivation. *Psychological Bulletin, 98,* 224–253.

Marsella, A. J. (1985). Culture, self, and mental disorder. In A. J. Marsella, G. DeVos, & F. L. K. Hsu (Eds.), *Culture and self: Asian and Western perspectives* (pp. 281–308). New York: Tavistock.

Marsella, A. J., DeVos, G., & Hsu, F. L. K. (Eds.). (1985). *Culture and self: Asian and Western perspectives.* New York: Tavistock.

McAdams, D. P. (1994). *The person* (2nd ed.). Fort Worth, TX: Harcourt Brace & Company.

McMullen, L. M. (1985). Methods for studying the use of novel figurative language in psychotherapy. *Psychotherapy, 22,* 610–619.

McMullen, L. M. (1989). Use of figurative language in successful and unsuccessful cases of psychotherapy: Three comparisons. *Metaphor and Symbolic Activity, 4,* 203–225.

McMullen, L. M., & Conway, J. B. (1994). Dominance and nurturance in the figurative expressions of psychotherapy clients. *Psychotherapy Research, 4,* 43–57.

Novaco, R. W. (1975). *Anger control: The development and evaluation of an experimental treatment.* Lexington, MA: Lexington.

Safran, J. D., & Segal, Z. V. (1990). *Interpersonal process in cognitive therapy.* New York: Basic Books.

Sampson, E. E. (1989). The deconstruction of the self. In J. Shotter & K. J. Gergen (Eds.), *Texts of identity* (pp. 1–19). London: Sage.

Shotter, J., & Gergen, K. J. (Eds.) (1989). *Texts of identity.* London: Sage.

Shweder, R. A., & LeVine, R. A. (Eds.). (1984). *Culture theory: Essays on mind, self, and emotion.* Cambridge, England: Cambridge University Press.

Siegelman, E. Y. (1990). *Metaphor and meaning in psychotherapy.* New York: Guilford.

Smith, M. B. (1985). The metaphorical basis of selfhood. In A. J. Marsella, G. DeVos, & F. L. K. Hsu (Eds.), *Culture and self: Asian and Western perspectives* (pp. 56–88). New York: Tavistock.

Triandis, H. C. (1989). The self and social behavior in differing cultural contexts. *Psychological Bulletin, 96,* 506–520.

Young-Eisendrath, P., & Hall, J. A. (Eds.). (1987). *The book of the self: Person, pretext, and process.* New York: New York University Press.

5

An Intensive Analysis of Metaphor Themes in Psychotherapy

Lynne E. Angus
York University, Ontario, Canada

Empirical studies (Angus, Hardtke, Pedersen, & Grant, 1991; McMullen, 1989) have established that irrespective of therapy outcome, clients use metaphors extensively in their conversations with therapists. Whereas the number and frequency of metaphor phrases occurring in therapy session transcripts can be readily identified by trained raters, what has been more difficult to determine is in what manner and for what purposes certain metaphors become salient over the course of a given psychotherapy relationship. Moreover, findings from studies investigating good-outcome therapy dyads (Angus et al., 1991; McMullen, 1989) seem to indicate that the presence of elaborated metaphor themes throughout the course of therapy may be an important marker of a productive therapeutic relationship. Specifically, it appears that in good-outcome dyads both the client and therapist are able to draw upon a primary set of metaphoric scenarios in which the ongoing events of the client's life can be thematically connected and understood (Angus & Lawrence, 1993).

Despite these empirical findings, and the extensive case study documentation of the power of metaphor in therapy (Siegelman, 1990), little is known about the processes entailed in generating and elaborating metaphor themes in psychotherapy. In an attempt to address this gap, two studies were undertaken to further our understanding of the roles and functions of metaphors and metaphor themes in the therapeutic discourse. In this chapter the quantitative research findings from an intensive analysis of metaphor use in good-outcome and poor-outcome Brief Dynamic therapy dyads is presented first. In order to explore the interface between metaphor use and the emergence of themes, the returns from an intensive qualitative analysis of one good-outcome Brief Dynamic therapy dyad is reported next. Finally, the interrelation between metaphor and the evolution of therapy themes in productive

73

psychotherapy is discussed and suggestions for clinical practice are put forward.

METAPHOR USE AND THERAPY OUTCOME

Although literary in origin, metaphor phrases are intrinsic to verbal discourse. They have an easily identifiable and stable form, two properties which are definite assets when conducting empirical research studies. In a series of studies focused on the intensive analyses of therapy session transcripts, we have identified the frequency and pattern of metaphor use by clients and therapists engaged in both good-outcome and poor-outcome Brief Dynamic therapy (Angus, 1992).

The sample of 18 transcripts used for this study consisted of an early (3rd), middle (5th), and late (15th) session from each of 3 good-outcome and 3 poor-outcome brief dynamic therapy dyads (Angus et al., 1991). The selection of the good- and poor-outcome dyads was based on the rank ordering of factor scores which had been derived from the clients' pre- and postscores on three symptom indexes (Beck Depression Inventory [BDI], Beck, Ward & Mendelson, 1961; Behavior Symptom Index [BSI], Derogatis, 1983; Social Adjustment Scale [SAS], Weissman & Bothwell, 1976).

For the purposes of this study, Lakoff and Johnson's (1980) conceptualization of metaphor was used as a guiding framework. They define metaphor as an episode of figurative language in which two separate items or concepts are juxtaposed. A Metaphor Identification Manual (Pedersen, 1991) was developed for this project and two raters were able to achieve an overall agreement rate of 82% for the identification of metaphor phrases in three sample therapy sessions.

The findings from these studies suggest that metaphors are used frequently by both clients and therapists, irrespective of outcome group. The good-outcome dyads produced 53 metaphors per session on average while the poor-outcome dyads had an average of 73 metaphors per transcript. Clients of both good- and poor-outcome dyads were more likely to contribute metaphor phrases to the therapy discourse than were their therapists (70% vs. 30%). Interactive and coelaborated metaphor phrases were found slightly more frequently in the good-outcome (23%) than in the poor outcome (20%) therapy transcripts. An unexpected finding emerged when the rates of novel metaphor production in the two outcome groups were compared. Contrary to popular belief, proportionally more novel metaphors (21%) were found in the poor-outcome than in the good-outcome (9%) therapy transcripts.

The trend evident in this discourse analysis of metaphor use, and reported in other published studies (McMullen, 1989), is that the more we talk, the more we speak metaphorically. As suggested by Lakoff and Johnson (1980), metaphorical concepts undergird much of our language, and are endemic to verbal discourse, irrespective of whether we find ourselves in a productive or nonproductive psychotherapy relationship.

The discovery that the good-outcome dyads had fewer novel metaphors was surprising and required further exploration. One possible explanation for this rather curious finding appeared in a subsequent study of narratives (Angus & Hardtke, 1994) and the generation of metaphor themes in psychotherapy sessions. An intensive sequential analysis of therapy sessions revealed that therapists and clients in the good-outcome dyads tended to cocreate and reuse a core set of metaphoric phrases or themes in their therapeutic conversations. Thus, novel metaphor phrases are less likely to be introduced in later sessions of the good-outcome dyads than in the poor-outcome dyads.

This finding in turn supports the critique of mainstream psychotherapy literature put forward by Stiles and Shapiro (1994). These authors challenged the widely shared assumption that the more a critical factor or event is present in a therapy relationship, the more likely it is that a productive outcome will be achieved. It is in this regard that the limitations of studies focused solely on investigating the frequency of variables in the therapy discourse are starkly evident. It would appear that as in the case of metaphorical expressions, a complex relation exists between processes of meaning generation and the therapy discourse. In response to these results, the findings from an intensive, sequential analysis of the emergence and generation of metaphor themes in the context of a good-outcome, Brief Dynamic therapy dyad, are addressed in the following section.

A SEQUENTIAL ANALYSIS OF METAPHOR THEMES IN BRIEF THERAPY

There seems to be broad support for the importance of metaphor themes in therapy. Pollio and Barlow (1975) reported in their case study analysis of figurative language that the novel metaphors produced in the therapy session could be grouped into categories on the basis of conceptual similarities. Shell, Pollio, and Smith (1987) described "radical" metaphors which had to do with ongoing dialogue and served as a focus over extended periods of therapy.

Additionally, McMullen (1989) also identified the existence of a central metaphor or metaphors in psychotherapy transcripts and considered this pattern to be a feature or discourse marker associated with good therapeutic outcomes. The intensive investigation of metaphor themes in this sample, supported by findings from other studies, suggested that therapists in good-outcome therapy relationships develop and carry forward metaphor phrases initially introduced by their clients. At the session level, one or two core metaphor themes—such as conceptualizing life as a journey on a sailboat and/or interpersonal relationships as war grounds—are then drawn on by client and therapist alike when linking separate events or episodes together to coconstruct an organized, comprehensive life narrative. It was in the context of overarching, conceptual metaphor themes that individual metaphor phrases, whether novel or cliché, seemed to take on special meaning in the good-outcome therapy sessions.

In the poor-outcome dyads, there appeared to be a clear lack of metaphor theme development within and across sessions. The absence of a core set of metaphor themes may in fact provide a cogent explanation for the finding that a higher percentage of novel metaphors were found in the poor-outcome dyads than in the good-outcome dyads in the previously described study.

For the purposes of this study, the intensive analysis of metaphor themes was undertaken in collaboration with Heather Lawrence, a York University undergraduate student (Angus & Lawrence, 1993). For this study all 20 sessions of one good-outcome, Brief Dynamic psychotherapy dyad were transcribed for intensive analyses. The overall story or narrative of the client's life as coconstructed by client and therapist across the 20 sessions was then identified and summarized. Once this overview was generated, the focus of the analysis shifted to the identification and elaboration of recurring metaphor phrases and themes across the 20 transcribed therapy sessions. It is these findings which we describe in the following section.

Drawing upon a number of published studies (Angus & Rennie, 1988, 1989; Brooks, 1985; Siegelman, 1990), metaphor may be conceptualized broadly as the evocative use of language which synthesizes and conveys meaning through implied comparison, and thereby elicits interpretation relative to the transition and transformation of contexts. Furthermore, based on the empirical results from qualitative analyses of in-session metaphor episodes (Angus & Rennie, 1988, 1989), it was anticipated that the metaphors initiated and elaborated in the therapy sessions would be conjointly developed by both client and therapist. Two raters identified the metaphor phrases included for analysis in this study and only those phrases in which a consensual agreement was achieved were included for further analysis.

The intensive analyses of the therapy sessions resulted in the identification of two elaborated metaphor themes. The first structural metaphor theme centered on a comparison of the development of a marital relationship to building, maintaining, and sailing a boat in which the client drew upon her extensive nautical experiences to flesh out her metaphoric representation. The second structural metaphor theme, which we focus on in this chapter, was based on the metaphor of life and relationships with significant others as a battle, fight, or war. This metaphor was repeatedly used throughout the therapy sessions, most noticeably within the context of the client talking about her relationship with her husband. Accordingly, the battle metaphor appeared to signify a "metaphoric scenario" (Angus, 1992) through which the client tacitly communicated her understanding of her marriage. The battle or fight metaphor was also particularly apt and evocative for the client, given her previous experiences of having been physically beaten by her husband.

The recurrent metaphor theme of life as a battle was initially introduced by the therapist in the first therapy session and then was elaborated further by the client in the same session. This coconstructive extension of a metaphoric scene suggests that both client and therapist were engaged in a collaborative interaction which in turn signified the development of a shared understanding between the therapist and client.

T: Have you ever lost a battle?
C: Have I ever lost a battle? (laughs)
T: Or is this the first one?
C: What kind of a battle? Yeah, I seem to spend half of my life losing battles. That's not true. I don't think I have won many battles with J, maybe that's a better way of putting it, I seem to have always been struggling, to stay on top of it, whatever it is at the time, working hard emotionally and physically, and I haven't been able to win a battle with him I guess that's it (laughs). Now, I don't think I've really lost, you know, this is the first big battle I've lost, but then this is the biggest battle.
T: This is the war.
C: (laughs) Yes.
T: You lost the war.
C: That's right, that's right

Later in the same session, the client returned to the therapist's war metaphor when further describing her marital relationship. She stated, "But you did tell me this isn't a battle this is a war (slight laugh)," and later, "Well, I think the war is really on, this one is not handling it very well." It appeared likely that this initial set of interactions around the metaphor of *"RELATIONSHIP AS WAR"* represented the coconstructive germination of a salient metaphor theme.

For the client, the metaphor of a *"lost war"* conveyed a great deal about how the client felt about herself as having been beaten in the battle for her husband's love. In later therapy sessions the client used the war metaphor to articulate a cross-cutting relationship pattern which she identified as occurring in a number of different relationships:

C: I've given quite a bit of thought to the question you raised earlier about, have I lost any battles before. And I do lose a lot of battles. We all do. And then I tend to retreat, battles at work and so on. But they always seem to be minor things. I suppose the largest things in my life have been my marriage, the children, and probably the boat.

This amplification and extension of the implicit pattern of battles and retreats across a range of interpersonal relationships is the first elaboration of what eventually became a core therapeutic theme. It is significant that it was the client, not the therapist, who took up the metaphor scenario and extended it to a variety of disparate relationships and life events. As a consequence, previously disconnected relationship events were linked together as apt exemplars of a recurring relationship pattern or theme.

Throughout the early and middle phases of the therapy relationship the client was clearly ambivalent about her separation from her husband. In her dialogue with the therapist she described feeling like she was caught in an emotional dilemma in which she shifted from wanting to end her marriage— she had been physically beaten and emotionally "brainwashed" by him for years—to wanting to give their relationship just one more try, that she has changed and he would find her less difficult to live with. A pivotal therapeutic turning point for the client occurred during sessions 13 and 14. In those sessions the client resolved to ask her husband to try to make the marital relationship work "one more time." In response to her invitation, he wrote a letter to the client in which he stated that he had no intention of ever returning to Canada or to the marriage. Additionally she was made aware of the fact that he had a new girlfriend whom he intended to marry. During session 14 the client returned to the theme of *"RELATIONSHIP AS WAR"* when she began the painful process of coming to terms with the fact that her marriage was over:

> C: When does it stop hurting? (It) just keeps tormenting me . . . it seems for years and years and years and all the wasted energy and weeping over him just for years. Always going against each other, always bashing . . . we never could make any progress really (sigh) I can't stand much more of this. (sighs) . . . I just want peace. And yet when I look six months ahead all I see is more battles, more battles, more battles . . . (sigh) I don't know how much more of this I can handle. Or do I just give up again? Or try and cope with all these battles . . . so that I get something or do I just give up and say "oh to hell with it"? I don't know. (sighs) . . . I just don't see why he should have it all . . . all his own way. (sigh/still sniffling)

At this moment in the session the client articulated an emerging awareness of her desire to simply let go of what had been a continually punishing and losing battle—which she anticipated would be most relieving— but was stopped further by the fear that in doing so she would be simply giving up and her husband would emerge the winner, the victor. The *"RELATIONSHIP AS WAR"* had always been cast as a winner-take-all competition in which struggling and fighting meant that one was gaining ground, while leaving the battle ground meant that one had been utterly and completely defeated. By session 17 the implications of this metaphor scenario were being intensively explored:

> C: And all through the years I've had good feedback from other people . . . um . . . but it doesn't seem to be important and that's unkind I don't mean it that way I do appreciate it but it doesn't have the significance and so what am I going to do over the next six

months? Have I got to learn? Maybe this is what I've got to do is learn to appreciate what I receive from all these other people . . . and that has got to be enough. And that's not a challenge because that's not difficult . . . and so it's just not enough to satisfy me. . . . It's almost like taking second best . . . it does sound unfair. (blows nose)

T: It doesn't count unless there's a fight in there?

C: That's right.

T: Some competition in it or . . . you're trying to put you down and you're trying to prove to him all the time that you're not as bad as you—he says you are . . . both J and your dad.

C: That's right.

T: And that gives you the energy or the

C: The drive.

T: The drive.

C: I mean I do—it sounds conceited—but I do do well at a lot of things and do get a lot of good feedback . . . and I just think "Oh, that's lovely, that's great" but it wasn't difficult to do and so it doesn't mean as much to get good feedback.

T: You've got to be put down. You've got to be fighting.

C: I've got to be fighting.

T: For your survival or something. . . .

C: Now how can I change that so that I don't always look for that? Or else I'm always going to be miserable aren't I? . . . maybe if there is somebody there and there is a challenge then as long as I'm—I've got the challenge then even if I am put down . . . it's what keeps me going I don't know—maybe it's like food.

This elaboration of the *"RELATIONSHIP AS WAR"* theme revealed that the client felt that she had experienced an intensity of feeling and focus in her life by engaging in the fight to win her husband's affection and the idea of giving that mission up left her feeling empty; as if her life had no direction or meaning. Engagement in a struggle was necessary to her being—like food or oxygen. Accordingly, praise, approval, and acceptance by others must be hard won in order to be of value and trustworthy.

A significant step towards finding a resolution for her marital problems appeared to occur when the therapist and client began to reframe the marriage as having been a challenge, a quest which was doomed from the beginning. The victory that she sought for so many years—to be respected, cared for and prized by her husband—would never be achieved because her husband was simply incapable of caring for another human being in that way. In essence, this goal was a lost cause. The client then tentatively began to explore the possibility that "throwing up her hands" and simply not fighting anymore may in fact be a form of "winning the battle." The therapist seized upon this budding realization and suggested further that the real victory for her might well be fully extricating herself from the embattled relationships with the men in her past—husband and father.

C: See in a way I think J just thought "Oh, I can't compete with all this competition any more," he'd had enough. Almost in the same way that I think I had too. We'd been competing with each other, we both sort of threw up our hands and thought "Oh, that's the end of it," and maybe I should just figure that was an achievement (laughing).

T: Well, it would be an achievement, wouldn't it? It would be that you could get out of that kind of a situation which you're in with your dad and then with J . . . and begin to look for yourself and then eventually perhaps select somebody for you that will complement you or you will complement and there will be not a negative put-down fight . . . who's winning this battle and pleasure only out of uh kind of up one-upmanship kind of struggle.

C: Mm.

T: And he seemed to always have the upper hand because he could make you feel guilty and make you feel as though you were worthless . . . and uh, therefore had you trapped.

C: Yeah, he did manage that. . . . I suppose a lot of that was my fault too . . . I always (wanted to). Yeah, I guess I mean I've said to you before that he was a challenge and um that next time around I'll probably look for another challenge which will be just as exhausting and it frightens me and depresses me. I couldn't handle it again (laughs). So maybe that's right I should use my energy and challenges in a physical direction instead of within a relationship with somebody (laughs). It should be a relationship should flower and blossom and . . . improve not diminish them.

Moreover, staying in the context of the battle metaphor in conjunction with ending her marriage, the client began to explore her fears of letting go and the different ways in which she might be able to find purpose, challenge, and satisfaction in life which does not include being physically or emotionally abused. In the following dialogue both client and therapist interwove the metaphor of the battle and struggle with a spatial metaphor of climbing a ladder of success. With this metaphoric coconstruction the therapist seized the opportunity to reframe the notion of the fight, and advancement on the ladder, from being a life and death struggle to one of choice, in which the client can choose whether or not she would like to take the next step and engage in the next fight.

T: It requires a considerable personality change doesn't it?

C: It does.

T: To be more content with what you are.

C: Yes, but how do I do that? (laughs) . . . or should I do that? Should I in fact say "Okay, you stay at this level because that's the level that you function well at" and I should be satisfied with that? It's almost like stopping climbing up a ladder in a career saying "Okay . . . (sigh) you can do this job perfectly well so you might as well stay here for the next thirty years." To me, that's suffocating.

T: But the thing was that with J and with your dad it seemed for years you just repeated and repeated and repeated and got nowhere. . . . You weren't going up the ladder it was just repetition at the same old place, until finally uh . . . .

C: I gave in.

T: This is where you got to.

C: (sniffling)

T: There must be a better way of using energy than that. . . . the idea of going up the ladder uh makes a lot of sense if you're just fighting to slip down into the—to get finally submerged.

The client then pursued a directed exploration of the different options she had for finding new, more satisfying challenges in her life, which did not include trying to win the love of her dad and husband.

C: I think that maybe now that I'm young and still got the boys I should at least channel my energy into something that I really want to do while I'm young enough to do it. And I've got their help too. Maybe that's it? Just um maybe that's what my dad was and what J was . . . just a channel for my energy. (mental and physical emotion) If I can channel for it may not matter so much if it's a whether it's a person or not. (pause) And that is something which will always be a challenge just (as the sea always is). . . . and it will keep knocking me down (laughing) literally. Maybe that's the kind of struggle it would be, a struggle with a human being and then maybe I could um eventually meet somebody—and have a relationship without having to have all this bloody struggle because I've got the struggle elsewhere. Because if I haven't got a struggle—there doesn't seem to be any point. . . . I mean in the past people have said, "Oh I don't know how you manage to do all this work and do a good job and have three small kids and baby-sit and all that stuff" but it was that kind of struggle that kept me going and I enjoyed it and did it well. And then the last few years building the boat and everything. "No, I enjoy it, I'm happy, it keeps me going, I thrive on it" . . . Last week um do you think that might help me if I take the sea as my challenge instead of a person?

A sense of having reached a resolution is conveyed in the 20th and final session by the client when she stated:

C: I think I am finally convinced that I don't have to take all of that punishment, maybe it has finally sunk in. . . . I've certainly got a lot more um confidence in myself in the last few months and I think that's partly due to our sessions here and partly through a couple of friends boosting me up encouraging me saying "Come on, P, don't keep putting yourself down," . . . taken an awful lot of that. It is like brainwashing, isn't it? Like I said earlier—you have years and years and years of being slapped down slapped down told you're useless stupid and all that stuff and it takes a long time to sort of work your way out of that.

In summary, a number of interesting patterns emerged from the intensive analysis of the development of core metaphor themes in brief therapy sessions. Firstly, it is quite clear from the examples selected from the therapy sessions that both the client and therapist coconstructed and elaborated the *"WAR"* theme.   The various components of this metaphor scenario used throughout the therapy sessions—*"the Fight," "Battles," "Brainwashed," "Beaten," "Painful," "Slapped Down," "Struggle," "To lose," "Battleground," "Throwing Up Our Hands," "Giving Up," "Competition," "Taking and Getting Advantages," "Winning"*—are all interconnected to the core theme. By remaining within this metaphor scenario, client and therapist build a shared network of meanings and develop a sense of shared purpose and focus in the therapy relationship.   Both of these outcomes are essential ingredients of what psychotherapy researchers term a working therapeutic alliance (Horvath & Greenberg, 1994).

Secondly, it appears that the intensive analysis of the development of the *"THE WAR"* theme provides a fascinating window into the steps involved in the client's eventual decision to let go of a longstanding abusive relationship. By tracing the development of the metaphor scenario in the therapy sessions we can track the client's growing awareness that loving relationships can be rewarding and collaborative, not competitive.   Additionally, a significant conceptual and experiential shift occurred for the client when she reframed the notion of life as a constant struggle, in which self-respect and love must be won from others, to the notion that challenges in life can be grounded in self-chosen pleasurable activities which are intrinsically, not extrinsically, rewarded and rewarding. In essence, the client realized that undertaking challenges can lead to pleasurable, not painful experiences and more importantly, she began to feel that she is simply deserving of respect from others and does not need to earn their love for her.

In conclusion, a few tentative recommendations can be made on the basis of the findings from this intensive single-case analysis of metaphor theme. For psychotherapy researchers, the selective analysis of recurring metaphor themes may be a particularly productive and meaningful method for tracing both the development of productive working alliances in therapy relationships as well as for tracing the specific conceptual and experiential stages entailed in the successful resolution of longstanding interpersonal problems.

In terms of treatment implications, it would be fascinating to trace whether shifts in core metaphor phrases are correlated with shifts in problem resolution as identified by clients and therapists in session evaluation reports. It would appear that an empathic attunement to client's metaphoric construals may be a particulary productive activity for practicing psychotherapists. Initially, the client's elaboration of experiences connected to the metaphor scenario seem to be of particular importance for the development of a shared sense of meaning and understanding between client and therapist. Throughout the middle phases of therapy the reuse of the metaphor scenario to connect new relationship episodes leads to the development of a shared focus in the therapy relationship and what I am terming a "core metaphor theme." In the later stages of the therapy it is the therapists' and clients' reflexive analysis, reframing and reconceptualizing of the original metaphor scenario in light of new evidence which appears to play an important role in the resolution of interpersonal problems.

As evidenced in the foregoing therapeutic interaction, it appears that a crucial factor in achieving resolutions to longstanding conflicts is the reframing and understanding of new possibilities inherent in the original metaphor scenario. In the therapy relationship under consideration, the client discovered that she could choose to either try to continue the war or choose to leave the battleground completely. To extend the metaphor, it is as if she chose the liberating option of becoming a conscientious objector in *"THE WAR"* with her husband. This step in turn led to the eventual rejection of the idea that relationships must be cast in terms of winning or losing propositions and facilitated the emergence of a new, more satisfying conceptualization of human relationships.

In terms of future research directions, the identification, tracking, and characterization of metaphor themes in sequential therapy sessions would seem to be a promising direction for future empirical studies. To this end, McMullen (1994) has demonstrated that figurative expressions selected from psychotherapy sessions can be reliably identified and categorized using an Interpersonal Circumplex Model (Kiesler, 1985). The challenge for future researchers will be to find methodological strategies which maintain the contextual richness of the phenomenon as researchers undertake empirical analyses which can lead to the identification of general properties and processes of metaphorical meaning making in psychotherapy.

ACKNOWLEDGMENTS

I would like to acknowledge the contribution of Rebecca Pedersen and Heather Lawrence to this manuscript. I would also like to acknowledge the generous support of the Nordic Association for Advanced Study (NorFa) for the support of a symposium on Semiosis in Psychotherapy (Joensuu, Finland), which stimulated the development of central ideas presented in this chapter.

REFERENCES

Angus, L. (1992). Metaphor and the communication interaction in psychotherapy: A multimethodological approach. In S. Toukmanian & D. Rennie (Eds.), *Psychotherapeutic change: Theory-guided and descriptive research strategies* (pp. 187–210). Newbury Park, CA: Sage.

Angus, L., & Hardtke, K. (1994). Narrative processes in psychotherapy. *Canadian Psychology, 35,* 190–203.

Angus, L., Hardtke, K., Pedersen, R., & Grant, K. (1991). *Metaphor in dynamic therapy: A dual code approach.* Paper presented at the meeting of the Society for Psychotherapy Research, Lyon, France.

Angus, L., & Lawrence, H. (1993). An intensive analysis of metaphor themes in brief dynamic therapy. In J. S. Mio (Chair), *Metaphor: Cognition and application.* Symposium presented at the 101st annual convention of the American Psychological Association, Toronto, Canada.

Angus, L. & Rennie, D. (1988). Therapist participation in metaphor generation: Collaborative and non-collaborative styles. *Psychotherapy, 25,* 552–560.

Angus, L. & Rennie, D. (1989). Envisioning the representational world: The client's experience of metaphoric expression in psychotherapy. *Psychotherapy, 26,* 372–379.

Beck, A., Ward, C., & Mendelson, M. (1961). An inventory for measuring depression. *Archives of General Psychiatry, 4,* 461–471.

Brooks, R. (1985). The beginning sessions of child therapy: Of messages and metaphors. *Psychotherapy, 22,* 761–769.

Derogatis, L. (1983). BSI administration and procedures: Manual 1. *Clinical Psychometric Research.* Towson, MD: Clinical Psychometric Research.

Horvath, A., & Greenberg, L. (1994). *The working alliance: Theory, research, and practice.* New York: Wiley.

Kiesler, D. (1985). *The 1982 interpersonal circle: Acts version.* Unpublished manuscript, Virginia Commonwealth University, Richmond.

Lakoff, G., & Johnson, M. (1980). *Metaphors we live by.* Chicago: University of Chicago Press.

McMullen, L. (1989). Use of figurative language in successful and unsuccessful cases of psychotherapy: Three comparisons. *Metaphor and Symbolic Activity, 4,* 203–225.

McMullen, L. (1994). Dominance and nurturance in the figurative expressions of psychotherapy clients. *Psychotherapy Research, 4,* 43–57.

Pedersen, R. (1991). *Metaphor in short-term dynamic psychotherapy: A preliminary analysis.* Unpublished Honour's Thesis.

Pollio, H., & Barlow, J. (1975). A behavioral analysis of figurative language in psychotherapy: One session in a single case study. *Language and Speech, 18,* 236–254.

Shell, J., Pollio, H., & Smith, M. (1987). Metaphor as mitsein: Therapeutic possibilities in figurative speaking. In R. E. Haskell (Ed.), *Cognition and symbolic structures: The psychology of metaphoric transformation.* Norwood, NJ: Ablex.

Siegelman, E. (1990). *Metaphor and meaning in psychotherapy.* London: Guilford.

Stiles, W., & Shapiro, D. (1994). Disabuse of the drug metaphor: Psychotherapy process-outcome correlations. *Journal of Consulting and Clinical Psychology, 62,* 942–948.

Weissman, M., & Bothwell, S. (1976). Assessment of social adjustment by patient self-report. *Archives of General Psychiatry, 33,* 1111–1115.

6

Metaphors in Child Custody Mediation: Utilizing Symbolic Language to Facilitate Agreements

Anne M. Rose
Mediation and Investigative Services
Superior Court of the State of California
County of Orange

The practice of mediation, an alternative form of dispute resolution, has recently increased in usage and application in many fields, particularly in the settlements of divorce and child custody disputes. The origin of mediation can be traced to ancient historical traditions. Mediation has evolved into a multi-faceted process, which in the case of divorce disputes, combines aspects of therapy or counseling, legal information, and negotiation processes in the settlement of problems with complex emotional and psychological facets.

In order to understand the development of what may be considered a relatively new derivative form of dispute resolution, a survey of the history of mediation is useful. The concept of negotiating family problems, according to Irving and Benjamin (1987), probably originated in China, Japan, Korea, and Ceylon under the influence of Confucianism. "Confucius (K'ung Fu-tzu, c. 550-479 B.C.), Chinese scholar and philosopher, emphasized persuasion and agreement as adjuncts to the natural harmony in human affairs" (Irving & Benjamin, 1987, p. 46).

The practice of dispute resolution has continued into modern times in the People's Republic of China and in Japan. The origins of mediation can also be traced to Judaism, specifically to the Beth Din, the Jewish religious court, which continues in the Israeli legal system today (Irving & Benjamin, 1987). Finally, the African "moot court," a tribal meeting in which issues were

85

resolved through the intervention of the "big man" or tribal chief or notable, served as another historical forerunner of modern dispute resolution (Irving & Benjamin, 1987; Milne, 1986).

Other more institutionalized types of dispute resolution developed with the changing demographics of the modern industrial society in the United States. "The Los Angeles County Conciliation Court, for example, was established in 1939 and was originally dedicated towards marital reconciliation" (Irving & Benjamin, 1987, p. 46). Around 1962, under the leadership of Meyer Elkin, the focus in the Los Angeles County Conciliation Court shifted to mediation of divorces.

Private sector mediation of a divorce first occurred in the early 1970's. O. J. Coogler, an attorney and counselor considered to be the father of private divorce mediation, conducted his first divorce mediation in 1975 through the Family Mediation Association, an organization that he founded (Coogler, 1978). Other organizations, such as the Academy of Family Mediators and the Association of Family and Conciliation Courts, have developed to address the issues and improve practices in private and court-connected divorce dispute resolution.

The process of mediation involves a neutral third party who works with two or more persons to facilitate the resolution of their dispute (Coogler, 1978; Emery & Wyer, 1987; Payne & Overend, 1990). By identifying the issues to be resolved, structuring the interactions between the parties, and maintaining a neutral stance, the cooperative process of mediation facilitates the mutual decision-making of the parties. Confidentiality within the process is also considered a necessary element and is often mandated by law (Payne & Overend, 1990). In some public sector practices of child custody mediation, the mediator is authorized by legislation and local court rules to recommend a decision to the court for custody disputes which are unresolved by the parties' efforts in mediation.

Mediation is not marital therapy, but it is one facet of the multifaceted process that a divorcing couple experiences, and it can assist them in resolving marital and parental relationship issues. Mediation differs from therapy in its goals, although at times, therapeutic results may be seen as by-products of the mediation session. The task in child custody mediation is to effect a resolution of parenting conflicts and issues in order to create a structure that defines the parenting responsibilities in the newly changed family structure (Milne, 1986). The benefits of mediation have been considered by many to be numerous. Mediation employs a problem-solving approach instead of the adversarial approach of the legal system, reduces interpersonal conflict, reduces additional future re-litigation, saves time and money, and most importantly for the parties involved, is a process of self-determination (Emery & Wyer, 1987; Saposnck, 1983).

Parents experiencing divorce and child custody mediation may engage in the process through private or public sector service delivery. The major difference between the sectors rests in the mandate held by court-connected programs. After California legislated "no-fault" divorce in 1970 and other states followed suit, accompanying legislation or local court policies have introduced mediation to the divorce and child custody process nationally (Emery & Wyer, 1987). Mandatory mediation became law in California in 1981 for custody and visitation disputes. The law (California Civil Code, Section 4607) proposed that mediation should reduce parental acrimony, develop an agreement that was in the best interests of the child, and assure the child of close and continuing contact with both parents.

Private sector mediation differs from public sector mediation in the voluntary participation of the parties and the flexibility of the mediation agenda. In the private sector, wider range of issues can be mediated, including child and spousal support, property settlement and division of community property debts, in addition to child custody issues. Private sector clients are involved in a lengthier process with potentially more mediation sessions. Private sector clients also incur expenses in the fee for service process.

Divorce and child custody mediation is different than marriage counseling or psychotherapy because of its goals and outcomes. Developing and finalizing a fair agreement, as mutually defined by the parties (parents), is the goal of mediation. Parties interested in reconciliation may propose terms for an agreement that would move the couple toward a renewal of their marital relationship. Mediators deal with emotionally laden, highly charged psychological issues, as do therapists. In public sector mediation, the clients' presenting problems may be more complex than those of clients in the private sector. For example, court-based mediators probably see a more diverse client population from a far wider range of economic and social backgrounds than do private sector mediators. As Irving and Benjamin (1987) noted in their court-based study, a proportionately larger group in their sample had problems of spousal abuse, alcoholism, and/or drug addiction. It should be noted that clients with undiagnosed or untreated mental illness were more likely to appear in court-based mediation settings.

The mediator needs to address these issues in the context of their impact on the conflicts between the parties and the safety concerns for both parents and child(ren). Resolution of these issues in negotiation often leads to the problem being addressed through negotiated solutions that are incorporated into the final settlement or agreement. The language of these agreements creates a figurative commitment by the parties to acting cooperatively and in good faith to uphold the personalized parameters of their settlement. Also, the agreement on paper becomes symbolic of their mutual goal to work together in a newly defined relationship as parents.

The mediation process is centered on problem-solving or creating solutions. Milne (1986) stated "[M]ediation does not focus on obtaining insight into the history of conflict, nor does it attempt to change personality patterns . . . mediation is not treatment. No diagnoses are made, and the parties do not analyze past behavior but reach agreement that provides for the future" (p. 200).

However, as Milne (1986) noted, the definition of divorce mediation is determined by the participants, the mediator, and the setting. Discussion and settlement of financial issues may not be seen as therapeutic, whereas negotiating parenting responsibilities and visitation issues may be.

MODELS OF MEDIATION

There is little agreement as to any one model or style of mediation as being the best suited to ensuring the outcome of a successful process and the development of a parenting agreement or settlement (Coogler, 1978; Emery & Wyer, 1987; Folberg & Milne, 1988; Haynes & Haynes, 1989; Milne, 1986; Payne & Overend, 1990; Saposnek, 1983).

The qualifications and training of the mediator influence the way in which mediation is practiced. Private sector practitioners are usually mental health professionals such as marriage and family counselors, clinical social workers, and psychologists. Perhaps 15% of mediators are attorneys (Kressel, 1985). Professional mediators may view their role as requiring a mixture of specialized skills. According to Haynes & Haynes (1989), one-third of the skills are taught in law school, one-third in graduate mental health programs, and one-third of these skills are unique to both fields not taught in either field.

The mediator's professional training usually lends a special focus to or emphasizes a particular model for the mediation process.

> Mediators whose expertise lies in psychoanalysis are more likely to adhere to a therapeutic model in which marital history and the family of origin are regarded as particularly significant in the search for solutions to current problems. Marriage counselors of a traditional persuasion who perceive their function as involving a "reconciliation" as well as a "conciliation" process may also look to the past in order to plan for the future. Social workers or family therapists, whose practice has centered on short term crisis counseling may be inclined to focus on the present and future, rather than on the distant past. Lawyers/mediators tend to emphasize a pragmatic approach to the resolution of the economic and parenting consequences of separation and divorce. (Payne & Overend, 1990, p. 27)

For a specialized aspect of mediation, such as working with resolution of child custody disputes, the mediator must have a repertoire of skills beyond general negotiation. These include knowledge of child development, children's responses to parental conflict, family dynamics, the various structures and schedules which benefit different ages, and psychological functioning (Saposnek, 1983).

STAGES OF DIVORCE

As noted, the process of mediation is one in which clients are self-determining in that the decision-making process is a function of the participants' mutual agreement on the issues (Neville, 1989). The ability to generate one's own solutions to personal family problems seems to enhance the likelihood of future success in implementation of the plan. This theory is borne out in assessing client satisfaction. For example, parents who developed their own plans were much more satisfied with those plans than were parents who were given a court-determined plan to implement (Slater, Shaw, & Duquesnel, 1992).

However, the complex array of emotional and psychological issues which may be intertwined with the parents' marital conflict often impede resolution of disputes and the design of parenting plans. The mediator needs to assess how the individual parties are progressing through the emotional stages of divorce. The loss of a marital relationship triggers intense feelings of grief and loss, which parallels Kübler-Ross' (1969) stages of grief over death and dying. The emotional stages are seldom experienced discretely or separately, and the parties rarely experience the same emotional stage(s) at the same time. If one party wishes reconciliation while the other party has decided the marriage is over, the bargaining/settlement process may be disrupted.

As Saposnek (1983) stated, "Among the many different feelings experienced are hurt, rejection, anger, loneliness, depression, anxiety, lowered self-esteem, and guilt. Although many of these emotions are transitory, there is a great deal of individual variation from one person to another in terms of the intensity and duration of each of these feelings" (p. 135).

In order for the mediator to successfully intervene in ways that foster cooperation between the parties, the structure of the session must be established. As Kressel (1985) explained, the mediator's task is "establishing a productive negotiating climate and addressing the substantive issues" (p. 179). The context or setting is also a determinant of the structure of the process. Although mandatory and voluntary mediation contrast in terms of the basis for participation, the mediator in either setting can discuss with the couple the options available for conflict resolution. As Milne (1986) noted, this reviewing of options helps clients to evaluate their commitment to mediation, and thus, if they choose to continue, negotiate their first point of agreement.

This sets the stage for the couple to become consumers in the mediation process. It is a symbolic experience of settling on mutuality. If clients are neither interested in nor committed to the process in order to attempt to negotiate, then they are not "customers" interested in obtaining the benefits of the process/service. Clients who do not or cannot consciously ascertain their committment to the process, and who do not discuss their options in conflict resolution, will usually resist agreeing to and effecting a final settlement.

ROLES IN THE MEDIATION PROCESS

In thinking of clients as "consumers," it is helpful to view the mediator not as a "salesperson," but rather someone in the role of "consultant" or "facilitator." Milne (1986) viewed the role as one held by an expert and compared it to the role of a sports coach who brings in plays and strategies to assist the players' game.

The mediator prepares the clients for the process by educating them on the parameters of negotiation. This includes clarifying the mediator's role, establishing what can be negotiated in the setting, the time frames, etc. Irving and Benjamin (1987) stated that there is a wide disagreement on the stages in the mediation process, ranging in number from 12 stages to 5 stages. They defined 5 stages as follows: (1) Introduction—information giving and eliciting a committment to the mediation process; (2) some form of assessment combined with delineation of the issues in dispute; (3) working through these issues through negotiation between the spouses and with assistance from the mediator; (4) nailing down and completing a final agreement; and (5) vetting of the agreement by the spouses' lawyers, and final signing of the agreement. In addition, Irving and Benjamin mention two other stages, "one in the form of therapeutic intervention following assessment—typically towards preparing one or both spouses for the rigors of negotiation—and either some routine form of follow-up or return to mediation if some aspect of the agreement causes later problems" (p. 52).

In opening discussion of the process, the mediator as consultant can facilitate the release of emotional tension when the parties express uncertainty as to how they can develop or formulate a schedule that is developmentally appropriate for their children. As a consultant, the mediator shares information from child psychologists and child development specialists about developmental guidelines for when parents will have the child(ren) going between two homes. Sometimes, referring to the parents as the "experts" on what is best for their offspring seems to ease tension. Other interventions might be supportive and even humorous, such as saying "Well, babies aren't delivered with an instruction manual," so that learning how to parent and finding out what is best for their child becomes a "trial and error" process.

The tasks of the mediation process can be guided by a formal structure such as written rules (Coogler, 1978) to specify exactly what can be addressed in the mediation. Public sector mediators, especially in mandatory mediation settings, have the tasks or issues clearly defined by statute, court rules, and the legal filings of the parties. For example, in California, court-based mediators work with child custody and visitation issues. Local court rules determine whether or not the mediator may recommend a custody and visitation plan to the court if the parents do not reach an agreement in mediation.

Once the parameters have been set in defining the issues to mediate, the mediator also begins to learn what might be in dispute. Typically, the parties will identify what they hope for as an outcome or solution to the dispute rather than identifying the issues in dispute, saying "What I want is just what is fair and equal—50-50 custody." Or a parent might say, "I want the children to live in a stable environment with me and see their father on weekends."

These types of statements reveal the party's positions on the issues. They do not state the issue itself. Positional bargaining does not address the underlying interests or concerns of the parties. Fisher and Ury (1983) suggested "principled negotiation" or "negotiation on the merits" by defining the points of negotiation: "People: Separate the people from the problem. Interests: Focus on interests, not positions. Options: Generate a variety of options before deciding what to do. Criteria: Insist the result be based on some objective standard" (p. 11).

Milne (1986) suggested that the mediator's task is one of organizing and validating topical issues (division of property, visitation, etc.), personal issues (internal conflicts and concerns), and relational issues (accumulated unresolved marital-divorce issues). These personal and relationship issues may become focal points overshadowing the topical issues. Saposnek (1983) postulated that the mediator's most significant intervention in developing cooperation between the parties is through controlling each phase of mediation. Further, agreements on topical issues require a minimum amount of trust between the parties. As Saposnek explained, mistrust needs to be accepted by the mediator as a given premise from the start of the mediation process. Mistrust cannot be argued against logically.

METAPHORS AND MEDIATION

In some cases, the inability of clients to acknowledge mistrust as causing their unsuccessful negotiations can be addressed metaphorically. The use of indirect figurative language may create an opportunity to open discussion and frame options for developing trust.

According to Combs and Freedman (1990, pp. 20–21), the skilled use of indirection facilitates therapy in several ways:

1. It allows therapists to bypass reflexive objections of clients.
2. It allows therapists to test client's responses to ideas without calling attention to them.
3. It allows therapists to build a careful foundation before being direct.
4. It encourages active mental search on the part of clients, which in turn:
    a. develops access to forgotten resources,
    b. stimulates new associative pathways,
    c. gives clients a greater sense of creativity in and responsibility for the therapy process.

The mediator, then, similar to the therapist can indirectly help parents to develop trust and work together. The central metaphor *"PARENTS ARE BUSINESS PARTNERS"* offers the introduction of several possible figures or symbols of developing co-parenting relationships (Ricci, 1980). Examples of metaphorical phrases describing this relationship might be *"parents are in a business together," "your child is the most important product of your relationship," "investments in the child are the focus of your relationship,"* and similar statements.

A more involved action metaphor or story might include comparing the parenting relationship to a bank account in which both parents have responsibility as account-holders. The central metaphor *"PARENTS HOLD A MUTUAL BANK ACCOUNT"* is another symbol of a co-parenting relationship. The conflicts of the marital-divorce relationship may have placed that *"bank account"* in an *"overdrawn"* status because of behaviors that have reduced the balance of trust and other positive feelings. If the level of mistrust between the parties is seen as being overdrawn, thus depleting the balance, the couple can *"make deposits"* toward rebuilding the balance in their parenting *"account."* These *"deposits"* can be quantified by exploring with each parent the kinds of behaviors that each would accept from the other as helping rebuild the trust in their relationship.

METAPHORS OF ENTRENCHMENT

When parents present competing proposals for resolving a custody battle (particularly in cases where each parent wants sole custody of the child) a central metaphor addressing the rivalry, competition, and energy involved may be helpful in moving the negotiations towards a more mutual solution. *"A CUSTODY BATTLE IS LIKE A FOOTBALL GAME BETWEEN RIVAL TEAMS"* is a metaphor that can illustrate the futility of parental rivalry. The parents become members of *"opposing teams"* and the child(ren) feel like a *"football"* that is symbolically carried to and fro, kicked back and forth by each parent and perhaps others such as attorneys and relatives, so that a *"goal"* can eventually be *"scored"* by one parent. Comparing the behaviors between the parties to the *"rivalry"* between teams points out the hostility and animosity of the *"game"* in that one side typically loses when a child becomes a pawn between adversaries. If either parent indicates a refusal to modify his/her position, the mediator can discuss how much time, preparation, and practice is required for a *"football player"* to participate in the game. Implying that a parent must be ready to play and participate suggests the potential demands and stresses on a parent who desires or elects to continue the *"sport."*

Frequently, a mediation session can evolve into a deadlock between parents on how to resolve a particular issue. The deadlock or impasse sometimes occurs prior to generating solutions or options for an issue. Couples can be unwilling to participate in discussion of future-oriented solutions, preferring to engage in repetitive, unproductive complaining. Or, the impasse can result from the parties' inability to agree on a single mutually acceptable solution. Arguing over the merits of a position or refusing to agree on a solution-driven outcome also results from the parents' repetition of old patterns of interaction as a couple. Marina Nichols, a supervisor in the Mediation and Investigative Services Department, suggests that a central metaphor describing the lack of momentum in this interaction could be *"AN IMPASSE IN NEGOTIATION IS LIKE A CAR THAT'S STUCK IN MUD."* Explaining that attempts to *"step on the accelerator"* and *"spinning the wheels,"* and just getting further *"stuck in the mud"* illustrate the futility of escalating the conflict using old, unsuccessful approaches. In order for a *"car stuck in the mud"* to *"move forward,"* it must *"get traction"* through a measured and calculated process. This is done by putting the transmission in forward and reverse gears, gathering momentum in a rocking motion. The process of *"grounding"* to find a *"centerpoint of gravity"* suggests that parents might go both forward and back, to and fro, in the development of solutions to effect a mutually satisfying momentum rather than applying a singular unidirectional force to their process.

Another central metaphor relating to the mediation process is the focus on the adversarial nature of the court system and the litigation process and the theme *"GOING TO COURT IS WAGING WAR AGAINST THE OTHER PARENT."* One of my colleagues, J. Robin Powell, often explains to clients that the court setting is *"a place where people throw stones at each other"* and where each party, especially if represented by legal counsel, *"wages war"* at the other party's emotional and psychological expense. These *"casualties"* and *"wounds"* are deeply felt and often hard to heal, setting the stage for future battles of an even costlier nature.

Besides the image of *"the courtroom is a battlefield"* is the central metaphor of *"MEDIATION IS A PEACEFUL WAY OF RESOLVING CONFLICT."* Contrasting the settings of court and mediation can ease tension between the parties and defuse many of the positional and adversarial comments that parents may have made in response to a pending hearing on contested litigation. The more cooperative aspect of mediation and the neutral setting are empowering to parents and support the goal of generating mutually acceptable, self-determined solutions for settlement.

Another metaphor which describes the competitive aspects of custody and visitation disputes centers on *"court litigation is a contest to decide which is the better parent"* (Ricci, 1980). This would seem to have as its root metaphor the idea that the whole process is a *"GAME."* Often, parents feel that they are trying to impress the court that their abilities, qualities, and experience are superior to the other parent's. The mediator reframes the competitive aspects of parents' statements with the metaphor that *"parenting is not a contest,"* and affirms the unique contributions each parent has for the child(ren)'s development to succeed and for the parent-child relationship to flourish. It is also helpful to emphasize, in the framework where parents express their competitiveness, that the child will undoubtedly be *"the loser"* if the parents' focus remains on *"the game to see who can be the better parent."*

USEFUL MEDIATION METAPHORS

In some cases, the stress and strain of parental conflict is directly visible in the behavior of one or all of the children involved. In a bitter and conflicted divorce, the child(ren) may manifest symptoms of distress in "acting out behaviors," depression, school problems, experimentation with drugs/alcohol, regressive behavior, problems in sleeping and eating, and even violent behavior towards siblings and authority figures. During the mediation session, one parent may discuss at length the child(ren)'s difficulties and attempt to enlist the other parent's cooperation in an intervention to help the child(ren). However, the parents together may be unable to agree on a plan to resolve the child(ren)'s crisis. When parents appear immobilized in their decision-making for the child(ren) in distress, or appear polarized in their choice of options, it falls to the mediator to help the parties mobilize for decisive action.

To impart a sense of urgency to the settlement process, a central metaphor of *"YOUR CHILD(REN)'S HEALTH IS AT RISK"* creates an impetus for treatment of the problem. Describing to the parents how the child appears to be *"in an emergency situation,"* just as if *"they are lying on the emergency room table"* and parents are being asked by medical personnel if they have permission to treat the child(ren)'s *"critical health problem"* right now imparts urgency and concern to the situation. This *"emergency"* emphasis often breaks the impasse of one parent's resistance to a role in implementing any decision-making that is cooperative in nature with the other parent.

When parents are newly separated, it is likely that one of the parties will continue to ruminate on relational issues, often bringing up past scenarios that generate unhappiness and discomfort for the other parent. If a parent persists in bringing up these issues, it is helpful to intervene by communicating to them how this return to the past interferes with current communication between them. Using the central metaphor *"SEPARATION AND DIVORCE CREATE A PAINFUL WOUND,"* the mediator can advise the parent that bringing up these historical issues is *"like picking off a scab covering an unhealed wound.* " Unless the parent deliberately desires to inflict pain, he/she will usually respond by eliminating further references to historical issues and will move on to the task of negotiating.

An area of frequent resistance by one or both parents relates to the possibility of generating any successful parenting agreement that will be adhered to by both parties. This interest is an outgrowth of the experiences since separation as frequent confusion and conflict have marred the cooperation on a schedule, and it carries over into efforts at settling on a plan. Many couples will express doubt that they can ever get to a point where they will feel trusting of the other parent's behavior and be willing to follow through on agreements. Using the potential agreement as a symbol, the mediator can help the parents to begin to think of a written, court-ordered plan as a *"guide"* or *"map"* that will bring them to points of mutual trust if they follow the parameters (Ricci, 1980). Implicit here is the central metaphor *"RESOLUTION INVOLVES SECURE BORDERS."* It is reassuring to parents to understand that they cannot individually and arbitrarily *"redraw the map"* to their own specifications once their agreement is entered as a court order.

Since indirection also facilitates association, other concepts can be introduced through the use of metaphors with humorous content. The humor can act as a vehicle for delivering interpretations or interventions that may impact impasse and resistance. For example, during a session that I co-mediated with a colleague, Nick Liberis, the mother expressed her response to the other parent in a metaphorical phrase. The mother appeared overwhelmed with the unexpected acquiescence of her ex-husband to her requests that he modify his lifestyle and enter a substance abuse treatment program. Nick and I were also aware that we were nearing the end of the time allotted for the session. The successful resolution of the agreement hinged on the mother's acceptance of the father's offer. She was quiet for a few moments and then said, *"I feel like I'm in the Twilight Zone."* Her comment underscored the difficulty she was having in accepting the father's unexpected response. Another short silence ensued, and then Nick, jokingly, said, *"Well, it will be time to turn off the T.V. soon."* Both of the parents started laughing. The tension was broken, and the mother was ready to complete the agreement.

On another occasion during a co-mediation with another colleague, David Lynn-Hill, the communication between the parents had become increasingly tense and strained in the session. One parent repeatedly made overtures of conciliation to the other parent, who seemed determined not to acknowledge a *"cease-fire"* and de-escalate obvious verbal hostility. After numerous attempts at reframing the conversation and supporting the conciliatory parent's overtures, David said, *"This brings to mind the image of a dove carrying an olive branch, flying back and forth, getting a sore head from banging it against the wall."* This symbolic interpretation of the conciliatory parent's frustration was acknowledged with a smile by the hostile parent, and the mediation process continued. These humorous metaphors imply that *"DIVORCE IS NOT A LIFE OR DEATH SITUATION,"* and that easing of tensions can be good for the process.

Frequently, the association of one or two words, "the smallest units of metaphor—words, objects, mental images, and the like," according to Combs and Freedman (1990, p. xiv), become a symbol in which the richness of meaning is crystallized. The use of the term "agreement" may be an irritant for one of the parties in a mediation. It holds possible negative emotional connotations due to the power issues in the dyad. So the terms "custody" and "visitation" may also hold negative implications for one parent, symbolizing the loss of his or her position and status in the family and devaluing of his or her role as an equal in the parenting relationship.

In order to neutralize the impact of these terms, other words or phrases can be substituted which become new symbols of the family restructuring. For example, as a reframing of the term "child custody and visitation order," the phrase *"parenting plan"* implies direction and goal orientation. When the child is with either parent, that time frame becomes *"time sharing"* rather than "custody" or "visitation."

CONCLUSION

Mediation in response to conflict resolution has roots in many cultural traditions. Its contemporary applications include the application of dispute resolution, involving negotiation skills, legal information, and techniques and approaches derived from models of counseling and psychotherapy to the resolution of divorce and child custody disputes.

The mediation process facilitates the settlement of interpersonal conflicts and affords the parties a vehicle for self-determination. The benefits of the process may be numerous, particularly as families can problem-solve together rather than litigate against each other.

Private and public sector mediation vary from each other in both setting and agenda. However, both arenas afford parents the opportunity to review highly emotional issues with a professional, neutral party acting as facilitator. The mediator's training and knowledge of issues related to family structure, child development, and psychological functioning provide the parties with important information in developing options for decision making.

The mediator's interventions, couched in their understanding of the dynamics of marital–divorce issues and conflict resolution assist the couple in expressing their interests and options for developing points of agreement. The complex emotional and psychological issues of the dyad in mediation lend themselves to indirect interventions created by the mediator. The use of metaphoric and symbolic language in reframing and facilitating communication can move the parties through impasse and resistance and enhance their opportunities to negotiate mutually agreeable settlements.

REFERENCES

California Civil Code. Section 4607. (1981).

Combs, G., & Freedman, J. (1990). *Symbol, story and ceremony using metaphor in individual and family therapy.* New York: Norton.

Coogler, O. J. (1978). *Structured mediation in divorce settlement.* Lexington, MA: Lexington.

Emery, R. E., & Wyer, M. M. (1987). Divorce mediation. *American Psychologist, 42,* 472–480.

Fisher, R., & Ury, W. (1983). *Getting to yes: Negotiating agreement without giving in.* New York: Penguin.

Folberg, J., & Milne, A. (Eds.). (1988). *Divorce mediation: Theory and practice.* New York: Guilford.

Haynes, J. M., & Haynes, G. (1989). *Mediating divorce: Casebook of strategies for successful family negotiations.* San Francisco: Jossey-Bass.

Irving, H. H., & Benjamin, M. (1987). *Family mediation: Theory and practice of dispute resolution.* Toronto: Carswell.

Kressel, K. (1985). *The process of divorce: How professionals and couples negotiate settlements.* New York: Basic Books.

Kübler-Ross, E. (1969). *On death and dying.* New York: Macmillan.

Milne, A. L. (1986). Divorce mediation: A process of self-definition and self-determination. In N. S. Jacobsen & A. S. Gurman (Eds.), *Clinical handbook of marital therapy* (pp. 197–216). New York: Guilford.

Neville, W. G. (1989). Mediation. In M. Textor (Ed.), *The divorce and divorce therapy handbook* (pp. 103–122). Northvale, NJ: Aronson.

Payne, J. D., & Overend, E. (1990). Divorce mediation: Process and strategies, an overview. *Family and Conciliation Courts Review, 28,* 27–34.

Ricci, I. (1980). *Mom's house, dad's house.* New York: Collier Books.

Saposnek, D. T. (1983). *Mediating child custody disputes.* San Francisco: Jossey-Bass.

Slater, A., Shaw, J. A., & Duquesnel, J. (1992). Client satisfaction survey: A consumer evaluation of mediation and investigative services, executive summary. *Family and Conciliation Courts Review, 30,* 252–259.

7

The Mental Image of the Human Body: Implications of Physiological Mental Models of our Understanding of Health and Illness

William P. Banks
Suzanne C. Thompson
Pomona College, Claremont, California

As we begin this chapter on metaphors of health and the human body we are reminded of Sontag's (1978) caution that, despite a rich literary and cultural tradition of metaphors for illness, illness itself is not a metaphor, but a real biological event with real biological consequences. Her warning is needed. As this chapter shows, people are incorrigible users of metaphors in thinking about sickness and health and the workings of the body, so much so that even our interpretation of biological events is infused with metaphorical thinking that owes little to scientific findings.

The anthropological study of medical beliefs shows that, although there is a broad array of cultural conceptions of disease and illness, people from all societies possess cultural norms that define categories of illness and disease and that signal when a condition is classified as a disorder requiring medical attention. These same norms are used in the negotiation of treatment and the definition of cure when an individual is seen by a medical practitioner. Practitioners of modern scientific medicine have acquired a set of concepts, and a whole treatment theory, that differs from the folk concepts of most potential patients and that is discordant in many ways. Not surprisingly, then, physicians and their patients come to have markedly different ways of viewing disease and illness (Barnlund, 1976). As Mishler (1984) put it, "The medical interview may be viewed as an arena of struggle between the natural attitude with its common sense lifeworld and the scientific attitude with its objectified world of abstract logic and rationality . . . I am proposing an interpretation of the medical interview as a situation of conflict between two ways of constructing meaning" (p. 123).

It is very much in the interests of both doctor and patient that information be accurately transmitted in both directions between the two of them. Such accuracy is needed to make sure that the diagnosis is accurate and that the patient will understand and remember the course of treatment and his or her role in it. If recall of instructions given in a medical consultation is accurate, patients are three times as likely to comply with the prescribed regimen (Svarstad, 1976). Communication between physician and patient is, however, often problematic. A large percentage (from 35% to 87%) of patients do not understand prescription instructions (Ley, 1983) and many report that they desire more information from their physician (Pendleton & Hasler, 1983). Patients, in fact, report more dissatisfaction with the information they receive than with any other aspect of a medical visit (Cartwright, 1983).

There are, undoubtedly, many factors that affect the quality of physician–patient communication, including poor communication skills on the part of physicians, patient anxiety, and the emotional tone of the interaction. Here we consider another factor that may also contribute to miscommunication between practitioners and patients—the patient's model of how the body functions. Doctors and patients often have very different conceptions of the anatomical position of bodily organs and different interpretations of commonly used medical terms (Boyle, 1970). Patients can appear to have the understanding the physician intends to communicate because both members in the conversation often use the same terms. However, with a different understanding of the terms the patient can appear to be noncompliant or can disastrously mismanage the treatment.

We find an excellent example of this sort of miscommunication in the literature on blood pressure management. One reason for the high frequency of noncompliance seems to be the belief of many patients that they can tell when their blood pressure is high (Bauman & Leventhal, 1985). One reason for the persistence of the belief that high blood pressure has symptoms and therefore must be detectable by the patient may be the underlying concept that pain is an indicator of damage to the body. If there is no pain (no apparent symptom) there is no damage. When no ill consequences in the form of symptoms are felt after doses are missed or reduced, patients would see no intuitive reason not to reduce the dose further or stop it altogether. The noncompliance is thus permitted because of the meaning of pain in the patient's mental model of the body.

This chapter investigates naive conceptions of how the cardiovascular system works and what causes it to malfunction. The approach taken here derives from the mental model literature (cf. Gentner & Stevens, 1983, for a broad selection of articles from this research). A "mental model" is itself a theoretical model, constructed by the investigator to account for the predictions subjects make about physical events. The physical events that constitute the domain of these models have generally been taken from physics, mechanics, electricity, or chemistry. The subjects in most of this research are not experts or professionals working in the domain under study; the intent is to understand the "folk" theories of people who have not learned the relevant scientific model. When experts are studied the intent is to understand and possibly formalize the model that underlies their expertise.

We concentrated on the cardiovascular system. Some specialization was needed because the body as a whole is clearly too large a system to tackle in an initial project. We chose the cardiovascular system because it has a structure that is, at some level, understandable in terms of physical relations among pipes and tubes carrying fluid and thus may lend itself easily to an analysis based on mental model research. Another reason is simply practical. Cardiovascular disease remains the leading cause of death in the U.S., and it is a disease strongly influenced by risk factors directly under the individual's control. These factors include diet, exercise, weight control, and smoking. One reason why more people do not control these risk factors may be that their mental models of cardiovascular disease do not have roles for these factors.

In this chapter, we examine only the "folk" models of nonexperts. The simple metaphors for understanding the cardiovascular system that lay people possess may be limited in utility and misleading when compared with complex and scientifically informed expert models. Although expert models are not the subject of this research, we need to refer to these models for comparison to naive models. However, the expert model of the complete cardiovascular system would be so complex that we cannot hope to characterize it here, and it is doubtful that more than a few, if any, experts can be assumed to keep a complete model of the cardiovascular system in mind when addressing questions about it. According to one physiologist, "The number of variables involved in cardiovascular function is so great, the regulation in living animals so efficient, that it is difficult to grasp the quantitative relation of any single element in the system to all the others" (Milnor, 1990, p. 18). In comparing the lay metaphors to scientific models, we have confined ourselves to well-established and relatively simple facts about the cardiovascular system. When some of the physiological processes included complex processes, as, for example, in factors that control blood pressure or the process of build-up of atherosclerotic plaque, we only researched as much scientific evidence as was necessary for evaluating the lay understanding of the process. As it turned out, not a single respondent made assertions about processes that forced us to consider any of the more esoteric aspects of the system, and the scientific comparison with the lay models was relatively simple medical models.

Readers interested in expert models and in attempts to create intuitive models of aspects of the cardiovascular system in a scientifically accurate manner may find Milnor (1990) of interest. Milnor frequently used physical models to illustrate how parts of the system function. He found models that represent the process accurately and that allow the reader to see the process in physical terms. For example, he described the Windkessel model, devised by Stephen Hales in the early 18th centrury (Fishman & Richards, 1964). This model explains how the discontinuous pumping action of the heart results in the relatively smooth flow of blood in the system. It likens the heart to the pump on an old-fashioned fire engine that fills an air compression chamber, the output of which is the more steady pressure on the stream of water. The model illustrates the interaction of arterial elasticity, resistance, and one-way flow in the circulatory system, and it forms an easily imaged and serviceable mental model. On the other hand, physical models of parts of the system that involve nonlinear interactions among various effects; for example, the control of blood pressure or the flow of blood through capillaries, are not easily captured by mental models and very difficult even for the experts to imagine. When the system is studied in its entirety and interactions among these more complex systems must be considered, it is clear that a mental model can be used only at a superficial level.

In our investigation of the conceptions people have of physiology and medicine we wanted to determine whether these conceptions are proper models or just loosely related beliefs. To make this distinction we need a working definition of a model, one that can successfully contrast it with a set of beliefs that may be unordered or, at best, associatively rather than logically organized. Of the various properties a model should have, we consider the following most central:

1. *Parsimony.* The model must contain a set of basic propositions smaller than the number of propositions applicable to the domain of the model.
2. *Structure.* There should be basic principles, a mechanism for generating predictions, and a way of identifying appropriate data. In contrast, a purely associative model connects causes and effects with no intervening mechanism, but by their degree of associative relation.
3. *Coherence.* The basic concepts must be at least superficially consistent; an obvious inconsistency between propositions A and B would require a choice between them. Purely associative structures can, on the other hand, have internal inconsistencies.
4. *Productivity.* A model must be able to cover new cases. While an isolated proposition retrieved from memory may "extend" to cover a new case by superficial similarity, extensions of a model come from predictions based on underlying structure rather than superficial resemblance.

While these four properties abstractly characterize a theoretical model, they also provide empirical diagnostic criteria to determine whether a subject's beliefs can be considered to form a model. The first two can be applied to models as revealed in questionnaires of interviews with subjects. For example, a subject's model should yield to descriptions by a few principles (parsimony), and these principles should be recognizable across cases, not changing from case to case (structure).

Coherence should also be observable in models taken from protocols. In addition, they provide a basis for using differences between subjects' reports to test whether they are based on a model structure or on a list of independent propositions. For deductions from the model, we should find a chain of reasoning based on the abstract properties of the model.

The productivity characteristic of models allows us to make diagnostic predictions about the responses of subjects to novel cases and situations. In this aspect of the research the subjects were given questions that should be given one answer by one model and a different answer by others. For example, subjects were told that a fictitious drug X had properties j and k. They then had to decide whether it would raise or lower blood pressure.

Perhaps the most important aspect of mental models is that they provide a schema for the intake and storage of information. A model therefore forms a person's understanding of information—everything from sensory information to information delivered by the media to a physician's advice—and determines what will be remembered, how information will be distorted, and what will be forgotten. We approach this aspect of models in several ways.

In the following section we report the results of our investigations of people's mental models of the cardiovascular system, their understanding of how it can fail, and some consequences of the models for health-related behavior. We emphasize that few models held by individuals have all of the characteristics that, ideally, models should have. Such a high standard represents a goal of description. Models that fall short of this still have the property of providing a mental schema that determines perception, memory, and action, even if it does not have all of the characteristics of the ideal, complete model.

STUDY 1: QUALITATIVE DESCRIPTIONS OF MODELS OF THE CARDIOVASCULAR SYSTEM

In our initial investigation we asked 26 Pomona College students (12 male, 14 female, mean age 18.9 years) to fill out a questionnaire. They were enrolled in an introductory psychology class and answered the questionnaire individually or in small groups, with the first author available to answer questions. They took from 15 to about 30 minutes to complete it. The main questions are listed in Table 7.1.

To determine the models we first read the protocols and came up with a number of hypotheses. As discussed above, the "mental model" is itself a model, inferred by the researcher, that accounts for the observations and reports given by the subjects in interviews and in responses to the questionnaires. We do not "find" the models in the questionnaires; rather, we construct plausible models and test them against the data provided by the respondents. Likewise, we do not depend on the subjects' own theoretical account of the system to determine the mental model. In most cases, we do not find such an account. In all cases, the "mental model" we propose is a result of inference, which is then supported by evidence we draw from the protocols. It is fortunate that subjects often have some insight into their own models and describe them in terms that are similar to those we use. This makes it easier for us to hypothesize models. However, subjects are often unaware of the basis of the deductions they make, and in fact may not realize that they are deductions. It is our objective to draw conclusions from across subjects and find the basis for their judgments, and to propose models when appropriate.

The Basic Plumbing of the Cardiovascular System

The students had a surprisingly consistent conception of the circulatory system in terms of "plumbing." All 26 characterized the heart as a "pump," and all had the blood leaving the heart on one set of vessels and returning on another. Despite this general model, only three mentioned the capillaries as the means by which the blood gets from the arteries to the veins (one additional subject responded that the blood "somehow" gets from one set of vessels in order to return on the other). In a later sample of Buildings and Grounds staff, we found a few respondents who carried the Galenic "ebb and flow" theory by which the blood flows out of the heart and returns on the same vessels on each stroke, but there was no evidence for this sort of model in any responses of these 26 students.

There were a number of differences between the folk models and the scientific model. These differences were suggested by a few characteristic flaws. One of these is a lack of appreciation of the massive parallelism of the circulatory system. Thus, for example, one respondent stated that the blood travels through the brain on the way to the rest of the body. Several others drew diagrams that had the blood feeding each organ in turn.

A second difference between the students' models and physiology was the pulmonary circuit, which many students omitted. Only 10 of the 26 respondents gave diagrams or statements that included the process of oxygenation, and of these only 6 had circulation going through the lungs. The rest had the blood simply returning to the heart and then being pumped back to the body. This is all the more surprising because in the answer to "What is blood for?" 23 of the 26 mentioned carrying of oxygen to the body. Transport of oxygen was the most frequently mentioned function for blood, followed by delivering nutrition (food, vitamins, protein, etc.) (17 of 26), carrying off of wastes (13), providing transport for the immune system (6), distributing hormones (2), and warming the body (1). It seems likely that respondents, in leaving out functions, simply did not complete their models; in addition to a majority not covering the method of oxygenation, none described how the nutrition, hormones, immune components, and so forth were picked up. On the other hand, these may represent gaps in the models that they would have been powerless to fill.

High Blood Pressure and Heart Attack

The subjects' understanding of malfunctions revealed additional details of how they thought the system worked. The two malfunctions about which we queried were high blood pressure and heart attacks. Our review of the answers the subjects gave led us to propose two models of blood pressure, and four models of heart attack.

Table 7.1
Questions 1-12 from Study 1

---

1. What does it mean to say that blood circulates? Be sure to describe the route the blood follows in circulating. Please illustrate with a drawing or diagram.
2. What is blood for? What functions does it play in the body?
3. What is blood pressure?
4. What is high blood pressure?
5. What are some of the symptoms of high blood pressure?
6. List as many factors as you know that cause high blood pressure.
7. For each of these factors explain *how* they cause high blood pressure: What is the *mechanism* in each case?
8. What is a heart attack?
9. What are the symptoms of a heart attack?
10. What are the conditions that would make it more likely that a person would have a heart attack? That is, what are the "risk factors?" Please list as many of these as you can think of.
11. For each response you gave for question 10, please explain the *physiological mechanism* by which the risk factor increases the chance of a heart attack. How does the risk factor operate to damage the heart?
12. Draw a picture showing a healthy artery, then one that has arteriosclerosis. Use cross-sectional diagrams or side views, or both, as illustrations.

Blood Pressure. The models we inferred about blood pressure were based on answers to Question 3 through Question 7 (listed in Table 7.1). Often it was necessary to survey a series of answers to find the best model because the direct answers were incomplete. For example, one respondent answer Question 3 with the ambiguous statement, "Keeps the blood moving." However, answers to the later questions clarified the conception the subject had in mind. In this case the answer to Question 4 was "Blood moves too fast," and one answer to Question 7 was "Stress speeds up the blood." These later answers allowed us to categorize this subject as having a "velocity" theory of blood pressure.

We decided that the subjects carried one of two models of blood pressure: (A) Essentially the *standard biophysical model,* in which blood pressure is the force of the blood against the artery walls, and (B) A *velocity model* in which blood pressure is determined by the rate of flow through the blood vessels. Both models assume an underlying "pump-and-tubing" conception of the circulatory system. Also, all else being constant, a faster blood flow in such a system would translate into higher pressure against the vessel walls; however, these two models are still quite different.

To verify our intuitions, we explained the two categories to two research assistants and asked them to use our definitions of the two models to classify all of the subjects, on the basis of their blood pressure/high blood pressure answers, as conforming to Model A, Model B, both, or indeterminate. We had them perform these judgments independently and then meet to resolve any disagreements. Because this process did not yield any measure of interrater reliability, the first author then also categorized the protocols independently and compared his results with theirs. There were disagreements on 2 of the 26 subjects. In both cases the research assistants had classified these subjects as indeterminate; the first author classified one as A and the other as B, and these were kept in the results reported here.

One major difference between the two models is the manner in which malfunctions might occur. The velocity model has no explanation for the role of salt in high blood pressure, nor for the effect of narrowing of the arteries with atherosclerotic deposits. Individuals who possess the velocity theory have limited mechanisms to use to select risk factors that can increase blood pressure. Essentially the factors are reduced to those that influence heart rate, which provides the only source of variation in rate of blood flow. In the pressure interpretation, rate of flow is one of many factors that influence pressure. Pressure theorists have a role for narrowing of arteries, for heart rate, and for those who understand osmotic equilibrium, a role for sodium consumption.

It was expected that the model of blood pressure held by the subjects would influence the risk factors subjects cited, as well as the mechanisms they gave for these risk factors. Consequently, we tabulated the risk factors and the reasons each subject gave for them according to the blood pressure theory they held. Of the 26 respondents, 17 (65.4%) held the pressure model, and 9 (34.6%) held the velocity model. Both groups frequently cited stress as a risk factor, and both thought that stress operated by speeding up the heart, but the speed theorists did this in greater proportion than the pressure theorists (67% versus 35%). Clearly, something that raises velocity is a sensible risk factor for the velocity theorists, but it is only a risk factor for the pressure theorists through the indirect effect of velocity on pressure. On the other hand, a large proportion of the subjects thought a fatty diet contributed to high blood pressure. The pressure theorists cited it 76% of the time whereas the velocity theorists cited it in 56% of the cases. In every case but 2 of the 18 citations of fatty diet the reason given was that a fatty diet clogs the arteries in some way. It would seem that the clogging of arteries makes sense as a risk factor for the pressure theorists because a narrow-bore pipe will create more resistance than an open one. It is a mystery to the velocity theorists, who cited fatty diet less often; clogging the tubes will only slow the flow of fluid.

Salt or sodium was cited less often than either stress or fatty diet, and there was near equality between the two groups, with 47% for the pressure theory mentioning salt and 56% for the velocity theory mentioning it. A possible reason for the lower overall rate of mention of this risk factor, and for the lack of difference between the two theories of blood pressure, is the subjects' inability to provide a mechanism for the effect of sodium. Of the 13 who listed salt, 8 either left off the mechanism for this risk factor or explicitly stated that they did not know what it was. In addition, the mechanisms subjects gave are often strained and ad hoc. Two of the five with explanations said that salt clogs the arteries, one said that it hardens them, one said that it constricts arteries, one that it causes an increase in the water content of blood (the heart has to pump faster to get the same effect from this less efficient, thinner blood), and only one said that the retention of water to equalize the osmotic balance raises blood pressure.

The earlier description of salt as a mechanism illustrates another property of these mental models, namely that they do not cover their domain completely. Subjects know that salt is a risk factor for high blood pressure; this is part of general knowledge, and it is cited in almost any source of information about blood pressure or general health and diet. However, the mechanism by which the effect of sodium is mediated is not part of the model of any but a very few people. Consequently, we find a model, sometimes tightly organized with clear predictions of which the subject is quite confident, combined with a list of additional facts that are not integrated into the model but simply stand beside it. The items in the list are sometimes given an explanation, but usually they are simply cited. When a mechanism is demanded, the usual response is "I don't know," but sometimes an explanation is given with a low degree of confidence, such as "Excess salt makes deposits in the arteries," or "Salt corrodes the arteries." We see the model-plus-list pattern in other factors as well. Many subjects, for example, cited heredity in our studies as a factor for both heart disease and high blood pressure, but only about half were able to think of a reason for it.

Exercise was mentioned by 54% of the respondents, with nine of the subjects saying that exercise strengthens the heart (and/or that lack of exercise weakens it), four that exercise "flushes" out fatty deposits, and one that exercise strengthens the arteries directly. In later studies reported here, "Exercise burns fat" is also given as mechanism. Smoking was mentioned by only four (15%) of the subjects. Their explanations were "Constricts arteries," "Weakens heart," "Reduces flow of oxygen," and "Don't know." These individual responses are similar to those made by subjects in our later studies.

The responses for smoking and exercise as risk factors, as well as for salt, illustrate a pervasive reliance on mechanical factors and a nearly total lack of understanding of biochemical processes. These models, whether based on pressure or velocity, are entirely mechanical. Malfunctions involve breakdown of the pump, clogging of the pipes, excess speed or pressure of delivery, and so on. Subjects are usually powerless to explain the role of salt, the effect of which is mediated by biochemical processes. In none of our protocols is the role of High-Density Lipoprotein (HDL) and Low-Density Lipoprotein (LDL) cholesterol ratios in arteriosclerosis mentioned. The risk factors for smoking are explained in terms of crude effects poorly integrated even into the mechanical model, such as "Weakens heart" and "Overloads body," and are never given biochemical explanations. Likewise, the effect of exercise was seen as "flushing" out the system, strengthening the heart muscle, and not once to lowering LDL cholesterol or otherwise modifying biochemistry.

Heart Attack. The models of heart attack fell into four categories: (A) A coronary artery becomes clogged, leading to the incapacitation or death of the portion of heart muscle it serves (this is the standard account of a heart attack, or infarction); (B) A coronary artery bursts (this we took to be similar to the first model); (C) A general clogging of arterial flow, or of flow of blood through the heart; and (D) Failure of the heart muscle from factors other than clogging of a coronary artery (this would include such authentic medical conditions as cardiac arrest, fibrillations, and arrhythmias, as well as conditions frequently listed by our subjects as muscular weakness resulting from heredity or lack of exercise). In this sample we found that eight respondents held Model A, 15 held Model D, two held Model C, and one was unclassifiable. No one in this sample adhered to Model B, but a few did in the other studies reported later. These classifications represented perfect agreement between the first author and the joint ratings produced by the research assistants.

The subjects' descriptions of these theories of heart attack give a colorful picture of their mental models, but we found that the models of blood pressure tended to predict other responses better than did the heart attack model. Nevertheless, there are some reasonable associations between heart attack theories and other responses in the data. For example, it might be expected that "muscle" theorists (advocates of Model D) would find the condition of the arteries a minor factor in the causation of heart attacks, and indeed only four of the 15 who held this theory mentioned clogged or hardened arteries as causative factors, whereas 6 of the 8 infarction theorists listed clogging of the arteries. On the other hand, 13 of the 15 "muscle" theorists listed factors that were assumed to affect the strength of the muscle directly: weakness through lack of exercise, overexertion, heart wearing out with age, and obesity or clogged arteries (forcing the heart to work too hard). Only one of the eight infarction theorists mentioned anything that could be classified as a direct muscle effect.

STUDY 2: RISK FACTORS FOR COLLEGE STUDENTS AND BUILDINGS AND GROUNDS STAFF

In order to get a larger sample of information on assumptions about risk and the connection between models of cardiovascular function and perceived risk factors, we gave a new questionnaire to two new samples of respondents. One was from the same population we sampled in the first study. This time we obtained responses from 55 students enrolled in introductory psychology. In addition, we gave the same questionnaire to members of the Buildings and Grounds crew for the Claremont Colleges, as well as to some members of the secretarial staff. This nonstudent sample, totaling 26 people, ranged in age from 20 to 56 years and from 8 years of education to possession of a B.A. degree. Some were nonnative English speakers, with Spanish as their first language, but all were able to read the questionnaires and respond in English.

The questionnaire asked respondents to define blood pressure, high blood pressure, and a heart attack. Instead of asking them to list risk factors and symptoms for high blood pressure and heart attack as in the first study, we gave them a list for each category and asked them to mark the three most important items in each case.

Descriptions of the circulatory system were similar to those of the first study. Both groups gave plumbing models, with the traits seen in the first study. The only interesting difference was the clear assumption of an ebb-and-flow model in four of the building and grounds staff members' responses. It seems possible that these models owe their origin to Galen's account of blood flow, possibly preserved in Mexican-American folk theories.

For the basic definition of blood pressure, 50 student and 15 nonstudents gave classifiable answers. Force theories were seen in 52% of the student sample and 47% of the nonstudent sample. The students gave speed definitions 44% of the time, and the nonstudents gave the same definition 33%

of the time. In addition, 20% of the nonstudents gave responses containing some of both positions.

Heart attack theories had 46 interpretable responses from the students and 19 from the non-students. Of these, 37% in both cases were muscle theories (17 and 7, respectively). The students gave 14 (30%) blocked path theories, 12 (26%) coronary artery blockage theories, and 3 (7%) combination theories. The staff members gave no path blockage theories, 4 (21%) coronary artery theories, and 8 (42%) combination theories.

The risk factors cited by the two groups are of interest. In the first study respondents had to produce risk factors, while here they checked them off of a list. For high blood pressure the most important risks for the college students were stress, salt, fat, and exercise, and for the staff they were obesity, salt, fat, and hardened arteries. For heart attack the students checked exercise, stress, obesity, fat, and diet as the most important, while the staff checked smoking, stress, obesity, fat, and exercise in that order. The greatest difference is in smoking, which not a single subject mentioned spontaneously in the first study, but here and whenever a checklist is used, it is cited. Salt also moved higher in the rankings when a checklist was used. Stress, fat, exercise, and obesity are cited whether free recall or checking is the mode of response.

STUDY 3: A "MIDDLE AMERICA" SAMPLE

It is obvious that our college sample is an atypical group of people, limited in age to the range of 17 to 22 years with few exceptions, and with all of the other selection and demographic peculiarities of college students. Our buildings and grounds staff is mainly blue-collar but drawn from very different populations. We therefore sought a broader sample and decided to use people waiting in an airport (Ontario, California). The questionnaire was substantially the same as the one we used in the first study. We approached people who were seated and briefly introduced this as a study about health and the heart. If they agreed to participate in the study, we had them fill out the personal information. They were then asked to give us their understanding of blood pressure and heart attack. In approximately half the cases the experimenter transcribed the participant's account, and the rest wrote it out themselves. The subjects then filled out the rest of the questionnaire.

We interviewed a total of 60 subjects. Their mean age was 37.6 years ($SD = 14.4$ years), and they had a mean of 13.8 years of schooling, ranging from 5 years to attainment of a PhD plus post-doctoral work ($SD = 2.7$ years). The sample included 32 males and 27 females.

We categorized their definitions of heart attack and blood pressure using the same categories that we had in the first study. The categories were applied to the single statements given by the subjects, rather than to the series of questions, but most subjects provided as much information as was given in the series of questions. For the definition of blood pressure, we found, as before, that the majority, 53.8%, had the concept that blood pressure was the force with which the blood pressed against the artery walls, while a smaller proportion, 46.2%, thought blood pressure was determined by the velocity of the blood passing through the vessels.

Definitions of a heart attack differed somewhat from those we found in the college sample. The muscle failure hypothesis (usually failure from stress or a sudden shock, lack of exercise, or overwork, and not from constriction of blood flow to the heart muscle) was held by 28.3% of the subjects (down from 39.1% in the college sample). The most nearly correct theory, that a heart attack is an occlusion in the coronary arteries, was proposed by 31.7% of the respondents. The idea that a heart attack is some kind of obstruction in the flow of blood through the heart was held by 33.3% of the respondents. In addition, we found two (3.3%) who believed that a heart attack was a bursting of an artery, and 2 who gave no answer at all.

The descriptions and explanations of the conceptions of blood pressure and heart attack were as dramatic and revealing as those we obtained from the college sample, and they suggest similar conceptions of the underlying mechanisms. While we did not ask them to describe mechanisms or risk factors, they frequently volunteered them. Fat or cholesterol clogging arteries or constricting blood flow was frequently cited both as a cause of heart attacks and of high blood pressure. The bad effect of arterial clogging was in most cases asserted to be from the extra work the heart had to do because of the increased pressure. Interruption of general blood flow because of clogging within the heart was the heart attack theory of 33.3% of the subjects, and many of these specifically described how they thought blockage took place in the valves or in the aorta. Stress was also frequently cited as a cause of high blood pressure and heart attacks, mainly because it forces the heart to work too hard or pump too fast. Being in a weak condition can exacerbate the effect of stress.

As these descriptions illustrate, these subjects worked with a pump-and-tubes model similar to that of the college sample. All processes were cast in terms of this model, with the bases of prediction found in blocking or narrowing of tubes, overworking of the pump, and so on. Biochemical explanations, or even citations of chemical risks, were nearly absent. Not one subject volunteered salt consumption as a risk factor for high blood pressure, or smoking as a risk for either high blood pressure or heart attack. In general, if a mechanism was given, it was based on a mechanical analogue to the cardiovascular system, with no recognition given to possible biochemical bases for functioning and malfunctioning. The only extended discussion of chemical risk is a bizarre account by a male of 29, who reported having taken courses in health, of how the failure of the body to eliminate noxious substances from the blood can lead to heart disease.

STUDY 4: TWO TESTS OF THE MENTAL MODEL APPROACH: MEMORY FOR HEALTH INFORMATION AND GENERALIZATION TO NEW CASES (PRODUCTIVITY)

Memory for Health Information. An important consequence of the models people hold is the way they acquire and retain information. Information that fits a person's model or schema for a domain is more likely to be perceived accurately and retained than information that does not fit. One consequence of practical importance for health is that compliance with treatment is greatly influenced by memory for instructions. Thus, we thought it important for practical as well as for theoretical reasons to determine whether we could show effects of the model a subject held on his or her memory for different sorts of facts from a passage on the topic of cardiovascular health.

We prepared a passage that gave information and advice on cardiovascular disease. All information in the passage was drawn from American Heart Association educational materials and thus presumably accurate in terms of current knowledge. A copy of one version of the passage is reproduced in the Appendix. Using procedures derived from analysis of the cognitive structure of stories and tales (Thorndyke, 1975), we divided the passage into 69 separate propositions. These are numbered from 1 to 69 in the Appendix. Subjects saw only a prose passage, not numbered, divided into paragraphs at the points noted in the Appendix.

The passage began with a short paragraph containing 5 propositions of general information, then a second paragraph with 11 propositions on the importance of blood pressure in the risk of a heart attack. Paragraphs 3, 4, and 5 contained the propositions critical to our study. These were reproduced in two different orders (3, 4, 5 and 5, 4, 3) to compensate for order effects. Paragraph 3 contained 17 propositions that described the effect of dietary lipids in the health of arteries. Paragraph 4 discussed the benefits of exercise with 14 propositions. Finally, Paragraph 5 gave 20 propositions on stress and stress management. The sixth paragraph covered a number of additional factors. Only 3, 4, and 5 were scored; the other paragraphs were placed as fillers to reduce primacy and recency effects on memory.

Subjects were taken from a section of Introductory Psychology. Subjects began by filling out a questionnaire containing items similar to those in Table 7.1, but with the additional questions seen in Table 7.2.

They filled out the questionnaire in small groups in a classroom with a research assistant and/or one of the authors present. When they were finished with the questionnaire, they turned to the last page of the handout, which contained the passage. They were told to read it carefully and be prepared to take a test on it later. Subjects were given 5 minutes to read the passage. When they finished they were given a verbal puzzle for 5 minutes At the end of the session they were asked to write out the passage as completely and accurately as possible. They were given the rest of the period, about 15 minutes, for this task, but most finished in about 5 minutes.

We began with 42 subjects, but two produced materials that were incomplete. The final sample had 40 subjects, 14 males and 26 females, mean age 18.6. We classified them separately by their theories of blood pressure and heart attack. For this classification we trained four research assistants, who independently classified the subjects in much the same way as in the first sample. However, we gave them more categories for heart attack so that differences between clogging of coronary arteries, clogging of the main path through the heart, and general clogging of arteries in the body could be distinguished. In addition, combination theories were allowed, such as: "muscle fails because general clogging wears out the muscle." For categorizing of blood pressure models, we used the following four categories: *pressure, velocity, both,* and *neither* (other).

Initial interrater reliability was fairly high for blood pressure, with a mean of $r = .76$. However, one rater differed greatly from the other two, and the mean rises to .93 when she is removed from the ratings. The four assistants met after the ratings were completed and discussed each case until they all agreed on the classification of each one. The first author independently classified all of the cases, and his ratings have an $r = .98$ with the agreed-upon final ratings.

Although the respondents' accounts of heart attacks usually seemed as vivid and clear as their accounts of high blood pressure, they proved more difficult to classify. Interrater reliability was only .64, and with the discrepant rater removed from the average, it rose to .79. The discussions of heart attack cases resulted in agreement on all but one case. The first author also independently classified the accounts of heart attacks, and his classifications correlated .69 with the final list of agreed-upon classifications by the research assistants.

We had a number of a priori predictions about memory for the passage, which are based on the factors that would seem most important (and memorable) for each of the theories. In order to make testable predictions with a sample this small we had to condense the categories to obtain more subjects per category. The heart attack theories were easily reduced to (1) Clogged or burst coronary artery (40%), (2) General Clogging or Clogging of main path through heart (22.5%), and (3) Muscle Failure unrelated to coronary artery disease (37.5%). The final Blood Pressure theory categories were (1) Pressure (50%), (2) Speed (35%), and (3) Both (15%).

For blood pressure theories we predicted that "Pressure" theorists should be better on the Artery Health items than the "Speed" theorists (because, as noted, "Speed" theorists had no way of explaining how narrowing the arterial passages would increase the speed of the blood), and that the "Speed" theorists should recall exercise and stress items better than "Pressure" theorists because their theory focuses on the overworking of the heart in having to pump too fast.

Two of the research assistants scored the recall sheets. They used a master list of the propositions in the passage to identify and classify propositions in the recalled material. They scored by the sense of the propositions rather than the literal wording, but we found little difference in the pattern of responses when we used a strict scoring that allowed little deviation from the words in the original. The correlation between the results obtained by the two raters was .96.

The recall differences for the two blood pressure theories were striking. Figure 7.1 shows the proportion of propositions in each of the three categories "Pressure" and "Speed" blood pressure groups recalled. For this analysis the subjects who seemed to endorse both positions were combined with the "Pressure" theorists, but the results are changed very little if they were left out altogether.

As the figure shows, the three types of information were recalled unequally, with $F (2,76) = 20.3$, $p < .0001$. However, this difference is not of great interest because item difficulty, rather than differences in the memorability of the categories, may account for the effect. The items contributing to a fatty diet were each counted as propositions, but they may have formed a coherent category for the subjects and have been easier to recall than the same number of separate propositions in the other categories.

The interaction between the "Pressure" and "Speed" groups and information category is, on the other hand, potentially revealing because items are the same for both groups, and differences may be attributed to the differential encoding of categories by the two groups. This interaction (Group by Category of information) is reliable, with $F (2,76) = 4.1$, $p < .02$. Tests of simple effects within this interaction show that the difference between the two groups is reliable for the lipid items, $F (1,96) = 8.65$, $p < .004$, where the "Pressure" group recalled approximately 50% more than the "Speed" group, and the two groups are statistically equal for the other two categories. Another way to look at this interaction is to test the "Speed" and "Pressure" groups separately. This analysis shows that the "Speed" group had statistically equal recall for the three categories, F (2,76) = 2.38, $p < .1$, while the "Pressure" group had differential recall, F(2,76) = 30.4, p<.01.

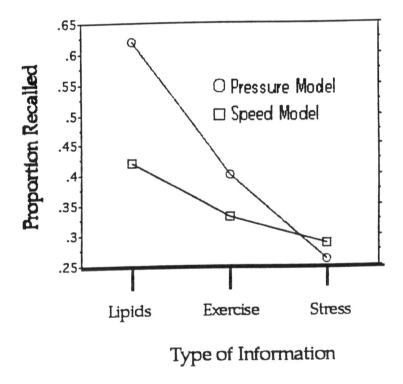

FIG. 7.1. Proportion of facts recalled in the three categories of information analyzed in recall of the passage on cardiovascular health and disease (see Appendix). Recall for subjects with Pressure and Speed theories of the meaning of blood pressure is plotted separately.

The heart attack theories did not predict recall reliability, even with several different groupings of the classifications of the theories. This lack of reliable effects renders tests of reasonable associations with different mental models moot. The problem in prediction may have been the difficulty of using reported heart attack theories to infer the underlying model. On the face of it, the muscle and artery theories seem distinct and clear, with clear predictions for memory and other measures. However, a person who reports an apparent muscle theory ("Muscle fails") may actually hold the theory that this failure results from an occlusion of a coronary artery—an *artery* theory—but did not fill out the model beyond the proximate cause of the heart attack. If this is the reason for the poor diagnostic success of the reported heart attack theories, then a structured interview or a very carefully constructed questionnaire might improve predictability.

Why did this same problem not also cause the blood pressure classifications to fail as predictors? The reason may be that the conceptions of blood pressure were not as rich as those of heart attacks. There may not be the layers of causality, and the distinction between underlying and proximal causes, that exist for conceptions of heart attack.

Productivity.   A crucial test of the mental model is the criterion termed *productivity* in this chapter. This is a characteristic that distinguishes a model from a list or a set of associative connections. A model covers new cases by application of underlying principles, which may not create any superficial similarity across the cases. An associative system would generalize to new cases through some associative link, which may or may not reflect the underlying principles. For example, a dolphin is a mammal on the basis of the underlying defining features, but associatively it would be classified as a fish. People with some knowledge of the biological basis of classification understand that it is a mammal, but children and others without the biological knowledge almost always assume it is a fish. They have no principle other than the associative one on which to base the classification.

Our test of the productivity of the subjects' mental models was the 10 "drug treatment" questions seen in Table 7.2. Each question contrasts the predictions of two models of blood pressure or of heart attack. Subjects were asked, for example, in Question 1, "Which is a better medication to reduce high blood pressure: one that decreases blood volume or one that slows heart rate?" The pressure theorist should select the first drug, and, in fact, diuretics, which can reduce blood volume, are used in blood pressure management. The subscriber to the speed theory of blood pressure, on the other hand, should have no prediction about volume, but slowing heart rate should reduce the velocity and thereby lower blood pressure according to this theory.

Table 7.2
Items Used in Productivity Study to Assess the Ability of the Mental Models
to Generate Predictions for New Cases

A physician is treating a patient for high blood pressure. Only one drug from each group can be prescribed at a time, and so the physician must choose which one from each set to use. Using your best judgment please describe which drug you think the doctor should prescribe for the patient. Just pick the drug from each group that you think might be the best for lowering someone's blood pressure.

Drug	Effect	Choice (please circle one)
1. A	Decreases blood volume	<u>A</u> or B
B	Slows heart rate	
2. A	Decreases speed of blood	A or <u>B</u>
B	Opens blood vessels	
3. A	Makes artery walls more flexible	<u>A</u> or B
B	Makes blood move more slowly	
4. A	Makes blood thicker	A or <u>B</u>
B	Makes blood thinner	
5. A	Reduces maximum pulse rate	A or <u>B</u>
B	Makes blood vessels wider	

Another physician is trying to figure out which drugs would be the best to use to reduce the risk of heart attack. Again, using your best judgment, please decide which of each pair would be MOST effective in reducing the risk of a heart attack.

Drug	Effect	Choice (please Circle One)
6. A	Strengthens the heart muscle	A or <u>B</u>
B	Increases blood flow to heart	
7. A	Makes blood less likely to clot	<u>A</u> or B
B	Prevents exhaustion of heart	
8. A	Slow pulse rate	A or <u>B</u>
B	Opens arteries	
9. A	Reduces stress on heart	A or <u>B</u>
B	Increases oxygen to heart muscles	
10. A	Clears arteries leading to heart muscle	<u>A</u> or B
B	Slows down heart rate	

Now you have a patient who is willing to follow either an exercise plan or a diet but NOT BOTH. This patient is at high risk for having a heart attack; which should the patient do, follow a diet or an exercise plan?

A	Safe exercise plan	or	B	Better diet

Note: For items 1-5 the choice corresponding to the pressure model of blood pressure is underlined. For items 6-11 the choice corresponding to the artery theory of heart disease is underlined.

To perform this analysis, each question was coded such that the drug choice corresponding to the pressure theory was given a score of +1 and that corresponding to the speed theory was given a minus 1. The heart attack choices were similarly scored, with choices derived from the muscle theory given a minus 1 and those derived from the artery theory a +1. Thus the total scores for each category could go from minus 5 to +5. In addition, the question of which is better for a patient who will only follow one regime, an exercise plan or a better diet, was scored with minus 1 for exercise, 0 for subjects who answered both or neither, and +1 for those who chose diet.

The mean scores across subjects and questions was 1.21 for the questions about blood pressure management, and it was 1.3 for questions about heart attacks. The standard errors were .29 and .259, respectively, and both means were different from zero, the chance expectation, at $p < .001$, by a z test. The mean for the diet/exercise question was .33, $SE\mu = .016$, and this was also reliably different from zero.

The mean scores indicate that the subjects tend to know, overall, the correct answers to the questions about medication. However, this knowledge did not vary reliably as a function of the theory of either blood pressure or heart attack that they held. Analyses of variance testing on the relation between theory of heart attack or blood pressure and scores on the blood pressure or heart attack questions, or on the diet versus exercise question, all turned out nonsignificant.

While the overall score on the drug questions was not predicted by the models the subjects held, analysis of individual items as part of an omnibus test did show that some items were reliably discriminating well above chance. The motivation for looking at individual questions is that the overall lack of significance in the omnibus test may have resulted simply from poor questions. This is one way to begin the search for better questions. The questions that turned out to be reliable for the blood pressure theories were 1 ($p < .05$), 9 ($p < .001$), and 10 ($p < .05$), all differences in the predicted direction.

GENERAL CONCLUSIONS

The models of the cardiovascular system that our subjects reported were all "plumbing" models, and when subjects provided a causal explanation, it was generally in the terms that follow from such a model. Vessel models have figured in thinking about physiology in many cultures and for many years. It was not until 1628 that William Harvey demonstrated that blood did not merely flow, but circulated. However, for most of our subjects it would not matter whether it circulated, moved in an ebb-and-flow manner, or simply flowed out from some central location and was absorbed in the body, because very few explained how the circulatory cycle is completed.

The models seem to be almost entirely mechanical. They do not contain any processes by which biochemical effects are modeled. The result is that some factors, such as clogging of arteries, are well understood and remembered, while others that depend on biochemistry, such as salt intake and smoking, are not understood and are not given the importance they deserve. Thus, while intake of salt in the diet and smoking are seen as risk factors, subjects were unable to give good explanations of how they might pose a risk.

There are individual differences in the models people hold. When subjects were asked to describe what happens in a heart attack, they came up with two different types of models: an "artery" theory, which divides into two varieties (infarction in a coronary artery and a general clogging of blood flow through the heart), and a "muscle" theory, which attributes the heart attack to a weakness, malfunction, or a sort of cramp in the heart muscle. These two theories of heart attack led people holding them to suggest different risk factors. The muscle theorists tended to emphasize lack of exercise as a risk factor, while the artery theorists emphasized diet.

Another individual difference was found in the theories of blood pressure. Two broad groups of theories were found, with some subjects defining blood pressure correctly as pressure on the artery walls, while others defined it as the velocity of blood flow. These two theories also led to differences in perceived risk factors and differences in memory for health information. In particular, the "velocity" theorists had poorer memory for correct dietary information than the pressure theorists. The results clearly show that this difference does not result from educational differences.

These models seem to play an important role in the cognition of bodily processes, understanding of risk factors, and memory for health-related information. There is clearly practical relevance for models in many areas, including dissemination of health information and communication between physician and patient. The idea that the patient's understanding of physiology and conceptions of illness is important has been noted by other authors. What we have sought to do is cast this understanding in the terms of a mental model. Two generalizations that resulted from this approach seemed of particular practical importance. One is that people hold different theories of blood pressure and the mechanism of a heart attack, and as a result they have different ideas about treatment and prevention, and furthermore, they remember different facts from the same passage of health advice. A second generalization is that risk factors that depend entirely on biochemistry will be poorly understood and probably ignored by all subjects.

How well does the mental model schema account for the conceptions of physiology we have described? Certainly, the majority of respondents have definite conceptions that fit the form of a mental model, and they generally describe the cardiovascular system as a coherent mechanical system in terms of fluid moving through vessels. This mechanical system also provides the appropriate theoretical context for the mechanisms they use to explain heart attacks, blood pressure, and a number of risk factors. In addition, the difficulty subjects have with biochemical factors may be attributed to the lack of chemical mechanisms in the model. Successes of the mental model approach are also seen in the prediction of memory for medical advice and in the differential predictions for risk given by the two major models of blood pressure.

Despite the success of the models in accounting for some results, there are a number of inadequacies. One is the limited success in demonstrating that the model could categorize new cases in selection of medications. The problem may have been some bad questions, or questions that were too difficult, but the fact is that the models did not achieve success in the objective test of the productivity criterion.

Another, and probably more important, lapse is the inability of the model approach to account completely for beliefs. Some of the risk factors that subjects hold to be very important do not follow from their models and may even be inconsistent with them. Salt, as a risk for high blood pressure, is one of these. Stress and exercise are two more. They are listed with high frequency, but causal explanations of their effects are weak and poorly related to the model when they are given. Cases such as these in which people's beliefs are not consonant with their models demonstrate that the mental model can not be the sole source of judgment about health beliefs.

While we have presented evidence that people use mental models in health decisions, we think it is necessary to conclude that the mental model is but one tool we use. It may be unrealistic to think that a mental model can in itself be adequate as the sole device for making health judgments. People need to be able to judge the acceptability of many things that they can not derive from their models.   While a scientist can list unanswered questions as interesting projects, individuals have to decide about things frequently in daily life. We must consider what other bases for decision may exist and how they are all coordinated.

Earlier in this chapter we suggested that the proper account of the mental representation of health information is "model plus list," where people have a mental model of the kind we describe but also have a list of beliefs, strongly held, that do not follow from the model. An elaboration of this proposal is seen in Figure 7.2, which might be characterized more accurately as "list plus model," or "list plus several different models."

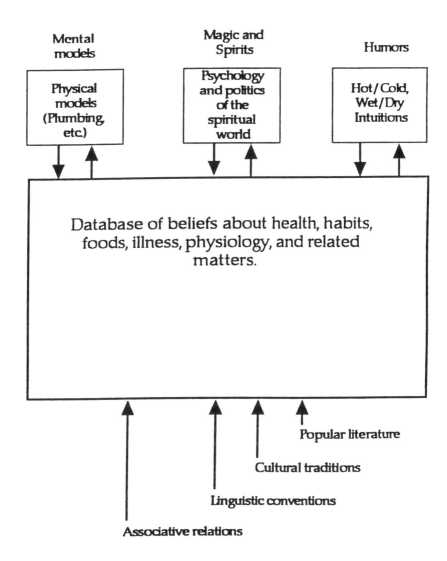

Fig. 7.2. Hypothetical relation between mental models and other cognitive structures and the memory database of beliefs concerning health and bodily function. Every item in the database has a valence indicating the degree to which it is good for or bad for a person. Arrows leading into the database show the origin of the valence information, which can be retrieved directly and automatically along with other information about the item in question when the item is accessed. Arrows leading out of the database show the more effortful process of evaluation by one of the three conceptual schemes that seem to be employed by subjects in evaluating items when needed.

The structure outlined in this figure has a large pool of health beliefs (the "list") that come from many sources. Each member of the pool—a concept, word, or thing—normally has a valence indicating the degree to which it is considered "good for you" or "bad for you." These valences could be qualified as, for example, "good for your liver," "bad for your blood pressure," and so on. When a decision must be made the pool is consulted as a sort of database in memory. Normally the mental model is not consulted when a question comes up. Rather, the information is retrieved with item information from the central pool. The mental model is only used when retrieval fails or contradictory information is found, or when people are asked to justify their beliefs, as when they are interrogated in this study. Once an item has been processed by the mental model, it may be returned to the pool with an associated valence, to be used upon future retrievals.

The other sources of valences for concepts in the pool include associations, received opinion, and tradition, and there are undoubtedly more sources. The effect of all of these sources is that a person will have available a ready-made set of intuitions about a great number of things. Ideally, for the sake of ease of the individual's decisions about things, retrieval of the valence "good for me" or "bad for me" is made effortlessly, and time-consuming mental model computations can be avoided. Since people simply retrieve the valence along with the item in question they normally have no knowledge of the origin of the valence. Thus they believe that stress is bad for the heart with no support from the model, and that fat is also bad, but with support from the clogging model. In both cases they assume that the beliefs are consistent with their conceptions of bodily function, but in neither case do they attempt to apply the model unless there is a good reason to do so.

Parallel to the mental model function we have included functions labeled *"MAGIC AND SPIRITS"* and *"HUMORS."* These are conceived as conceptual tools much like mental models that can operate on the database of health beliefs, evaluating, comparing, and assigning valences. Like mental models, they are associated with a process of conscious evaluation, but they may also operate so rapidly as to be cognitively transparent. These two functions were considered necessary because a broad segment of humanity uses these systems to evaluate health factors, or more generally, to evaluate whether something is "good" or "bad."

"MAGIC AND SPIRITS" is the realm of what Westerners dismiss as superstition, but it is a powerful realm for many, and none can claim to be completely free of it. We see it commonly in faith healing, in the use of protective or healing amulets, and perhaps in the power of the placebo effect (see Moerman, 1991). In some cultures, this is the dominant source of theories about health (see, e.g., Unschuld, 1985). Illness may be caused by a curse, by an offense against an ancestor, by a spirit that dwells in trees, and so on.

Health beliefs are imbedded in a larger world system that includes spiritual theories of physics, weather, dreams, and so on, just as in fact our plumbing models are so imbedded. The system will differ from culture to culture, but some constants can be seen. There are invisible forces, sometimes animate and willful, sometimes simply forces lacking anthropomorphic motivation, sometimes benign and sometimes aggressive. Illness is caused by these forces, and healing often involves an expert, or shaman, who counteracts or propitiates these forces in a form of allopathic medicine. Healing may also be sought through individual prayer, rituals, lighting of candles, group prayer, and so on.

"HUMORS" represents a cognitive system similar to mechanical mental models, but based on the concepts of wetness versus dryness and heat versus cold. Familiar examples of this system are seen in the concept of "catching a cold" or the practice of avoiding "mucous-forming foods" when in the midst of the "wet" condition of the common cold. Westerners trace this thinking to Galen's system, but very similar systems were developed, apparently independently, in Indian Ayurvedic medicine and in traditional Chinese medicine (Leslie, 1976; Unschuld, 1985). These systems may have arisen from observation of fevers and chills, the "wet" conditions that often accompany infections, and such "dry" conditions as dry mouth or skin. Whatever the reason, the similarity of these systems from widely separated geographical areas and very different cultures is remarkable. They have many things in common, including a concept of health as a balance of the elements, illness as an imbalance, medical treatment as a process designed to restore the balance, and some agreement about the nature of the elements (hot, cold, wet, and dry) themselves.

These three theoretical systems are shown with a set of arrows going both ways. This indicates that they do not simply provide valences for retrieved items that need them but also add valences to items in the pool. The behavior of subjects in retrieving the information suggests that the valence is attached to the item without any indication of its origin. Thus our subjects would apparently recall very easily that salt is "bad" for blood pressure, but they then encountered difficulty in finding a reason or explanation for this categorization.

The two-way arrows also suggest that confirmation bias may help make belief in the system stable and strong. When an item is retrieved after it has once been considered, the evaluating process will find that it agrees with the valence the item has, even though the valence was attached in the previous evaluation by the same process. Because the origin of the valence is lost, this appears to be confirmation of the evaluation process the second and subsequent times.

Finally, we assume that all three systems can co-exist, and probably do, in most individuals. For example, in Taiwan many people maintain belief in both traditional Chinese medicine and Western scientific medicine, choosing the practitioner on the basis of the nature of a given illness, sometimes going to practitioners of both persuasions for the same malady (Unschuld, 1976). This pattern is seen in many cultures. The main differences seem to be which system is seen as dominant, and which particular version of each system is held by the individual or culture.

We began this research looking for coherent metaphors people hold that govern their organization and recall of health-related information. Clearly, the picture we found is more complex than a set of simple metaphors or mental models. Most individuals do appear to have a model of cardiovascular functioning, but one that is limited in a number of ways. Two of the most important limitations are that the models are strictly mechanical and can not handle biochemical functions, and the models do not cover all of the health-related beliefs a person has. The likely picture is that people have a large set of beliefs about health-related items, and there are many sources for these beliefs. Physical metaphors serve as a way of deciding about health-related beliefs and may be an important source of beliefs in some circumstances, but they do not serve as a complete theory of the domain of propositions relevant to health.

Finally, we should ask what strategies our results suggest for health care professionals. How might they improve communication and compliance? One suggestion would be to attempt to teach patients the correct model, or at least the part of the model that applies to the case at hand, to make sure that they encode advice and communicate symptoms properly. However, the correct model requires understanding of biochemical and other processes that essentially none of our respondents incorporated in their models.

A more feasible approach might be to recognize that most patients have a folk model of blood pressure and heart disease that differs from the scientific one in important respects, and that they are not going to understand the correct explanation of the basis for many recommendations without literally years of education. This folk model, however wrong, is simply seen as "common sense" to them. An effective strategy might therefore be to use the results of research like that reported here to determine just what the beliefs are, then to use these beliefs to support the recommendations. For example, a physician could ask the patient a few questions to find out what he or she believes blood pressure and high blood pressure are. The advice might then be something like this, for a patient who thinks high blood pressure is excessively fast blood flow: "You should think of this medication as slowing the blood down, and if you do not take it, the blood will go too fast and you will not even know it." It would be unethical to portray this as the scientific explanation, but it could be presented as a way to visualize the process. Research extending the present work would be needed to determine what models people have that relate to specific treatments and recommendations. Research is also needed to find efficient ways for a health care provider to learn what a given patient's model is and how to tailor the recommendation to that model. Finally, research would be needed to determine whether this approach works and, if so, to refine it so that it might become a useful part of standard treatment modalities.

APPENDIX

Passage on Cardiovascular Health Given to Subjects in Study 4

First Filler Paragraph

1. Heart attack is the leading cause of death in the U.S. 2. Everyone is potentially at risk. 3. There are some factors that make a heart attack more likely. 4. There are many things you can do to decrease your personal risk 5. and increase your overall level of health. 6. High blood pressure is often correlated with heart attacks. 7. It is a good idea to avoid things that raise blood pressure. 8. Salt and salty foods are important causes of high blood pressure. 9. Some drugs and medications can also influence blood pressure. 10. Check with your physician about anything you may be taking. 11. Race, heredity, age, and gender are often predictors of high blood pressure. 12. These factors can only be used to attempt to identify people at risk 13. and try to protect them from associated risks.

Paragraph Containing Artery Risk and Lipid Information

14. Another major risk factor for heart disease is a high fat or cholesterol content in the diet. 15. Saturated fats, such as those found in animal meat, can cause arteriosclerosis, or hardened arteries. 16. Foods that should be avoided include 17. eggs, 18. red meats (even if visible fat is removed), 19. butter, 20. bacon, 21. cheese, 22. pork, 23. lamb, 24. ice cream, 25. fried foods, 26. pizza, 27. hot dogs, 28. cold cuts, 29. sour and whipped cream, and 30. organ meats.

Paragraph containing exercise advice

31. Exercise is beneficial for the cardiovascular system 32. and strengthens the heart muscle. 33. It also helps people handle stress 34. and can help control weight problems. 35. The amount of exercise adequate to strengthen your heart is about 20 minutes of sweat-inducing exercise 36. three times a week. 37. Overexertion can put undue strain on the heart, 38. so knowing one's physical limits 39. and designing a safe and effective program is important. 40. Aerobic exercises such as 41. jogging, 42. dancing, and 43. swimming are particularly good for your heart. 44. Isometric ones such as weight lifting do not strengthen the heart.

Paragraph Containing Information About Stress

45. Stress may also be a factor in causing heart attacks. 46. There is support that "type A" personalities run a greater risk of having a heart attack. 47. These are people who have a highly stressful lifestyle 48. and can best be described as uptight. 49. People who are angered easily might also have a slightly higher risk of heart disease. 50. Staying relatively calm may be quite important. 51. Caffeine may also cause problems. 52. Sufficient sleep and relaxation can help relieve tension. 53. Particularly effective are relaxation techniques such as meditation, a few minutes of quiet time in the middle of stressful activities, and guided fantasies. 54. Stress can also be alleviated by avoiding tense situations. 55. Being well prepared for an exam or an interview 56. and learning to anticipate and deal with anxiety are a few ways this can be done. 57. Sudden shocks have been known to trigger heart attacks. 58. Even animals like birds have been known to have heart attacks from the shock of being captured. 59. There is often no way to avoid shocks, but 60. being prepared to deal with emergencies 61. and knowing how to control your emotions can help.

Final Filler Paragraph

62. Obesity (being excessively overweight) is also a risk factor. 63. If your weight is more than 20% over the average for your height, age, and sex, you should lose weight. 64. Alcohol should be consumed in moderate quantities (10 or fewer drinks a week). 65. Smoking should be completely avoided. 66. It is also a good idea to get regular medical checkups. 67. A person with diabetes is also at greater risk than average for heart disease 68. and should carefully avoid the other risk factors. 69. If this advice is heeded the risks for having a heart attack can be dramatically reduced.

REFERENCES

Barnlund, D. C. (1976). The mystification of meaning: Doctor-patient encounters. *Journal of Medical Education, 51,* 716–725.

Bauman, L. J., & Leventhal, H. (1985). "I can tell when my blood pressure is up, can't I?" *Health Psychology 4,* 203–218.

Boyle, C. (1970). Differences between patients' and doctors' interpretations of some common medical terms. *British Medical Journal, 2,* 286–289.

Cartwright, A. (1983). Prescribing and the doctor–patient relationship. In D. Pendleton & J. Hasler (Eds.), *Doctor-patient communication* (pp. 177–191). London: Academic Press.

Fishman, A. P., & Richards, D. W. (Eds.). (1964). *Circulation of the blood: Men and ideas.* New York: Oxford University Press.

Gentner, D. & Stevens, A. L. (Eds.). (1983). *Mental models.* Hillsdale, NJ: Lawrence Erlbaum Associates

Leslie, C. (1976). *Asian medical systems: A comparative study.* Berkeley: University of California Press.

Ley, P. (1983). Patients' understanding and recall in clinical communication failure. In D. Pendleton & J. Hasler (Eds.), *Doctor-patient communication* (pp. 89–107). London: Academic Press.

Milnor, W. R. (1990). *Cardiovascular physiology.* New York: Oxford University Press.

Mishler, E. G. (1984). *The discourse of medicine: Dialectics of medical interviews.* Norwood, NJ: Ablex.

Moerman, D. E. (1991) Physiology and symbols: The Anthropological implications of the placebo effect. In L. Romanucci-Ross, D. E. Moerman, & L. R. Tancredi, (Eds.), *The anthropology of medicine* (2nd ed., pp. 129–143) New York: Bergin & Garvey.

Pendleton, D., & Hasler, J. (Eds.). (1983). *Doctor–patient communication.* London: Academic Press.

Sontag, S. (1978). *Illness as metaphor.* New York: Farrar, Straus & Giroux.

Svarstad, B. L. (1976). Physician-patient communication and patient conformity with medical advice. In D. Mechanic (Ed.), *The growth of bureaucratic medicine: An inquiry into the dynamics of patient behavior and the organization of medical care* (pp. 220–238). New York: Wiley.

Thorndyke, P. (1975). Conceptual complexity and imagery in comprehension and memory. *Journal of Verbal Learning and Verbal Behavior, 14,* 359–369.

Unschuld, P. U. (1976). The social organization and ecology of medical practice in Taiwan. In C. Leslie (Ed.), *Asian medical systems: A comparative study.* Berkeley: University of California Press.

Unschuld, P. U. (1985) *Medicine in China: A history of ideas.* Berkeley: University of California Press.

III

Metaphors and Politics

8

Metaphor, Politics, and Persuasion

Jeffery Scott Mio
California State Polytechnic University, Pomona

Imagine yourself in a debate. Your opponent builds her argument around an incisive metaphor that has the potential of convincing the audience of her position. Do you ignore the metaphor, thus not drawing attention to it, hoping the audience will be swayed by the weight of your arguments? Do you respond by attempting to defeat your opponent's metaphor by using a metaphor in response? Do you respond by extending your opponent's metaphor, thus turning her own metaphor back onto her? These are real-life dilemmas facing politicians attempting to convince a skeptical public of the proper course of action.

As most observers of politics know, the use of metaphor is a common rhetorical device. Do these devices work? Is the public manipulated so easily by simplistic symbolic representations of complex matters? Under what circumstances is the public more susceptible to such manipulations? Among their many uses, metaphors are applied to convey policies, convince or persuade the public of a plan of action, or to characterize political opponents. In this chapter, I propose to limit my scope to questions involving persuasion as opposed to communication or characterization. In so doing, I will attempt to integrate areas of social psychology, political psychology, political science, and communication.

PERSUASION

As most social psychologists know, the contemporary field of persuasion owes its roots to Carl Hovland's Yale Communication Research Program (e.g., Hovland, Janis, & Kelley, 1953; cf. Baron & Byrne, 1994; Fishbein & Ajzen, 1975; Myers, 1993; Sabini, 1992). In their studies, the Yale group identified four central areas influencing the persuasiveness of a message: the communicator, the content of the message, the medium or channel of communication, and the audience. As many in the field (e.g., Myers, 1993) like to say, the four areas can be summarized in the question: *Who* says *what* by *how* to *whom*?

Factors involved in communicator influence upon persuasion include credibility and attractiveness of the speaker. If the speaker is perceived to be an expert on a particular topic, he or she will be perceived to be more credible, thus more convincing (persuasive) than a nonexpert counterpart. Similarly, trustworthiness affects the credibility of the speaker. Attractiveness of the speaker is also positively related to persuasiveness of the message. Either a physically attractive speaker or a person perceived to be similar in attitudes, values, or physical appearance to the audience can be attractive. Thus, product manufacturers generally try to get an attractive female or male actor to endorse commercial products. In political commercials, there is generally an attempt to get "average voters" as actors endorsing a candidate or policy position. In the 1993–1994 health care debate, opponents to President Clinton's health care proposal used a series of "Harry and Louise" commercials, where Harry and Louise were supposed to be "average citizens" who would be negatively affected by the proposed changes in America's health care system. This political campaign was widely credited with the defeat of President Clinton's health care proposal.

The content of the message involves factors such as reason versus emotion, one-sided versus two-sided appeals, primacy versus recency, and discrepancy of new information. As I will be spending a great deal of time on the reason versus emotion factor, I will only mention here that some messages are logically constructed and are convincing because of the weight of the arguments put forth. On the other hand, there is also evidence that messages that stir emotions can also be persuasive. One-sided arguments seem to be effective in reinforcing the opinions of those who already agree with the position of the speaker. Two-sided arguments seem to be effective in convincing uncommitted or well-informed audiences. Moreover, two-sided arguments seem to have a more enduring effect (Lumsdaine & Janis, 1953). The primacy effect has been known at least since the time of Asch's (1946) classic study, where a list of descriptors of a person were identical except that half of the subjects received the descriptors in one order while the other half received the descriptors in reverse order. Subjects' assessment of the speaker were greatly influenced by the first items in each list. Thus, information given early has greater influence than information given late. Miller and Campbell (1959) found support for the recency effect, where later messages are more convincing than earlier messages. This occurs when there is a long enough time period between the two messages, and an assessment must be given soon after the second message is delivered. Finally, Aronson, Turner, and Carlsmith (1963) found that if a highly credible source delivered a highly discrepant message from the audience's original position, it was more persuasive than a message that was minimally discrepant. However, if a source with low credibility delivered a minimally discrepant message, it was more persuasive than a message that was highly discrepant.

The medium or channel of communication involves factors such as active versus passive reception and personal versus media influence. When people are active participants in message construction, they are more convinced than if they simply passively receive the information. Thus, typical classroom lectures may not be as persuasive as we in academia might hope. As Myers (1993) stated, "Ask college students what aspect of their college experience has been most valuable or what they remember from their first year, and few, I am sad to say, recall the brilliant lectures that we faculty remember giving" (p. 278). With respect to the personal versus media factor, while the media is an important influence, personal appeals seem to be most convincing (e.g., Eldersveld & Dodge, 1954).

Finally, audience factors include the age of the audience and what they are thinking at the time of the communication. Quite clearly, age is an important factor in receptivity to certain messages. As Erikson (1959) pointed out, different age groups deal with different life tasks and questions. Thus, messages crafted for one age group will not be as persuasive when delivered to another age group. With respect to what the audience is thinking at the time of the communication, Freedman and Sears (1965) found that those forewarned about a counterattitudinal message were much less persuaded by the message than those who were not forewarned about it. Others (e.g., Festinger & Maccoby, 1964) found that distracting the audience just enough to prevent them from developing counterarguments to the main thrust of the message rendered the message more persuasive.

RECOGNITION OF THE IMPORTANCE OF METAPHOR IN POLITICS

Graber (1993) asserted that political communication is "the lifeblood or mother's milk of politics because communication is the essential activity that links the various parts of society together and allows them to function as an integrated whole" (p. 305). She suggests that political reality is created by images (metaphors) conveyed by political rhetoric. "Freedom fighters' halos may tarnish when they are dubbed 'terrorists.' When opposition to the state is called 'treason' it is treated differently than when it bears the label 'civil disobedience'" (p. 311).

        This theme of political reality created by political rhetoric is resonant
throughout the literature. Thompson (Chapter 11, this volume) suggests that
this is because average citizens do not know enough about the complexities of
most political events to participate fully or even render an opinion. Metaphors
are useful in simplifying such events to make them accessible and
understandable to the general populace. "Until and unless that metaphorical
leap of understanding is made, there is no participation in politics nor political
discourse" (p. 186). Thompson further states, "Metaphors do more than
simplify complexity for the analyst or decision maker. They clothe the
intangible, giving life to abstractions" (p. 188).

Information Processing Aspects of Metaphor

As alluded to previously, political events are inherently complex, given the
many competing voices that want to be heard on the issues. Thus, for average
citizens, there is too much information available to be integrated, so that
opinions cannot be formed without help of political "elites" to guide the way.
Most political theorists (e.g., Graber, 1993; Neuman, Just, & Crigler, 1992;
Sniderman, 1993) have relied upon cognitive psychology's general information
processing model to characterize perceptions of political events. As most
psychologists know, this model suggests that there is a wealth of information in
the environment. This wealth is actually too much to be examined in its
entirety, so it needs to be pared down by either eliminating most of the
available information or by collapsing elements so that the information comes
in fewer separate elements. These theorists suggest that average citizens
employ cognitive short-cuts, such as heuristics or metaphor, in order to achieve
the goal of paring down the information if a political decision or opinion must
be rendered. Metaphors can act as both filters that screen out much of the
available information, leaving only the core ideas consistent with the
metaphors, and as devices to collapse disparate information into smaller, more
manageable packets.
        Edelman (1964, 1971, 1977, 1988) has long written about the use of
symbolism in politics for the purpose of collapsing information. He stated that
metaphors, symbols, and other linguistic cues are employed in order to provide
the motivation or justification to think or behave in a particular manner.[1] His
position is that we all have latent beliefs about matters arising in the political
arena, and politicians attempt to use symbols to bring those beliefs to the
surface. For Edelman, metaphors are primarily important in their part-to-
whole functions in that certain smaller events can become metaphors for larger
political events. "Vivid metaphors . . . can create benchmarks that shape
popular judgments of the success or failure of specific programs" (Edelman,
1977, p. 36). In recent political years, Republicans and Democrats have been

arguing about the success or failure of President Lyndon Johnson's "Great Society" program. Republicans have used the funding of a handful of controversial arts projects as a metaphor for the failure of the entire National Endowment for the Arts program, and, by extension, the Great Society vision of Johnson. Democrats have used the success of the Head Start program as a metaphor for the success of the Great Society vision.

Metaphors as Solutions

As stated earlier, the focus of this chapter is a discussion of how metaphors are used as persuasive devices in politics. The implication of this is that metaphors offer solutions to political problems or events. They offer a course of action, and politicians hope their metaphors persuade the public to follow the prescription suggested by the metaphors. Stone (1988) connects political problems and story narratives. Both have elements such as heroes, villains, and victims, and both involve some sort of transformation. "Metaphors are important devices for strategic representation in policy analysis. On the surface, they simply draw a comparison between one thing and another, but in a more subtle way, they usually imply a whole narrative story and a prescription for action" (p. 118).

Miller (1979) identified two prevalent views of metaphor in the political arena: the verificationist view and the constituitivist view. The verificationist camp views metaphors as predictions of the future, or working hypotheses. These can then be verified (or falsified) by subsequent political events. Thus, when President Ronald Reagan took office in 1981, he proposed the notion of *"trickle-down economics"* to solve the country's problems. A verificationist would have evaluated the economy after President Reagan left office to determine if in fact *"trickle-down economics"* solved the country's problems.

On the other hand, a constituitivist would have asserted that *"trickle-down economics"* actually determined Reagan Administration policy. Economic advisors to this administration used the metaphor as justification for actively seeking out opportunities to give massive tax cuts to businesses and the richest individuals in the country in order to stimulate the economy. The theory was that if such individuals and companies were to receive such tax cuts and other increases in their wealth, some of them would reinvest it back into the American economy. This wealth would then *"trickle down"* to those less fortunate. Although this policy has since come under attack because of the quadrupling of the debt of the government, and there are those on both sides who argue about the effectiveness of the policy, it is unquestionably true that *"trickle-down economics"* drove U.S. government policy during that era. The metaphor was the driving force behind the government's economic policy, influencing policy whenever decisions had to be made regarding which economic paths to follow. Thus, in this case, the constituitivist view would seem to have characterized the *"trickle-down"* metaphor better than the verificationist view.

Miller (1979) proposed his own view, a manifestationist view, which combines the elements of the verificationist and constituitivist views. Miller reasoned that since political events cannot be directly perceived by the senses, metaphors must be used to help us define the relevant issues. These metaphors are then subject to evaluation to find the best predictive model.

Metaphors may offer solutions because they are fundamentally ambiguous, so people can take from metaphors what they interpret them to mean. Stone (1988) asserted that the essential ambiguity of metaphor allows for cooperation and compromise among a wide array of people. The ambiguity allows politicians to give rhetoric to one side of an issue while voting for the other. The ambiguity allows the general populace to reconcile their own inconsistent, ambivalent attitudes.

Stirring Emotions

Finally, a major impact of metaphors and other forms of symbolic political communication is achieved by stirring emotions. Gross (1983) suggested that metaphors in the political arena are designed to stir emotions, as opposed to those that occur in science, which are designed to analyze situations and to ultimately lead to formulas which calculate specific relations and predictions among variables. Certainly, Edelman's writings (1964, 1971, 1977, 1988) underscore the importance of connecting to latent symbols which stir emotions in the general populace. Writing from a psychoanalytically oriented perspective, Edelman (1971) discussed how curbs on firearms raised fears of impotence and/or castration. Thus, any discussion of curbs on firearms automatically raises the emotional pitch on both sides of the argument. He further suggested that even literal language on this particular topic can be interpreted as metaphorical, symbolic language, for any such language resonates to these latent symbolic (and emotional) issues.

Others have written about how metaphors invite the receivers to make a connection with the speaker by evaluating the speaker's claims, motives, and intentions (e.g., Bronowski, 1972; Goodall, 1983). Goodall (1983) claimed that the use of metaphor and other analogical discourse established a relationship between the speaker and the listener, as the speaker subtly asked the listener to agree with the premises behind the metaphors suggested by the speaker.

Earlier, I discussed aspects of persuasion, where messages are either logically or emotionally presented. This was the old school of thought (e.g.,

Hovland et al., 1953). More recently, theorists in this area have been examining how metaphors fit into this logical–emotional dichotomy (e.g., Chaiken & Stangor, 1987; Jamieson, 1985). They have come to the conclusion that metaphors do not fit into either camp and are, in fact, able to bridge the gap between logic and emotion. Jamieson (1985) asserted, "Metaphors provide a good example of the possible intertwining of the rational and the non-rational, they permit a vagueness which enables them to carry cognitive and emotive potential within the one framework" (p. 73).

Chaiken and Stangor (1987) discussed how it was that metaphors may bridge the gap between the logical and emotional camps. They suggested that people strive to be logical, but because of the wealth of information potentially available, they cannot be maximally logical. They thus need to rely upon metaphors, cognitive heuristics, and other condensations of information. When these are employed, there is a pseudodeducative reasoning process. Users can introduce a heuristic decision-making rule, assume it to be true or reasonable, and come to conclusions based upon metaphors referring to this process. Stone (1988) also suggested this pseudodeducative reasoning process to be an important part of why metaphors may be persuasive. For example, in the aforementioned health care debate, "Harry and Louise" were used as metaphors for every citizen in the country. The pseudodeducative reasoning process might be something like:

Major premise: The Clinton health care proposal will hurt many people.
Minor premise: Harry and Louise (who are just like me) will be hurt by the health care proposal.
Conclusion: Therefore, the Clinton health care proposal will hurt me, and I should be against it.

If Harry and Louise were successful metaphors for everyone concerned about health care, then this reasoning process would be widely shared. As mentioned earlier, they did appear to be effective metaphors, as this "Harry and Louise" ad campaign was widely credited for defeating the Clinton health care proposal. Republicans later asserted that this plan was a metaphor for the very essence of Bill Clinton, as it portrayed him as a "big spending liberal Democrat whose first impulse was to offer big government solutions to every problem," as opposed to the "New Democrat" candidate Clinton had promised to be in the 1992 presidential campaign.

EXPERIMENTAL EVIDENCE FOR THE EFFECTIVENESS OF METAPHORS AS PERSUASIVE DEVICES

Although the theoretical support for the use of metaphors as persuasive devices is strong, the experimental research supporting these theories is sparse and equivocal. Most people cite John W. Bowers as the first researcher to experimentally manipulate metaphors in political discourse for the purpose of measuring the effectiveness of the communication (Bowers, 1964; Bowers & Osborn, 1966). He discussed a notion in social psychology called "psychological reactance." This notion suggests that extremely intense language used for the purpose of convincing someone of a certain position can actually have the opposite effect upon the receiver. He termed this reactance the "boomerang effect." For example, if parents disapprove of the boyfriend their daughter has chosen and sternly lecture her about this, setting down ultimatums and sanctions against her seeing him, she may instead run away from home and elope with this offending boyfriend. However, if her parents were to soften their tone against him, expressing reasons why they were against him but leaving the ultimate decision up to her, she may listen a bit more to her parents' warnings and ultimately discontinue seeing him.

Bowers and Osborn (1966) felt that metaphors had the ability to maintain the intensity of language without causing the boomerang effect. Bowers and Osborn used root metaphors of *"SEX"* and *"DEATH"* as the basis of persuasive speeches. Overall, the researchers found that those speeches containing root metaphors were more persuasive than their literal counterparts. However, upon closer inspection, Bowers and Osborn found that only the *"SEX"* speech was more persuasive. They concluded that the *"DEATH"* speech stirred up questions about the speaker, and that subjects who were more interested in trying to figure out this strange speaker who was obsessed with death would be too preoccupied to receive the basic message of the speech. Overall, however, Bowers and Osborn (1966) maintained their support for metaphors as effective persuasive devices.

What little experimental evidence collected since those early Bowers studies that exists has shown similar equivocal findings. Reinsch (1971) found evidence supporting the persuasive effectiveness of metaphors over that of their literal counterparts. Furthermore, Reinsch found that similes fell somewhere in between metaphors and literal discourse in their persuasiveness (see Glucksberg, 1989, for a discussion of subtle differences between metaphors and similes). Johnson and Taylor (1981) also found support for the persuasiveness of metaphors, but they found this to be true only for subjects who were politically sophisticated. This ran counter to their predictions, as they predicted that politically unsophisticated individuals would be more susceptible to metaphorical manipulations, whereas the politically sophisticated would not be so susceptible, as their knowledge of the topics being discussed would innoculate them from simplistic characterizations. Their conclusions about the effectiveness of metaphors was taken from Fiske and Kinder (1981), who stated that politically sophisticated individuals had developed schemas about political events. When metaphors are used, they can rearrange their political knowledge about these metaphors. Those who were politically unsophisticated did not have knowledge enough to be organized about such metaphors.

Bosman and his colleagues (Bosman, 1987; Bosman & Hagendoorn, 1991) have found mixed results for the effectiveness of metaphors as persuasive devices. Their studies found evidence which contradicted the other's results. The Bosman (1987) study found that metaphors were effective persuasive devices. Questionnaires regarding subjects' opinions about racist political groups in the Netherlands were greatly influenced by introductory metaphors, indicating that the groups *"should be unmasked"* for their racist policies or that the groups *"sprout from the fertile soil"* of adverse social conditions. Note that in this study, metaphors were compared against one another. In the Bosman and Hagendoorn (1991) study, these metaphors were compared to a literal equivalent. Although the results from the Bosman (1987) study were replicated in that introductory metaphors influenced responses to the questionnaires the subjects were given, the results did not differ from those obtained from the subjects who read the literal introduction. In fact, there were indications that the literal message was even more convincing than the metaphorical one:

> Summarizing these results, it seems safe to conclude that, when a suitable paraphrase is available, metaphorical language has no special persuasive advantage over ordinary literal language. On the contrary, the evidence is in favor of literal language, for although not statistically significant, effect sizes for literal language are twice as large. (p. 278)

The Bosman and Hagendoorn (1991) study found even more inconsistencies with past research. Contrary to Johnson and Taylor (1981), there was a trend for *less* politically sophisticated subjects to be persuaded. Moreover, whereas the Bosman (1987) study found women to be *more* influenced by metaphors, the Bosman and Hagendoorn (1991) study found women to be *less* influenced by metaphors.

Finally, Read, Cesa, Jones, and Collins (1990) found evidence supporting metaphors as effective persuasive devices. Additionally, subjects recalled more of the metaphorical passages than their literal counterparts. However, in my own work (e.g., Mio, 1993), I could not find evidence supporting this memorability aspect of metaphors. Interestingly, subjects in the Read et al. (1990) study also attributed positive characteristics to speakers using metaphors. Subjects rated the speakers as "more interesting, persuasive, memorable, and having a better command of language" (p. 139) than those speakers not using metaphors.

A METAPHOR EXTENSION HYPOTHESIS

Given the seemingly contradictory findings regarding the persuasiveness of metaphors, it would seem that no conclusive statements can be made at this time. Perhaps this is due to the disparate areas that researchers are investigating.   Thus, I have restricted my efforts to a fairly limited area: political debates.   In 1986, after Ferdinand Marcos was overthrown in the Philippines, then President Corazon Aquino visited the United States, asking for more foreign aid to help rebuild her country.   She addressed a joint session of Congress to make her case—an honor bestowed upon very few foreign leaders.   Then Speaker of the House, Tip O'Neill, was quoted in the press that it was the best speech he had ever heard.   Senator Bob Dole was also impressed with the speech, and as President Aquino was leaving, Senator Dole said to her, *"Madam President, you just hit a home run."*   President Aquino replied, *"I hope the bases were loaded!"*   This little exchange led me to contemplate how metaphors may be effective in exchanges such as these.   One example of such an exchange is a political debate.   What President Aquino had essentially done was to use Senator Dole's metaphor and extend it.   The impact of her return statement, I felt, was quite strong.   It certainly seems that it would have been much less strong if she had simply given a literal retort, such as "Thank you. I hope we receive more aid from the United States."   Thus, I began formulating what I call "the metaphor extension hypothesis."   What this hypothesis suggests is that metaphors that extend someone else's metaphor are more effective persuasive devices than those that do not.   What is meant by "do not" could either mean a literal statement or a nonextending metaphorical one.

As many of you may recall, Lithuania was attempting to break away from the Soviet Union in the spring of 1990.   That year, they became more and more insistent regarding their freedom, prompting President Mikail Gorbachev to send in tanks and other heavy equipment to quell the uprising.   On a *Nightline* program that spring, a Soviet and a Lithuanian representative were presenting their positions.   The Soviet representative asked that the world be patient with the separation of the two countries.   He likened the relationship between the Soviet Union and Lithuania to a *"divorce,"* where the two sides needed to still be formally married, but there would be a time of separation to see if the two sides really could live without one another.   He then went on to describe how the two countries had been together since World War II, and their economies were interwoven.   To have a divorce immediately would be too radical a solution, for both countries would undergo much pain in stabilizing their economies independently.

After the Soviet representative spoke, the Lithuanian presented what I consider to be a classic example of my metaphor extension hypothesis.   He said that the two sides were *"not going through a divorce because we were never married, Lithuania was simply raped."*   He went on to describe how Lithuania was defeated by Nazi Germany.   Because Lithuania bordered Russia, the Russians were afraid of being drawn into the war.   Because Germany wanted to keep Russia out of the war so that it could concentrate all of its war efforts on the Western front, Germany gave Lithuania over to Russia to serve as a buffer zone. Thus, Lithuania felt *"raped"* first by Germany, then by Russia. This is why Lithuania wanted its independence immediately, for one would not ask someone who has been raped to spend more time with the rapist than necessary.

The reason why I felt that the Lithuanian response was a classic extension of a metaphor is that prototypical divorces are generally considered to be negative relationships between men and women. Prototypical rapes are even worse relationships between men and women. Thus, the Lithuanian used the Soviet's metaphor and extended it, turning the Soviet's metaphor against him. This exchange served as the basis for two experiments.

EXPERIMENT 1

Method

Subjects. We employed 167 subjects from the Human Subject Pool at Washington State University's Department of Psychology. Subjects were divided into three groups: One group heard a political speech derived from the Soviet position likening their situation to a *"divorce,"* with the Lithuanian position being presented without the *"rape"* metaphor. A second group heard both metaphorically derived positions. Finally, a third group heard control speeches, where neither metaphor was used.

Materials. Speeches were constructed around both metaphors along with corresponding control speeches. Thus, there were four speeches altogether, a Soviet *"divorce"* metaphor speech, a Soviet literal speech, a Lithuanian *"rape"* metaphor speech, and a Lithuanian literal speech. All speeches were approximately equal in length, and second halves of the speeches were the same for each country's position. In other words, although the first part of the Lithuanian speeches differed in that one started with a *"rape"* theme and the other with a literal transmission of the same information, both of these speeches provided the exact same information about Germany's takeover during World War II, the deal Germany made with Russia, and the demand for immediate separation from the Soviet Union. Two males recorded all speeches, with the recording times all being between 80 and 90 seconds. These speeches were re-recorded so that the speakers were counterbalanced to control for speaker effect. In other words, half the subjects heard Speaker A read the Soviet speeches, with Speaker B reading the Lithuanian speeches, and the other half heard Speaker B reading the Soviet speeches, with Speaker A reading the Lithuanian speeches. The speeches were pretested to make sure that the metaphor speeches and their corresponding control versions transmitted the same information.

Procedure. Subjects heard the speeches, then they indicated which speaker they believed the most by circling a number on a 6-point Likert scale. Since the natural sequence of the speakers was the Soviet speaker going first with the Lithuanian speaker responding, we always had the Soviet speaker at the "1" end of the scale, with the Lithuanian speaker at the "6" end. All numbers had verbal anchors associated with them. We predicted that subjects would be more persuaded by the Soviet speaker if he presented the *"divorce"* metaphor with the Lithuanian speaker not responding with a metaphorical retort. However, subjects would be more persuaded by the Lithuanian speaker if he responded with the *"rape"* metaphor. Subjects should score somewhere in between these two positions if neither speakers gave metaphorical speeches.

Subjects were then given an intervening task for 20 minutes. After the 20-minute period, subjects were asked to recall as much of the speeches as they could. Their responses were scored for idea units.

Results

The present study was a 2 (sex) x 3 (metaphor condition) factorial design. An analysis of variance (ANOVA) was performed with speaker ratings as the dependent variable. This result yielded nonsignificant but suggestive results, $F(2,161) = 2.45$, $p < .1$. Table 8.1 displays the means and numbers of subjects in each speech condition. In examining these results, we found that they followed exactly along the lines of our predictions. Note that there was generally a slight bias in favor of the Lithuanian position, as suggested by the 4.15 mean for the control speeches.

TABLE 8.1
Means and Numbers of Subjects for Metaphor Conditions, Study #1

Condition	Males	Females	Overall
Soviet Divorce	$M = 3.85$	$M = 3.88$	$M = 3.86$
Lithuanian Control	$n = 26$	$n = 33$	$n = 59$
Soviet Control	$M = 4.24$	$M = 4.05$	$M = 4.15$
Lithuanian Control	$n = 25$	$n = 22$	$n = 47$
Soviet Divorce	$M = 4.31$	$M = 4.32$	$M = 4.32$
Lithuanian Rape	$n = 29$	$n = 31$	$n = 60$

Because of this strong trend, and because we were primarily interested in comparing the metaphor extension versus a nonextension, we conducted a 2 x 2 ANOVA, eliminating the control speeches from the analysis. We were left with 119 subjects, with 59 in the Soviet-only metaphor condition and 60 in the condition where both speakers used their respective metaphors. This analysis yielded statistically reliable results, $F(1,115) = 5.15$, $p < .05$. Our results did not yield any gender differences, $F(1,161) = .269$, ns.

Independent judges attained excellent reliability in identifying idea units (Pearson $r = .94$). However, an ANOVA on these data did not reveal statistically reliable results. Metaphors did not seem to have an effect upon memory for the speeches. All groups yielded mean recollections of about four idea units per speech (i.e., eight idea units for the two speeches).

Discussion

Results are consistent with the metaphor extension hypothesis. The condition where the Lithuanian representative extended the Soviet representative's metaphor yielded higher convincingness scores for the Lithuanian position than the condition where the Lithuanian representative responded to the Soviet representative's metaphor with a nonmetaphorical speech. The fact that such speeches did not improve subjects' memories for the speeches is disappointing and inconsistent with Read et al.'s (1990) findings. Reyna (personal communication) suggested that this latter result is consistent with the Brainerd and Reyna (1993) fuzzy-trace theory. This theory asserts that memory for events typically does not follow verbatim traces but rather retrieves gist information (see also Reyna, Chapter 3, this volume).

As one might notice, although results from Experiment 1 are consistent with my metaphor extension hypothesis, they do not provide definitive evidence. There are two alternative explanations for the superiority of the *"rape"* metaphor speech. First, it could have merely been the case that metaphors following metaphors are more persuasive. The only comparison we have here is that the *"rape"* speech following the *"divorce"* speech was more persuasive than a nonmetaphorical speech following the *"divorce"* speech. Second, *"rape"* is an emotionally evocative concept. Perhaps subjects were merely swayed by the emotional argument posed by the Lithuanian speaker, and extension had nothing to do with the persuasiveness of the presentation. Experiment 2 was designed to address these issues.

EXPERIMENT 2

Method

Subjects. We employed 455 subjects from the Human Subject Pool at Washington State University's Department of Psychology. None of these subjects participated in the Experiment 1, as the present experiment was conducted a year after the first experiment. Subjects were divided into five groups, each consisting of 82–96 individuals. One group heard the Soviet *"divorce"* metaphorical speech, with the Lithuanian speech being nonmetaphorical. A second group heard the Soviet *"divorce"* metaphor, followed by the Lithuanian *"rape"* metphor. A third group heard the Soviet *"divorce"* metaphor followed by a Lithuanian speech likening their relationship with the Soviet Union to *"two ships passing in the night."* A fourth group heard the Soviet *"divorce"* metaphor followed by a Lithuanian speech likening their relationship with the Soviet Union to *"a prisoner being held captive by an evil Soviet regime."* Finally a fifth group heard control speeches, where neither speaker used metaphorical language to present their positions.

  Materials. Speeches were developed similarly to the way they were developed in Experiment 1. The two new speeches, which I will refer to as the *"ships"* and *"prisoner"* speeches, were pretested and determined to yield approximately the same amount of information as the previous speeches did. Moreover, the root metaphors of *"divorce," "rape," "ships passing,"* and *"prisoner"* were presented among a number of other words and phrases. A different set of subjects rated these words and phrases on a 5-point Likert scale for their abilities to evoke emotions. Although we were hoping that "prisoner" would evoke about the same amount of emotion that "rape" did, it did not. "Rape" evoked the highest amount of emotion ($M = 4.5$), "divorce" the next ($M = 4.1$), then "prisoner" ($M = 4.0$), and finally "ships passing" ($M = 1.2$). Notice, however, that even though notions of a "prisoner" did not evoke the same amount of emotion that "rape" did, it still evoked a great deal of emotion, especially in comparison to "ships passing," and about the same amount as "divorce."

  In selecting the two new metaphors, we reasoned that *"ships passing in the night"* was a reasonable metaphor that was fundamentally different from the *"rape"* metaphor. We wrote a speech that started out, "We in Lithuania do not see our relationship with the Soviet Union as a divorce. Instead, we see it more like two ships passing in the night." We went on to discuss how the ships shared common water at one time, but now that the ships have passed, it is time for the world to recognize that the two countries no longer shared common goals and that the world should allow this passage to take place. With respect to the *"prisoner"* speech, it was seen as different from a *"rape"* metaphor in that rape is prototypically seen as a bad relationship between a man and a woman, whereas notions of prisoners prototypically conjure up images of a bad relationship between a man and a man. Thus, we deemed it to be a nonextension of the *"divorce"* metaphor presented by the Soviet speaker. This speech started out, "We in Lithuania do not see our relationship with the Soviet

Union as a divorce. Instead, we are prisoners in an illegal Soviet regime." We went on to discuss how this imprisonment had gone on for far too many years, and that now that the truth had come out, it was time for Lithuania to be set free. As in Experiment 1, both second halves of these speeches concluded in exactly the same manner as the Lithuanian *"rape"* metaphor speech and the control speech.

As in Experiment 1, these two new speeches were recorded, and they both fell within the 80–90 second time frame that the other speeches did. We also counterbalanced the recorders.

Procedure. Procedures followed those of Experiment 1 with the only difference being that there were five groups of subjects instead of three.

Results

The present study was a 2 (sex) x 5 (metaphor condition) factorial design. An ANOVA was performed with speaker ratings as the dependent variable. This ANOVA yielded reliable differences among the metaphor conditions, $F (4,445) = 2.86$, $p < .05$. Table 8.2 presents the means and numbers of subjects for each condition.

We conducted a series of planned comparisons for pairs of groups, based upon predictions from the metaphor extension hypothesis. This involved comparing the condition where the *"rape"* speech followed the *"divorce"* speech with the conditions where the control, *"ships,"* and *"prisoner"* speeches followed the *"divorce"* speech.

We were able to replicate results from Experiment 1. Subjects in the *"rape"* condition clearly were more persuaded by the Lithuanian speech than subjects in the control condition, $F (1,183) = 5.63$, $p < .05$. Moreover, subjects in the *"rape"* condition were also more perusaded than those in the *"ships"* and *"prisoner"* conditions, $F (1,174) = 10.85$, $p < .001$; $F (1,179) = 5.38$, $p < .05$, respectively. Thus, it is clearly the *extension* of the Soviet's metaphor that made the Lithuanian's speech more persuasive. Finally, the *"rape"* versus *"prisoner"* comparison was the only pair-wise comparison that yielded gender differences. Female subjects seemed less convinced by the Lithuanian metaphor than their male counterparts, $F (1,179) = 4.87$, $p < .05$. In examining the means for all conditions, this appears to be a slight tendency in our overall findings, although it was not a reliable difference, $F (1,445) = 1.83$, *ns*). The largest male–female disparity was seen in the *"prisoner"* condition.

Technically, it is not proper to exceed the degrees of freedom (4) in conducting pair-wise comparisons, so we restricted our main analyses to conditions related to the *"rape"* speech. However, as a check for any differences among other pair-wise combinations, we conducted such analyses. No other pair-wise conditions yielded statistical differences.

TABLE 8.2
Means and Numbers of Subjects for Metaphor Conditions, Study #2

Condition	Males	Females	Overall
Soviet-Divorce	$M = 3.77$	$M = 4.04$	$M = 3.93$
Lithuanian-Control	$n = 39$	$n = 56$	$n = 95$
Soviet-Control	$M = 4.06$	$M = 3.98$	$M = 4.02$
Lithuanian-Control	$n = 48$	$n = 47$	$n = 95$
Soviet-Divorce	$M = 4.45$	$M = 4.19$	$M = 4.31$
Lithuanian-Rape	$n = 42$	$n = 54$	$n = 96$
Soviet-Divorce	$M = 3.83$	$M = 3.58$	$M = 3.67$
Lithuanian-Ships	$n = 30$	$n = 52$	$n = 82$
Soviet-Divorce	$M = 4.18$	$M = 3.66$	$M = 3.90$
Lithuanian-Prisoner	$n = 40$	$n = 47$	$n = 87$

Discussion

Overall, we found support for the metaphor extension hypothesis. When the Lithuanian representative's speech extended the Soviet representative's metaphor, subjects seemed much more persuaded by the Lithuanian position than when the Lithuanian representative's speech was a nonmetaphorical speech, a nonextending metaphor, or an emotionally evocative nonextending metaphor.

Unlike the Bosman (1987) and Bosman and Hagendoorn (1991) studies, we did not find any gender differences in most of our conditions. Perhaps this is not an important point, as their studies actually contradicted one another, with Bosman (1987) finding that women were *more* affected by metaphor and Bosman and Hagendoorn (1991) finding that women were *less* affected by metaphor. Although our set of studies did not find support either way, one condition in Experiment 2 did find a slight tendency for women to be *less* affected by metaphor. Chantrill and Mio (Chapter 10, this volume) contend that women *should* be less affected by metaphor per se but more affected by metonymy. None of our conditions included metonymic passages in these studies.

GENERAL CONCLUSIONS

Metaphor and other forms of symbolic language have long been assumed to be effective persuasive devices. Numerous authors have written about the persuasiveness of this metaphor or that one, and they have developed elaborate theories about *why* metaphors are effective. These theories have centered around information processing principles, where it is assumed that we are information processors attempting to integrate a great deal of information. This information exceeds our processing capacities, so we need things like heuristics, metaphors, and other devices that collapse the large set of information around us. Moreover, metaphors carry with them emotional arguments that motivate us into action, or at least to support those who use them. Finally, metaphors are seen as devices that bridge the gap between logical and emotional arguments. As such, they give us the sense that we are behaving rationally, although this may not be the case. As Chaiken and Stangor (1987) and Stone (1988) might say, we are behaving pseudologically.

Although theorists are numerous, empiricists are few. The effectiveness of metaphors in persuasive communication has not been consistently demonstrated empirically. Studies have found contradictory evidence with respect to the persuasive efficacy of metaphor. Some have found support for the persuasiveness of metaphor (e.g., Bowers & Osborn, 1966; Read et al., 1990; Reinsch, 1971), while others have found that metaphors are *less* persuasive (e.g., Bosman & Hagendoorn, 1991). Still others have found that metaphors are effective persuasive devices for subsets of people (e.g., Bosman, 1987; Johnson & Taylor, 1981).

Results from our studies suggest that there is some basis for assuming that metaphors are persuasive, at least in the limited circumstance of a debate format. Metaphors seem to need to extend opponents' metaphors in order to be persuasive in this debate format. Nonextension metaphors did not differ from literal language in terms of their persuasive powers. Unfortunately, this did not seem to translate into memorability, at least as measured by recall of the speeches containing metaphors. This differs from the Read et al. (1990) study, which found support for metaphors contributing to the memorability of their respective speeches.

Gender differences in response to metaphors have been inconsistent. Bosman and his colleagues (Bosman, 1987; Bosman & Hagendoorn, 1991) found contradictory evidence with respect to gender differences. Our findings found a slight tendency for women to be less affected by metaphorical appeals. This is consistent with assumptions by Chantrill and Mio (Chapter 10, this volume), who suggest that metaphors per se are more resonant with men, whereas metonymies are more resonant with women. Women seem to be more attuned to the type of language that invite them to join as one, which metonymy does, whereas metaphor asks people to keep the topic and vehicle separate while finding commonalities between them.

Because of the contradictory evidence coming from the metaphor and persuasion literature, future studies should concentrate on limited areas of concern. Our own studies have concentrated on the area of political debates. Besides the studies we reported here, we have preliminary evidence supporting our metaphor extension hypothesis in other contexts. For example, when subjects heard a speaker extolling the virtues of California, calling it the *"California dream"* despite the recent problems of riots, fires, floods, and earthquakes, subjects overwhelmingly preferred a second speaker's response, saying *"the dream has turned into a nightmare"* as opposed to the literal response of "the dream has turned into something horrible" or the nonextension metaphor response of *"the dream has turned into a horror show."* Such studies could then suggest *where* metaphors might be more persuasive, instead of general conclusions of *whether* metaphors are persuasive or not. As we pursue this course, we will follow the course of many findings in social psychology. The typical pattern is as follows: A phenomenon is discovered, the phenomenon is overapplied, then researchers specify when and where this phenomenon is most evidenced.

ACKNOWLEDGMENTS

Most of the work for this chapter was conducted while I was in the Department of Psychology at Washington State University. I appreciate the support of my colleagues and my department while I was there. I also appreciate the hard work of students who worked with me there to collect and analyze the data. These students include Joanna Bernard, Ty Brown, Marci Cook, Shannon Guilory, Daniel Hayes, Sandee Hunt, David Jones, Kevin Osborn, Reino Tanttila, Bradley Watts, and Brandie Worden.

ENDNOTE

[1]It has been my observation that political scientists, like Edelman, use the term "symbol" to be the more inclusive term, whereas cognitive psychologists use the term "metaphor" to be the more inclusive term. In politics, all language, actions, and settings are considered to be symbolic of a deeper level of understanding. Thus, in the 1988 presidential election campaign, candidate George Bush would deliver speeches in front of American flags. This was taken to underscore his patriotism and to contrast his level of patriotism with that of Michael Dukakis, whose veto of a bill requiring school children to recite the Pledge of Allegiance was suggested by the Bush campaign as a

symbol for Dukakis' lack of patriotism. Thus, actions and settings are used as symbol, as opposed to spoken as metaphor. Edelman reserves "metaphor" to be used strictly as the formal linguistic expression understood by most lay people. On the other hand, cognitive psychologists use the term "metaphor" as the more inclusive term because of cognitive psychology's interest in how the mind is organized. "Metaphor" is a linguistic act that provides some insight into this organization. Among all terms referring to figurative language (e.g., simile, analogy, metonymy), "metaphor" seems to be the most general and inclusive (Pollio, Hoffman, & Smith, 1986). To the extent that actions and settings can be expressed verbally, they can be transformed into a metaphorical expression.

REFERENCES

Aronson, E., Turner, J. A., & Carlsmith, J. M. (1963). Communicator credibility and communicator discrepancy as determinants of opinion change. *Journal of Abnormal and Social Psychology, 67*, 31–36.

Asch, S. (1946). Forming impressions of personality. *Journal of Abnormal and Social Psychology, 41*, 258–290.

Baron, R. A., & Byrne, D. (1994). *Social psychology: Understanding human interaction* (7th ed.). Boston: Allyn and Bacon.

Bosman, J. (1987). Persuasive effects of political metaphors. *Metaphor and Symbolic Activity, 2*, 97–113.

Bosman, J., & Hagendoorn, L. (1991). Effects of literal and metaphorical persuasive messages. *Metaphor and Symbolic Activity, 6*, 271–292.

Bowers, J. W. (1964). Some correlates of language intensity. *Quarterly Journal of Speech, 50*, 415–420.

Bowers, J. W., & Osborn, M. M. (1966). Attitudinal effects of selected types of concluding metaphors in persuasive speeches. *Speech Monographs, 33*, 147–155.

Brainerd, C. J., & Reyna, V. F. (1993). Memory independence and memory interference in cognitive development. *Psychological Review, 100*, 42–67.

Bronowski, J. (1972). *Science and human values.* New York: Harper Torchbooks.

Chaiken, S., & Stangor, C. (1987). Attitudes and attitude change. *Annual Review of Psychology, 38*, 575–630.

Edelman, M. (1964). *The symbolic uses of politics.* Urbana, IL: University of Illinois Press.

Edelman, M. (1971). *Politics as symbolic action: Mass arousal and quiescence.* Chicago: Markham.

Edelman, M. (1977). *Political language: Words that succeed and policies that fail.* New York: Academic Press.

Edelman, M. (1988). *Constructing the political spectacle.* Chicago: The University of Chicago Press.

Eldersveld, S. J., & Dodge, R. W. (1954). Personal contact or mail propaganda? An experiment in voting turnout and attitude change. In D. Katz, D. Cartwright, S. Eldersveld, & A. M. Lee (Eds.), *Public opinion and propaganda* (pp. 532–542). New York: Dryden Press.

Erikson, E. H. (1959). Identity and the life cycle. *Psychological Issues* [Monograph 1], 1(1). New York: International Universities Press.

Festinger, L., & Maccoby, E. (1964). On resistance to persuasive communications. *Journal of Abnormal and Social Psychology, 68*, 359–366.

Fishbein, M., & Ajzen, I. (1975). *Belief, attitude, intention and behavior: An introduction to theory and research.* Reading, MA: Addison-Wesley.

Fiske, S. T., & Kinder, D. R. (1981). Involvement, expertise, and schema use: Evidence from political cognition. In N. Cantor & J. Kihlstrom (Eds.), *Personality, cognition, and social interaction* (pp. 171–190). Hillsdale, NJ: Lawrence Erlbaum Associates.

Freedman, J. L., & Sears, D. O. (1965). Warning, distraction, and resistance to influence. *Journal of Personality and Social Psychology, 1,* 262–266.

Glucksberg, S. (1989). Metaphors in conversation: How are they understood? Why are they used? *Metaphor and Symbolic Activity, 4,* 125–143.

Goodall, H. L., Jr. (1983). The nature of analogic discourse. *Quarterly Journal of Speech, 69,* 171–179.

Graber, D. (1993). Political communication: Scope, progress, promise. In A. W. Finifter (Ed.), *Political science: The state of the discipline II* (pp. 305–332). Washington, DC: American Political Science Association.

Gross, A. G. (1983). Analogy and intersubjectivity: Political oratory, scholarly argument and scientific reports. *Quarterly Journal of Speech, 69,* 37–46.

Hovland, C. I., Janis, I. L., & Kelley, H. H. (1953). *Communication and persuasion: Psychological studies of one on one.* New Haven, CT: Yale University Press.

Jamieson, K. H. (1985). *Communication and persuasion.* London: Croom Helm.

Johnson, J. T., & Taylor, S. E. (1981). The effect of metaphor on political attitudes. *Basic and Applied Social Psychology, 2,* 305–316.

Lumsdaine, A. A., & Janis, I. L. (1953). Resistance to "counterpropaganda" produced by one-sided and two-sided "propaganda" presentations. *Public Opinion Quarterly, 17,* 311–318.

Miller, E. F. (1979). Metaphor and political knowledge. *The American Political Science Review, 73,* 155–170.

Miller, N., & Campbell, D. T. (1959). Recency and primacy in persuasion as a function of the timing of speeches and measurements. *Journal of Abnormal and Social Psychology, 59,* 1–9.

Mio, J. S. (1993, August). Responding to metaphors in the context of a political debate. In J. S. Mio (Chair), *Metaphor: Cognition and appreciation.* Symposium conducted at the 101st annual convention of the American Psychological Association, Toronto, Canada.

Myers, D. G. (1993). *Social psychology* (4th ed.). New York: McGraw-Hill.

Neuman, W. R., Just, J. R., & Crigler, A. N. (1992). *Common knowledge: News and the construction of political meaning.* Chicago: University of Chicago Press.

Pollio, H. R., Hoffman, R. R., & Smith, M. K. (1986). Editorial. *Metaphor and Symbolic Activity, 1,* 1–4.

Read, S. J., Cesa, I. L., Jones, D. K., & Collins, N. L. (1990). When is the federal budget like a baby? Metaphor in political rhetoric. *Metaphor and Symbolic Activity, 5,* 125–149.

Reinsch, N. L., Jr. (1971). An investigation of the effects of the metaphor and simile in persuasive discourse. *Speech Monographs, 38,* 142–145.

Sabini, J. (1992). *Social psychology.* New York: Norton.

Sniderman, P. M. (1993). The new look in public opinion research. In A. W. Finifter (Ed.), *Political science: The state of the discipline II* (pp. 219–245). Washington, DC: American Political Science Association.

Stone, D. A. (1988). *Policy paradox and political reason.* Glenview, IL: Scott Foresman.

9

Economic Metaphors: Ideology, Rhetoric, and Theory

Warren S. Gramm
Washington State University

> Conventional economics—after over a century of the Great Debate with Marxist socialism—has developed a number of bad habits of mythical and metaphorical thought, particularly when applied to the capitalist firm (Ellerman, 1991, p. 546).

Economic metaphor permeates political dialogue as well as economic commentary and thought. *"THE INVISIBLE HAND," "the marketplace of ideas, "the free lunch," "the safety net," "the golden parachute," "the glass ceiling"* are commonplace. Regrettably, their significance remains essentially unrecognized. Regrettable, because metaphors can be dangerous as well as useful. They can be a source for inspiration of new ideas, "a distinctive mode of achieving insight" (Max Black in McCloskey, 1985, p. 77). Schumpeter (1954, p. 41) applied the metaphor pre-analytic *"Vision"* in identifying the creative intellectual process. "In formulating [his] views about the role of metaphor in theory change . . . [Boyd argues that] there exists an important class of metaphors which play a role in the development and articulation of theories in mature sciences" (1979, p. 357). (c.f. Shulman, 1992, pp. 443-448, "The Relevance of Metaphors.")

There is danger in metaphor insofar as metaphors may trivialize important political and economic relations, and may become a digression from or substitute for serious thought and debate. "They dropped through the *"safety net"*; she hit the *"glass ceiling,"* you say! So what have you said? Like the meaning of politically sensitive words, metaphor readily provides ideological cover for existing power relations.

The political use of economic metaphors ranges from the obvious to the subtle and, often coincidentally, from ready, short-run political impact to long-run ideological influence. The *"trickle-down"* effect (of the depressed 1930s and the Reagan-Thatcher 1980s), the *"safety net for the poor,"* and *"golden parachute for the rich,"* are examples of the immediate, political use. They identify elements of macroeconomics, of aggregate resource allocation, and income distribution. In providing figurative illustration of problems of economic welfare and the appropriate extent of poverty and riches, their derivation and use is relatively clear.

This is not the case with the second—the subtle—long-run group. Here the metaphor tends to originate outside politics; it appears first in the writing of economists, in textbooks or theoretical analysis. Typically, both at such a beginning and during subsequent political application, the metaphor's use is supportive of capitalism, of the private market system. Thus, these metaphors provide integral ideological reinforcement of the dominant economic and political power base.

The strongest example here is the mechanical metaphor of "*EQUILIBRIUM.*" It was introduced in the late nineteenth century as the conceptual base of price theory—the logical grounding of economics as science. Linked with other metaphors, it has become an anchor of free market ideology of the belief that capitalism is the "best of all possible systems"; that, left to its own resources, the private market will generate acceptable growth and welfare.

Discussion of the immediate, politically clear-cut metaphor is mostly descriptive. The analytical, ideologically evolving metaphor is more complex and controversial. It cuts to the core of the socially sensitive issues of economics as apologetics and metaphysics (versus scientific generation of testable hypotheses), and the nature of ideology and power structures. Table 9.1 classifies these metaphors in order to reduce these difficult distinctions down to manageable proportions.

Two other somewhat overlapping classifications have been developed by McCloskey (1985) and Bicchieri (1988). Less concerned with political associations of economic metaphors, they apply a two-dimensional approach wherein directly economic-analytic metaphors are contrasted with all others. Their focus, like that of the present chapter, is on analytically grounded metaphors, those considered under Part IV of Table 9.1 under the heading, "Politically Indirect." In the introduction to Table 9.2, which follows, the three approaches are compared.

SOME INTERPRETATIVE ISSUES

The last two categories in Table 9.1, those metaphors with clearly supportable political applications or implications, are the primary topics considered here. Those whose political associations seem minimal, or are difficult to establish, are considered briefly as an extended introduction to the dimensional differences in economic metaphors.

Several economic metaphors are fundamentally non- or apolitical. Though, even here (like any piece of language or exposition) they can be used in a politically directed way. The *"pie chart,"* for example, is used in many contexts to illustrate allocating, or "divvying up" with respect to income distribution (wages, rent, interest and profits), government expenditures (welfare, military, general and miscellaneous), and government income (taxes, interest and fees).

TABLE 9.1
Economic Metaphors: Political Gradations*

I. Non- or Apolitical
    pie chart
    circular flow
    accounting
    economic man (Robinson Crusoe)

II. Politically Indeterminate
    Wizard of Oz (yellow brick road, tin woodsman)
    cash value (William James)
    invisible hand

III. Politically Direct
    trickle-down   glass ceiling
    free lunch   war (drugs, poverty)
    safety net   free market (system)
    golden parachute

IV. Politically Indirect**
  A. Primary
    mechanics
    physics
    equilibrium
  B. Secondary
    organics
    the firm
    capital

* Illustrative selection (in order of appearance in text).
** See Table 9.2 for greater detail.

The *"circular flow"* diagram, illustrating the movement of resources and money payments between "households and firms," in itself is politically neutral. Still, anticipating the major theme of the later section, Economic Metaphors that Are Politically Indirect, the gross simplicity of the basic model carries question-begging implications that, arguably, have political-ideological significance. Characterizing the "household" as *the* source of saving denies the central role of *accumulation* of the capitalist firm; the *"closed circle"* gives implicit reinforcement to the anti-Keynesian, Say's Law apologetic that full employment is the natural state of the capitalist economy.

Perhaps most important in this category is the accounting metaphor. Klamer and McCloskey (1992) asserted that "of economics' many metaphors

. . . its leading one, is the making of a set of accounts" (p. 158). Given its functional link to economic rationality and the governing maximization assumption, the *"accounting"* metaphor may well be the most pervasive, but not the "master metaphor," in terms of being most important. Similarly, the *"rational maximizer," "economic man"* (*homo economicus,* Robinson Crusoe) has been identified as the dominant economic metaphor (Browne, Bergeron, & Quinn, 1994).

The political relevance of some nonanalytic metaphors may be debatable. Interpretations of the purpose and content of a given metaphor can change at widely varying rates and to widely varying degrees. Sometimes the politicized interpretative transformation of a metaphor is rapid and complete. When Nikita Khrushchev said "We will overtake you" in economic production, the United States' immediate cold war inversion translated the statement to "We will bury you," making it a palpable military threat. More commonly the transition is gradual, partial, and opaque. After more than two centuries economists differ widely in their interpretations of Adam Smith's *"INVISIBLE HAND."* Some regard it as poetry, others find the metaphor to be a theory. Smith wrote, "every individual . . . intends only his own gain, and he is in this, as in many other cases, led by an invisible hand to promote an end which was not part of his intention. Nor is it always the worse for the society that it was no part of it" (Smith, 1776/1937, p. 423).

The metaphorical intent of a given author may be debatable[1]; there can be a fine line between purposeful metaphor and instructive or entertaining parable or simile. What was Smith's intent? Some judge it to be conflict resolution (Gramm, 1980, p. 129), reflecting the "Adam Smith problem" of ameliorating the tensions between social interest (sympathy) and self-interest (greed). The orthodox neoclassical economist tends to see it as a precursory insight concerning market equilibrium theory. Smith's strongly qualified observation can be interpreted as a metaphoric "it is" statement or as a tentative "as if" simile. (The transformation of Smith's socio-organic metaphor into the idea, the new market metaphor, of mechanistic, competitive *"market equilibrium"* is elaborated later in this chapter.)

Consider a somewhat tangential, similarly debatable case. *The Wonderful Wizard of Oz* (Baum, 1900), was written as a fairy tale for children. Yet, its substantive political essence is a descriptive caricature of the working conditions of Midwestern farmers and Eastern industrial workers and of the politics of the 1890s gold/silver standard controversy, a "Parable on Populism" (Littlefield, 1964, pp. 48-50).

The Wonderful Wizard of Oz can be seen as an assemblage of metaphors: the political theme presents the Populist, Midwestern farmers against the financial-industrial "East." The leading metaphor, *"the yellow brick road,"* which leads nowhere, represents the gold standard. Oz is the abbreviation for ounce, the standard measure of gold. Whatever Baum's intent, there is significant economic, metaphorical content in *The Wonderful Wizard of Oz* for late twentieth-century adults. As an institutional process, although a metaphor may originate on such general grounds as entertainment, noneconomic parable, or economic-analytic insight, it can readily evolve into a politically relevant, even ideologically effective proposition.

Two important interpretative relations are the interaction between metaphors and the relation between new, creative metaphors and other modes of thought and communication. The latter include mathematics, model building, and the use of analogy, anecdote, simile, or other tropes to explain complex, nonfactual social and economic phenomena. "One attraction of metaphorical reasoning is the capacity to make ready use of already developed and elaborated structures from another sphere" (Mirowski, 1989, p. 179).

Vertically, metaphors can be regarded as building blocks. Horizontally, they can illustrate Friedrich Nietzsche's vision of truth as "a mobile army of metaphors" (Ellerman, 1991, p. 546). Such breeding can be constructive, like the creation of Dorothy's little squad in *The Wonderful Wizard of Oz*. But it also can be negative. At the extreme, "Metaphors are like lies: one metaphor requires others to round out the picture" (Ellerman, 1991, p. 559) to complete the story that might be fiction (Bicchieri, 1988, p. 109).[2] More generally, in the compounding of layers of metaphorical abstraction, it is likely that contact will be lost with the limited initial insight of each one. Thus, we have the methodological metaphors of *"building on sand"* or *"castles in the air."*

POLITICALLY DIRECT METAPHORS

The most widely used and generally recognized economic metaphors are generated in the rhetoric of politics. Some are simply serviceable in calling attention to a sensitive issue in political or social economy. For example, fluctuations in the level of business activity in the past century have been characterized as *"cycles"* or *"crises,"* which, in turn, present the submetaphors *"depression,"* *"entropy,"* *"exhilaration,"* *"turning points,"* *"rolling readjustments,"* and *"stagnation."* Others, for example *"the trickle-down,"* *"the free-lunch,"* and *"the all-encompassing free market"* present altered meaning and ideological refinement in relation to distribution of income and wealth and the role of government in the economy. They illustrate the use of economic metaphor as political apologetics, for the essence of these changes is reinforcement of the desirability (necessity, inevitability) of great inequality in income and wealth and the undesirability of government action in restraint of business.

The *"trickle-down"* principle first took on modern metaphoric effect in the Great Depression of the 1930s,[3] a sardonic comment on government subsidies for business. Funds for people at the "top" create employment and eventually redound to improvement of those at the "bottom." The 1930s present a preview of the *"trickle-down"* of Reaganomics in the 1980s. The tensions of *"trickle-down"* are presented in workers' impatience, in turn-of-the-century slogans: the AFL's "more, more, now," and the IWW's metaphorical song line, "pie in the sky in the great by and by." [4]

The *"free lunch"* is a second metaphoric staple. It presents the transition in meaning from economic to political-ideological use. The standard formulation is "There's no such thing as a free lunch." Consonant with the physics principle of conservation of matter, its initial usage, over a half-century ago, served to emphasize the scarcity truism in relation to efficient resource allocation. Goods or services (in terms of opportunity cost) put to one use cannot be used for something else. From the outset it served the political purpose of demonstrating that public (government-based) goods and services are not free.

With cold war reinforcement of capitalism, the meaning of *"no free lunch"* shifted to the field of equity in the distribution of income and wealth. It reinforced the casual, popular belief that under capitalist production and distribution everyone gets what they deserve. The late twentieth-century capitalist economy is saturated with distributive *"free lunches,"* with income that has little or no connection to provision of a useful good or service. The term is most commonly, and casually, applied to welfare programs for the lower classes. At least of equal relevance are examples in the worlds of business and finance: in junk bonds, direct and indirect public grants, and unprosecuted fraud. A most general alleged basis for institutionalized *"free lunch"* is exploitation of workers, but this has been outside the bounds of economic or political discussion in the capitalist world for over a half century.

In the 1980s, new metaphors were found to avoid serious discussion of fundamental problems of economic welfare and inequality. The *"safety net"* was invoked to suggest that there was adequate provision against malnutrition and other spin-offs from poverty. The *"golden parachute"* made light of the opposite provision of relief for redundant or ineffective corporate executives. The *"glass ceiling"* presented a similar caricature of the problems of "gender equity." The overarching econo-political metaphor was the invocation of *"WAR."* Metaphorical *"WARS"* on drugs, poverty, inflation, and so on became the substitute for action that would ameliorate the fundamental causes of these elements of social crisis.

The *"free market"* as metaphor for the capitalist economic system has burgeoned since the break-up of the Soviet Union. Factually, capitalism is a private market system, private property is its base; its relation to freedom and open markets can be understood only in terms of the history of Western liberalism and the factual-functional base of the nature and extent of market monopoly. These relations are illustrated in Gelber's (1992) presentation of stamp collecting as a "free market metaphor." He encompasses a wide range of issues in product market development in the early industrial capitalist economy. He describes a new *"open market"*; but, the *"free market"* is a term that only appears at the beginning and the end.

ECONOMIC METAPHORS THAT ARE POLITICALLY INDIRECT

These metaphors are the most analytically challenging and politically important. They are at the core of formal economics. They are politically indirect because they appear initially in the analytic work of professional economists. The challenge here is to sort out and integrate their economic-analytic and socio-historical elements. They are important because of their disguised (subtle) apologetic role; their political-ideological function is overlaid with the prestigious aura of science. The central, integrating metaphors are *"market equilibrium"* as extension of one element of Smith's *"INVISIBLE HAND."* [5]

There is wide and deep disagreement concerning the role of metaphor within the academic field of economics. Metaphors exist. Everyone "recognizes" the *"INVISIBLE HAND."* But economists who believe that their enterprise can be essentially the same as hard science ignore or deny the importance of metaphysics in general, and metaphor in particular. With casual, habitual use, metaphor's origins and initial significance are sublimated or forgotten. This is one of many topics omitted from *The New Palgrave Dictionary of Economics* (Blaug, 1988). A significant exception to such denial is de Marchi (1993); the critical analyses by twelve contributors of Mirowski's (1989) *More Heat than Light* include exhaustive consideration of his and related uses of metaphor.

Table 9.2 is an extension of Part IV in Table 9.1. This classification is oriented to the challenge of finding a useful base for interpretation of the analytic and ideological role of economic metaphors. Emphasis of the *"EQUILIBRIUM"* chain reflects McCloskey's observation that "each step in economic reasoning, even the reasoning of the official rhetoric is metaphoric" (1985, p. 75).

As indicated above, the classifications of McCloskey and Bicchieri are less inclusive. Their focus, like the emphasis here, is on the contrast between metaphors with economic-analytic content and those having essentially terminological connotations. McCloskey distinguishes between ornamental and nonornamental metaphors. Drawing on and extending McCloskey, Bicchieri's classification can be termed idiomatic and cognitive. The former, with "words like *equilibrium, depression* . . . [involve] *catachresis,* the use of an idiom to fill a gap in the lexicon" (1988, p. 106). Both writers associate their analytical metaphors (nonornamental and cognitive) with building economic models. The major interpretative thesis presented later parallels this perception.

TABLE 9.2
Politically Indirect Analytic Metaphors: Discrete,
Overlapping, or Interconnected

Primary	Secondary
MECHANICS	ORGANICS
physics: energy (utility)	
equilibrium chain:	supplementary to chain:
demand, supply functions,	the firm, factors of
marginal revenue, cost	production, production
elasticity	function
macro equilibrium	capital

It is important to emphasize, parenthetically, that classification systems are not correct (true) or incorrect (false). They are useful or not useful. Given a necessary ground of logical coherence, they reflect the writer's interest and focus. Thus, the additional classification elements of Table 9.2 are oriented to the hypothesis that the *"equilibrium"* model is orthodox economics' dominant metaphor and that in its development it has served ideological as well as analytical ends. McCloskey's terminological trivialization of nonanalytical economic metaphors reinforces the importance—the usefulness—of the analytical, the nonornamental; it serves his interest in sympathetic reinforcement of the continued relevance of orthodox economic analysis. The present classification is oriented to demonstration of its obsolescence.

In analyzing "Models and Metaphors" Gudeman (1986) distinguishes between "primal" ("focal" or "axiomatic") metaphors and a "local" model; models may consist of "several primal metaphors or contain elements which are not strictly metaphoric" (pp. 40–41). His social, anthropological focus presents a qualification, not necessarily a rebuttal, of Leamer's (1987) statement that "Models . . . are merely metaphors. The basic conceptual error that is made by econometric theorists is their failure to recognize that in practice probabilities are metaphors" (p. 1). The economist's master (primal, dominant) methodological metaphor is the *"tool kit."* "Not only are concepts, assumptions, and models considered . . . to be tools; so too are theories" (Samuels, 1993, p. 15).

The key discussion here begins and ends with the political implications of primary metaphors in economic analysis. But first it is necessary to recognize the distinction between mechanical and organic metaphors.[6] Organic metaphors are important, but secondary. They lie outside formal, orthodox economics, the economics of *"equilibrium price."* They sharply identify the limits of the price paradigm. They appear in the contexts of dynamics, growth, motion, long-run, and capital relations; these elements, as we will see, are handled metaphorically, and alongside the formal *"price-auction"* model.

The modern use of metaphor in economic analysis essentially begins with the contributions of Alfred Marshall, with brief supplementary flashbacks into the preceding decades and century. Marshall (1890/1949) provides a direct comparative statement of organics and mechanics in economic analysis: "economic problems are imperfectly presented when they are treated as problems of statical equilibrium, and not of organic growth"[7] (p. 461). Necessarily, the metaphors for economic growth and capital theory are organic. The metaphors for market equilibrium are drawn from Newtonian physics, classical mechanics, and mathematics, especially calculus and simultaneous equations.

In their introductory statement Ingrao and Israel note the economic lyricism of Arrow and Hahn in *General Competitive Analysis* (1971):

> Just as an "invisible hand" places in equilibrium a pendulum oscillating around its center or sees to it that a liquid flowing between connecting chambers finds its own level, Adam Smith's invisible hand "is a poetic expression of the most fundamental of economic balance relations, the equalization of rates of return, as enforced by the tendency of factors to move from low to high returns." (Ingrao & Israel, 1990, p. ix)

Here we have a *"pendulum"* (mechanics), and a *"liquid"* (organics), and the scientific economists Arrow and Hahn reconciling *"poetry"* (art, metaphysics) and mathematically grounded *"economic abstraction."*

Market Equilibrium: Pseudoscience and Apologetics

The central position of metaphor in economic science is reflected in Mirowski's (1991) observation on "the almost neurotic concern of orthodox mathematical economics with the physical metaphor of equilibrium" (p. 577). The dominant position of *"EQUILIBRIUM"* is seen in the historical extension of the market equilibrium of Marshall—the *"particular equilibrium"* of *"price"* and *"quantity movement"* for the individual firm—to the idea of *"general equilibrium,"* first formulated by Leon Walras. In the late twentieth century, this has become "The Grand Neo-Classical Synthesis." This "GNS provides the intellectual justification for capitalism and operates as an apologetic for this system" (Arestis, 1992, p. 2).

The founding "microeconomic equilibrium" metaphor is Marshall's *"scissors"* analogy. With this he integrated the supply-side, production economics of Smith with the demand-side marginal utility of the early neoclassicists. Each side, independently, is a *"knife."* Their interaction as blades of a pair of scissors illustrates the two dimensions of market forces. The *"demand curve"* became a metaphoric symbol for the elements of choice that underlie the consumption process. The conventional *"upward-sloping supply line"* (based on the assumption of diminishing returns and increasing costs) became a metaphor for the multiplicity of processes, social relationships, and decisions that comprise the production of goods and services.

"Elasticity" presents perhaps the major economic insight of the *"demand-supply curve"* metaphor. This is the logical, quantitative relation between the relative change in price and the relative change in the quantity of a given commodity that is demanded or supplied. How much would the amount produced (supplied) or purchased (demanded) *"stretch"* with a change in price?

Before presenting the subsequent *"supply-side building blocks"* of the metaphorical *"pyramid"* of price theory it is important to recognize the strategic applications of late nineteenth century physics in the construct. Mirowski has argued that orthodox economics is essentially a metaphorical transplantation of physics, that the "original inspiration for the 'marginalist revolution' came from the physics of the mid-19th century" (1988, p. 178). "Neoclassical economic models seem to have a bare skeleton of applied mathematics (various models of constrained optimization) with an overlay of [obscurant] shifting metaphors . . . 'truth' [in] much of neoclassical economics . . . [may be seen as] 'a mobile army of metaphors'" (Ellerman, 1991, p. 546).

With truth in quotations, a metaphorical economics provides us with insights, but not scientifically grounded theory or fact, that can sustain a useful understanding of economic value. Neoclassical microeconomics is price theory. *"Market price"* is a metaphor for value.

Rounding out, closure of the *"market equilibrium"* paradigm required analytical incorporation of markets on the supply side, the markets for resources of production (land, labor, and capital). The necessary, essentially metaphoric formalisms, the marginal productivity theory, and the production function were established in the first half of this century. The now dominant *"general equilibrium"* metaphor, considered later, has been a major preoccupation of neoclassicism since the 1950s. A major sociopolitical effect of such extension of the *"EQUILIBRIUM"* metaphor has been the dehumanizing of formal economics. It is clear that mechanical analogies and metaphors portray people as things; more subtle is the requisite for *"general equilibrium"* analysis that everyone and everything must have commodity status, must be a private good or service for sale in a market.[8]

With his *"scissors"* Marshall formulated the economics of exchange and, implicitly, of production. With the *"marginal productivity"* theory, John Bates Clark provided the logical basis for imputation of figurative costs (prices of labor and capital) into the supply function.

The *"marginal productivity"* theory presented two new metaphors. The marginal product (the analogue to its predecessor, marginal utility) stood for the incremental output of land, labor, and capital, the resources of production. In general, as metaphor, the marginalist principle avers, the consumption and production processes can be divided into infinitely small increments—utils of satisfaction, microseconds of labor, and minute units of capital. With piece work, the theory has minimal contact with reality with respect to labor. The assumption of divisibility is pure fiction for industrial technology, joint inputs, and the general case of capital goods.

The second, dehumanizing, more ideologically functional metaphor, is analytical employment of the "factor" of *"production."* With acceptance of the marginal productivity relation as a theory of income distribution, the concept of socioeconomic classes was replaced by the abstract, depersonalized metaphor of workers, farmers, and businessmen as factors of production. Classical political economists Smith, David Ricardo, and Karl Marx associated the income shares of wages, rent, and profits to laborers, landlords, and merchants; the factors of production approach associated the shares of wages, rent, profit, and interest to the abstractions, labor, land, entrepreneurship, and capital, respectively. Schumpeter (1954) observed that from a political-ideological stance "any attempt to form economic categories other than social classes is bound to appear as an attempt to leave out or obscure the very essence of the capitalist process or, to use a phrase current among Marxists, to 'rob economic theory of its social content.' Such an attempt is . . . tainted with 'apologetics'" (p. 551).

The metaphorical essence of contemporary economics is perhaps best illustrated by Solow's invention of the *"aggregate production function"* in the late 1950s. With this metaphor he "asserts that the making of our daily bread is like a mathematical function. The jumble of responsibility, habit, conflict, ambition, intrigue, and ceremony that is our working life is supposed to be similar to a chalked curve on a blackboard" (McCloskey, 1985, p. 84).

McCloskey shows how the political-ideological, as well as analytical, uses of metaphor can be supplemented by the interaction of four master tropes of rhetoric: metaphor, metonymy, synecdoche, and irony. In Solow's mathematical expression of the production function, $Q = A(t) f(K,L)$, elements in the marginal productivity theory are formalized. The symbols K and L stand for capital and labor respectively. They "are metonymies, letting a thing merely associated with the thing in question stand as symbol for it, as the White

House does for the presidency. The L reduces the human attentiveness in making bread to an hour of work. The hour is a mere emblem, no more the substance of the matter than the heart is of emotions, or a bottle is of the wine. The K reduces the material inheritance of the workplace to a pile of shmoos" (p. 84). "The identification of A(t) with 'technical change' is . . . a synecdoche, taking a part for the whole; . . . Critics of the calculation . . . have called it a mere 'measure of our ignorance'" (p. 85).

Irony, the fourth, nonperspectival trope, is used to close the pseudo argument. Its most tangible form is in the use of quotation marks. They first are employed, then disappear. "The synecdoche of 'technical change' is protected when in doubt by ironical quotation marks, though the marks fall away as the doubt fades" (p. 85).

The Anomaly of Aggregate Equilibrium

With the reclassification of economics into micro and macro fields in the late 1940's, it was necessary to extend the microequilibrium metaphor to the new aggregate relations. The first step was invention of a "Keynesian cross." But placement of aggregate demand and supply on two-dimensional economic space presented problems analogous to the *"demand-supply equilibrium"* for the individual firm. The *"aggregate demand"* function has the theoretical and empirical grounding of the Keynesian *"consumption"* function. The Keynesian *"aggregate supply"* function is another tautology: business firms produce that which promises to be profitable. The purely abstract, definitional essence of the *"aggregate equilibrium"* of the 1980s New Classical school is seen in the observation which follows concerning the nonadditive nature of supply functions of the firm.

The analytic, putatively quantitative units of macroaggregative data are essentially metaphoric: the gross and net national product, national, personal, and disposable income. There are a number of macro-related metaphors that relate essentially to the problems of unemployment and inflation. Earliest perhaps is Marx's *"reserve army of the unemployed."*[9] Now there are the ideas of full employment and frictional and structural unemployment. Inflation metaphors are in abundance. Directly related to macroeconomic policy discussion are *"demand pull," "cost push,"* and *"psychologically-based inflation."* Others, *"runaway"* and *"galloping inflation,"* extend the initial *"horse racing"* metaphor for *"market competition."* The literature on business instability has given us a *"cobweb theorem," "business cycles," "bubbles,"* and *"crashes."*

Having considered the *"micro-"* and *"macroequilibrium"* metaphors, it would be logical at this point to discuss their extension—their connections, if any—to the *"general equilibrium"* metaphor. However, it has long been recognized that there is no empirical, economically relevant analytic way to move from the firm to the industry, far less to the economy as a whole. Demand for the product of firms is "horizontally" additive, in principle at least, to provide a demand curve for the industry. But this is not possible for the supply side, for costs of production.

So, *"general equilibrium"* is considered later as a secondary metaphor, essentially ornamental in McCloskey's term. Built on the Walrasian base, its essence is mathematically imbued storytelling. The following metaphors have evolved "outside" the dominant micro/macro models. As noted, these *"nonequilibrium"* metaphors and the relations for which they stand highlight the limitations—the omissions, oversimplifications and errors—of the standard paradigm.

Non-Equilibrium Metaphors: Behavioral, Institutional, and Organic

Orthodox, equilibrium-based economics does not deal analytically with human organization or behavior. It treats them as assumptions, often as metaphorical constants. Organic metaphors are most important here. They serve as cover for the vital relations of long-run process and motion (dynamics) from which the *"EQUILIBRIUM"* metaphor is analytically divorced.

The foundation of microeconomics is rational decision-making by individuals. Since inside economists regard psychology and sociology as second-class social science, they are content with a formal theory that deals with abstract, metaphorical "individuals": the consumer or the family on the demand side and the "firm" on the supply side.[10] The individual consumer is a *"calculating machine."* In 1898, in an early response to the *"marginal utility"* metaphor, Thorstein Veblen wrote: "The hedonistic conception of man is that of a lightning calculator of pleasures and pains . . . an isolated, definitive human datum, in stable equilibrium except for the buffets of . . . impinging forces" (Veblen, 1898/1984, p. 232). The metaphorical family is a combination of such *"hedonistic men."*

The business firm is the metaphoric *"person"* on the supply side. Again, Marshall (1890/1949) presents the initial entry. He contemplated the existence of a "representative firm" (p. 317). This is preceded by a more literal, metaphorical description of the survival problems of a business enterprise, where "we may read a lesson from the young trees of the forest as they struggle upwards through the benumbing shade of their older rivals." It is buttressed by a detailed Darwinian story, reinforced by natural law: "Nature still presses on the private business" (p. 316). Contemporary metaphoric treatment of business—*"the business system"*—is seen in "The metaphor of the firm as a 'nexus of contracts.'" One is asked to imagine the stocks and flows of property in a corporation as merely a set of contracts (Ellerman, 1991, p. 549).

As maximizing entities, there is no economic analytic difference between the consumer (family) and the firm. The household must be as profit-oriented as business, "free" consumer choice determines output. Noting the role of consumer preferences as the "guiding metaphor" of price theory, Stigler (1966) ironically observed: "It would of course be bizarre to look upon the typical family—that complex mixture of love, convenience, and frustration—as a business enterprise. Therefore, economists have devoted much skill and ingenuity to elaborating this approach" (p. 21). The family and especially the worker are notably absent in orthodox economic analysis. Leibenstein (1976) developed the concept "X-efficiency," essentially a metaphor for human labor, to fill a large gap in orthodox economics that is limited to allocative efficiency. "A commonplace to anyone who observes the creation of goods is that it takes effort, yet effort [labor] is not a key notion of contemporary economic analysis" (p. viii). Thus far, his circumspect effort to reincarnate the classical (Smith, Ricardo, Marx) emphasis on labor as a source of value has failed. The worker appears later in discussion of the *"human capital"* metaphor.

The most important organic metaphors appear in discussion of capital, and various attempts at a capital theory. The generation and application of capital goods is the strategic basis of economic improvement; growth depends on real investment. Metaphoric discussion of capital also can begin with Marshall (1890/1949). In his introductory comment (p. viii), related to the general problems of organics and growth, he distinguished between *"floating"* and *"sunk"* capital. *"Floating"* capital is "money-credit" (finance capital) looking for profitable investment; *"sunk"* capital is the actual investment, the transformation of money into "real" capital[11] that encompasses the tides of human emotion and perception, the hopes and fears of Keynesian-Robinsonian *"animal spirits."*

Buildings, tools and other machinery are solid stuff, yet marginalism dictates that they must be divisible. In attempting to overcome this methodological dilemma, controversy on capital theory in the 1960s evoked a series of metaphors, images of materials that are solid, yet malleable: butter, clay, putty, or shmoos. In 1936, Keynes characterized the stock market as a *"casino."* The role of the speculator becomes "serious when enterprise becomes the bubble on a whirlpool of speculation. When the capital development of a country becomes the byproduct of the activities of a casino, the job is likely to be ill-done" (p. 159). This Keynesian metaphor was revived in Bianco's (1985) *Business Week* cover story characterization of United States' financial economy as a *"casino society."*

The metaphor of *"human capital,"* introduced by Theodore Schultz in the 1960s was elaborated upon by Gary Becker. In Becker's extension of the humans as machines perspective: "Among the least bizarre of Becker's many metaphors . . . is that children are durable goods, like refrigerators" (McCloskey, 1985, p. 76). Here, human capital analysis illustrates the good-news, bad-news aspect of metaphor. On the positive side, "the field in economics treating human skills was . . . unified with the field treating investment in machines" (McCloskey, 1985, p. 77). But, simultaneously, it reified the general theme of people as commodities (Makgetla, 1992).

Nature, the idea of a "natural condition," has provided Newtonian, metaphorical underpinning for *"private market"* economics and ideology since Smith's *Wealth of Nations* (1776/1937). Philosophically, what is natural carries the connotation of normality, satisfaction, and goodness. Apologists of private enterprise often repeat Smith's observation on the desirability of minimalist government when "all systems either of preference or restraint [have been] completely taken away, the obvious and simple system of *natural liberty* establishes itself of its own accord" (Smith, p. 651, emphasis added). This corollary of the *"INVISIBLE HAND"* builds on the many specific natural elements embedded in his preceding discussion of private markets: natural talents, natural prices in general, and natural rates of rent, wages, and profit. It underlies the ongoing vision of market utopia, (Polanyi, 1944, pp. 102, 211) the present standing of the free market as metaphor for capitalism. We will see in closing how the *"nature"* metaphor, the notion of a natural social state, has culminated in the ideology of capitalism (and its alleged natural counterpart, democracy) as the only natural socioeconomic system.

Here, the metaphor of the *"tragedy of the commons"* has played an influential role. In yet another perversion of history, "like yesterday's nobility, contemporary social scientists often take a jaundiced view of common-property institutions, again making the commons an object of derision and 'reform.' Theorists decrying the 'tragedy of the commons' rely on the arid reasoning of the 'prisoner's dilemma' to demonstrate the impossibility of long-lasting voluntary cooperation or effective collective action" (Bromley, 1992, p. ix).

Supermetaphors and General Theories As Legitimizing Myth[12]

It is posited here that the master metaphor of *"orthodox economics"* is mathematized general equilibrium: "Walrasian economics is obsessed with the mathematical metaphor of simultaneous equations" (Blaug, 1988, p. 39). It is a blend of the submetaphors of *"market equilibrium"* and the modernized *"INVISIBLE HAND."* The strategic metaphoric combination is presented in Arestis' introductory summary: "In the absence of any structural, informational and other rigidities the price mechanism ensures a generalized market-clearing equilibrium. This is the very well known invisible-hand theorem. Divergences from a perfect allocative or full-employment equilibrium can only be due to a failure of one or more requirements of the invisible-hand theorem" (1992, p. 2). The transformation of Smith's invisible hand from poetic, socially grounded metaphor to scientific theorem is described below.

The modern economist's quest for a general theory, and associated physics envy, begins with ". . . Leon Walras—the first economist to construct a theoretical system based on the idea of economic equilibrium—Paul Samuelson, with equal enthusiasm, places him on the same level as Newton" (Ingrao & Israel, 1990, p. ix). Consider a parallel (a caricature) of physics and general equilibrium: "Is there an ultimate theory of nature [economics]—a 'Final Theory'—from whose principles all laws that govern the working of the physical universe [the economic system] may be deduced?" (Penrose, 1993, p. 78).

Keynes insisted on the strategic nature of expectations. Emphasizing the uncertainty of the capitalist process, in the vein of Einstein's relativity (Galbraith, 1994, p. 83), Keynes sought a general theory that would explain unemployment and depression. Also, he wanted to lift the "veil of money" (Boianovsky, 1993), to integrate money and market analysis, something that logically cannot be done.[13] Like Marx, the useful insights of Keynes, and later, Piero Sraffa (Blaug, 1988, pp. 23, 27–29) have not jelled into the desired general theory. These failures rest alongside the successful metaphors of *"economic man"* and *"general equilibrium."*

Consider in this light an historical metaphor, a comparison of contemporary *"EQUILIBRIUM"* economics with development of eighteenth century chemistry. The theory of "phlogiston" could be a metaphor for *"general equilibrium."* There is a thinkable parallel between the impact of the former on maturation of scientific chemistry and the influence of the latter on economic theory, thought, and policy in the post-Keynesian decades. "'Phlogiston' was, it was believed, an immaterial substance given off by burning bodies; it was the material of heat" (Sacks, 1993, p. 50). It stood for the unknown material that disappeared. In 1661 Robert Boyle (in parallel with Newton's physics)

> founded the equally new science of chemistry and disentangled it from its alchemical precursors . . . [introducing the analysis of elements]. But a peculiar confusion attended the isolation of [the] new elements. . . . These misinterpretations arose from a strange, half-mystical theory which had dominated chemistry throughout the eighteenth century, and, in many ways prevented its advance. (Sacks, 1993, p. 50)

This was the theory of "phlogiston." The mathematical theory of *"general equilibrium"* may have played a similar role in dominating economic analysis for the past generation. Economics seems to have built on the wrong physics metaphor. *"Relativity"* integrated with uncertainty and expectations could be the basis for a historically and institutionally relevant economics.

"*The Big U-Turn,*" a metaphor from the 1980s (Frazer, 1988), is useful in explaining the analytic success and apologetic power of "*general equilibrium,*" the withering away of humanistic, social economics. It portrays the shift from socially oriented to privately dominated economics and politics in the United States—the Reagan-Thatcher revolution that lives on with more than a half-life.

Facilitating, perhaps necessary, precursors were analytical-ideological "*U-Turns*" in the meaning of Smith's "*INVISIBLE HAND*" and Keynes' fundamental argument and program. In both Smith and Keynes, moderately radical, socially oriented propositions have been transformed into conservative-reactionary politico-economic doctrine. The "*U-Turn*" on Keynes was termed "*bastard Keynesianism*" by Joan Robinson. The similar turn on Smith could be paraphrased as the "*metastasized invisible hand.*"

In Smith's two books he passingly presented the "*INVISIBLE HAND*" metaphor.[14] He observed that, on occasion, landlords or businessmen will act to benefit others, rather than fully exploit their power position. Recognition of the cooperative nature of market exchange was implicit in its use in the *Wealth of Nations*. But, alongside this single reference one must place his recurring recognition of the conflict element in the capitalist class system (Gramm, 1980). In general, the weight of Smith's thought was that the interests of the masters ran counter to those of workers and consumers; the masters' natural selfishness, in Adam Smith's world, is checked by sympathy engendered by a metaphoric "*impartial spectator,*" by the Deity, the Author of nature, and small-scale, face-to-face economic and social relationships.[15]

The "*apologetic U-Turn,*" the reinterpretation of the "*INVISIBLE HAND*" from restrained to unqualified support of the private market system, was consolidated first in its equation with the economic metaphor of "*perfect competition.*" Then, some fifty years ago, F. A. Hayek pointed out the obvious association between the uncertainties of the invisible hand and the truism of *unintended consequences* in human behavior.[16] He used this as a primary rhetorical line in his argument against social (socialistic) planning.

Continuing, casual proliferation of economic metaphor reflects the poverty of creative thought, the dearth of new ideas and unthinkability of earlier, relatively radical ones. Metaphor is particularly useful in the exercise of cover-ups and lies. Parody appears in a metaphor of the absurd, especially on the sports and financial pages of newspapers. With the 1993 decline in interest rates: "The uptick seems to have tipped many buyers '*off the fence*' of indecision and into the housing market," still "There is no hint that things will '*fall out of bed*'" (Skidmore, 1993). The series of metaphors in a given article can compound the minimization of thought and analysis. Blake (1993) found that firms get a "*leg up*" with "*re-engineering,*" by redefining "*fat,*" making productivity "*soar,*" thus getting on "*firm footing,*" so now what can we do to *"slam the door"* on the Japanese?   Sportswriting presents continuing interaction between sports and the economist and businessman's metaphor of *"GAMES,"* and of *"GAMES AS WAR"*; losing opponents are *"buried,"* *"destroyed,"* *"massacred,"* *"ravaged,"* or *"whipped."* Legitimate athletic moves become *"cheating."*

The Need for New Ideas, Metaphors, Paradigms, Programs

Complaints about orthodox economics as a dead-end have been commonplace for at least a half-century. Arguably, they are just another aspect of the end of modernism in general and positivism in particular, and of the judgment that the individualist-rationalist-scientific dominance of the past century must be effectively balanced by humanistic, social, and historical "metaphorically conscious" understanding.

If metaphoric *"equilibrium economics"* is essentially empty as a medium for dealing with major problems, what is to be done? The simple answer is discovery and acceptance of new metaphors, of a socially oriented paradigm. "The Walrasian and mechanistic assumptions at the hub of orthodox economics have to be replaced: . . . A theoretical revolution is required at the core of economics itself" (Hodgson, 1992, p. 760). A major element here will be the extension of the Veblenian *"evolutionary"* metaphor. Hahn (1991) envisages "a return to the Marshallian affinities to biology" (p. 48). The successors of Marshall will not be diverted by the physics-like quest for a "grand unifying theory [what is needed instead is] The uncertain embrace of history and sociology and biology" (p. 50). Hicks "affirmed theoretical pluralism. . . . Our theories, regarded as tools of analysis, are blinkers. . . . Or it may be politer to say that they are rays of light, which illuminate a part of the target, leaving the rest in the dark" (Samuels, 1993, p. 22).

A socially relevant economics will require more than improvement of the rhetoric of orthodoxy (McCloskey, 1985) or a watered-down grafting of X-onto orthodox allocative efficiency. New organic, social, and time-grounded metaphors will become primary; mechanics-based equilibrium will become secondary. The generating base for new metaphors and subsequent analysis, building toward an historically conscious, humanistic social economics will involve strange bedfellows, past, present, and future. It will build on the late 19th-century understanding of Marshall, Marx, Veblen, and Friedrich von Wieser. It will incorporate the recent and ongoing arguments of Amitai Etzioni, Nicholas Georgescue-Roegan, Robert Kuttner, Leibenstein, and Paul M. Sweezy, a small sample of dissenting contributors from across the political-ideological spectrum.

A new metaphoric landscape, like the present one, will be at least two-dimensional. It will incorporate interaction between the relatively ephemeral, short-run, politically direct metaphors and the generation of new analytic paradigms. The former can enhance the latter's movement from vision to applicable analysis. An organic metaphoric base will be inclusive, expansive, and dynamic. The economy is *"animate,"* a living thing characterized by overlapping institutional and technological *"life-cycles."* Organic metaphors will incorporate the realities of dynamic process and *"disequilibrium."* Recognition of old metaphors that presented this reality can be *"stepping stones"* to their extension. For example, the *"cobweb"* theorem in agricultural markets showed how the price-quantity relation could *"explode"* (or *"implode"*) rather than converge in a natural, stable, or static *"EQUILIBRIUM."* It anticipated the mathematics of chaos, the disquietude of entropy.

Orthodox economics, in its pre-math, pre-general equilibrium period, used the secondary, organic *"river-dam"* metaphor to illustrate the general significance of stock-flow relation and the specific problem of capital formation. Wearing their static *"equilibrium blinders,"* economists did not deal with the outflow, the spillover. A full, holistic *"river-dam"* metaphor presents the microcosm of the hydraulic cycle. With water as the fundamental life-sustaining resource, the *"hydrological cycle"* can be a metaphor for the problem of mankind's unity and interdependence. Social entropy, an extension of Georgescue-Roegan's work, can provide a *"bridge"* linking social and resource analysis. Boulding (1970) has presented a stimulating metaphoric overview. "In the *spaceship economy* . . . the social system has to maintain itself in the middle of a *circular flow* of materials. . . . [in] the *throughput economy* . . . the *crocodile of human activity* [eats] the exhaustible resources in front . . . filling up the pollutable reservoirs behind" (p. 43, emphasis added).

New energy metaphors oriented to labor and nature would be central to useful socioeconomics. In technics, *"photosynthesis"* can be a metaphor for solar energy and the reality of renewable energy alongside renewable water. In economic analysis human *"labor"* (and human *"capital"*) can be a metaphor for animate, animal energy, the generating base of production. Orthodox economics' energy metaphor of *"utility"* reifies its solipsistic fixation on the individual. Human labor is social in its biological origins, in its fruitful mixture with other physical resources, and in the bulk of its application in production of goods and services. Intellect work as *"brainpower"* is the strategic *"vehicle"* on the *"information highway."*

What new, politically direct metaphors might sharpen our recognition of deep-seated socioeconomic problems of the late 1990s? The 1990s, Clinton-embellished metaphor of *"change"* embodies an optimistic message while masking the negative reality of change for many. It illustrates the dangers of

"Using Metaphors to Guide Public Policy" (Champlin & Olson, 1994, p. 456).
Culmination of the cold war has been a *"dark victory"* all around. The *"lost
horizon"* has come home to the United States in the rise of homelessness and
hopelessness, in the insecure *"down-sized"* workplace and society. The
average family, the *"common 'man'"* still needs an *"open door"* to a decently
"furnished room," one in which health and general well-being are
"embedded." The rungs of *"Horatio Alger's"* nineteenth century farm and
city *"ladder"* are broken. The *"escalator"* is a more serviceable metaphor for
the 1990s, for the parallel downward drift of the middle class, alongside the
necessity of an up-side for rural and urban ghettos.

    With primary organic metaphors, an organic-grounded economics will
build on living things, on creation, degeneration, death, and renewal. This is
holistic. It is not limited to the hedonistic, acquisitive bent of humans. The
domestic private market metaphor is extended internationally in the *"global
marketplace"* wherein citizens of each nation are in the *"same large boat"*
comprising a *"grand flotilla"* of competing national economies *"sailing in the
same wide sea"* (Reich, 1991, p. 5). Such privatized *"homogenization"* will be
a barrier, not an opening toward realization of the ideal of a commonwealth-
oriented *"global village."* A *"fruitful path"* would be illuminated by the
broad, humanistic vision of Mill (1848/1965) and Keynes (1933/1963),[17] not by
Benthamite narcissism.

ENDNOTES

[1]There is continuing controversy concerning William James's *"cash-value"*
metaphor in relation to his pragmatist philosophy and personal politics: One
may "surmise that at the time James was employing his cash-value metaphor
the term was suspended in two worlds of meaning": the ephemeracy of value
versus the durability of real worth (Cotkin, 1985, p. 40).

[2]Thus, "the Arrow-Debreu model of general equilibrium [and others] do not
pretend to be realistic. They are *fictional* descriptions, in that they attribute
to objects . . . properties of convenience [that bring] the objects modeled into
the range of mathematical theory" (Bicchieri, 1988, p. 109).

[3]The *"trickle-down"* principle has long been the linchpin of capitalist
apologetics. Its first, most notable appearance is in Nassau Senior's mid-
nineteenth century "economics of the rich" (Rogin, 1956, pp. 254–256).

[4]Another religio-economic metaphor of the same era was coined by the
legendary retailer John Wanamaker. In 1906 he called his new store the
"Garden of Merchandise." Metaphors of the Almighty recur in Adam
Smith's major works. Ferdinando Galiani, a contemporary of Smith, posited
that "the economic process is guided by a 'Supreme Hand'" which presents

directly the religious component of Smith's *"INVISIBLE HAND"* (Martin, 1990, p. 274).

[5]See Gramm (1980) and note 15 for a more inclusive discussion of the reinterpretation of Smith, for "the transformation of his usages of the invisible hand and behavioral competition into a new metaphor—the mechanistic, short-run, competitive equilibrium market model" (p. 120). Also, see Martin (1990).

[6]Sometimes mechanical and organic metaphors are mixed. Hirschman (1970) introduced the metaphors *"exit"* and *"voice"* to clarify and explain acts of protest. Their essence is organic; however, his link to orthodoxy is reflected when he asks, "What is the comparative efficiency of the two options as mechanisms of recuperation?" (p. 5).

[7]Still, Marshall feared that too much emphasis on the biological view of economics would detract from "the notions of economic law and measurement . . . as though such notions were too hard and rigid to be applied to the living and ever-changing economic organism. But . . . vertebrate organisms are the most highly developed. The modern economic organism is vertebrate; and the science which deals with it should not be invertebrate . . . it [must] have a firm backbone of careful reasoning and analysis" (1890/1949, p. 769).

[8]"A market economy must comprise all elements of industry, including labor, land and money. . . . But labor and land are no other than the human beings themselves. . . . To include them in the market mechanism means to subordinate the substance of society itself to the laws of the market" (Polanyi, 1944, p. 71).

[9]Analysis of the metaphors of Marx (e.g., the *"mode,"* *"forces,"* and *"relations"* of production, *"accumulation,"* and *"surplus value"*) and Marxism would require another paper. The master Marxian metaphor was small "c" *"communism,"* representing an idealized yet thinkable life. Its political inversion occurred in capital "C" Communism, Soviet metaphoric cover for a police state, the opposite of the Marx-Engels vision.

[10]Leibenstein (1976) introduced the extension of his X-efficiency argument with a physics metaphor: "Atomistic versus Molecular Economics." Orthodox economics' conventional units, the *"household"* and the *"firm"* are "viewed as molecular units. They are basic social and legal units but they are not *the* basic units" (p.3). They are composed of individuals, as atoms. This distinction serves his emphasis on the humanistic, behavioral elements of economics, the thoughts and actions of individual persons.

[11]Later (pp. 415-421), Marshall introduced the metaphor of a *"meteoric shower of stones sharper than diamonds,"* first in the context of tax policy and then extending it to include issues of distribution—rent, interest, profits—in relation to capital.

[12]The term is taken from Hobsbawm (1993, p. 64) concerning "the way in which the genocide of the Jews by Hitler has been turned into a *legitimizing myth* for the existence of the state of Israel" (emphasis added).

[13]"The analog of Newtonian time, in the classical [neoclassical] economics, is money. Just as time is absolutely separate from space, money is absolutely separate from the market. Prices and wages may be measured in money terms, but this is only a convenience. The prices that count are relative prices . . . Like time, money is an invariable standard" (Galbraith, 1994, p. 64).

[14]Earlier he had referred to the invisible hand of Jupiter in his essay on "The History of Astronomy." The term was virtually commonplace with Smith's contemporaries (Martin, 1990, p. 274).

[15]The significance of the *"INVISIBLE HAND"* of the *Wealth of Nations* is its meaning as a metaphoric statement of actual socioeconomic governors on greed, relevant for his time. These may be characterized as the *"three fingers"*: the Protestant ethic (the desirability of work and saving), small-scale, face-to-face human relationships (community), and market competition. All of these had atrophied by the early twentieth century (Gramm, 1980).

[16]With Hayek, the secularization of Smith's economics and sociology was complete. Gone was the recognition that "In Smith's system God's I-H [invisible hand] was the necessary and sufficient force compelling a beneficient order throughout the universe, including the marketplace. Masking God behind the invisible hand [had drawn] upon a long tradition" (Martin, 1990, p. 274).

[17]Mill envisioned a world wherein the production pay-offs from industrial technology would allow a shift from endless material acquisition to human improvement in the *"art of living"* (1848/1965, pp. 746–751). Similarly, almost a century later, Keynes amplified this prospect in Part V, "The Future," "Economic Possibilities for Our Grandchildren" (1933, pp. 363–366).

REFERENCES

Arestis, P. (1992). *The post-Keynesian approach to economics*. Hants, England: Edward Elgar.
Arrow, K., & Hahn, F. H. (1971). *General competitive analysis*. San Francisco: Holden-Day.
Baum, L. F. (1986). *The wonderful Wizard of Oz*. Berkeley: University of California Press. (Original work published 1900).
Bianco, A. (1985). Playing with fire. *Business Week*, No. 2912, 78–90
Bicchieri, C. (1988). Should a scientist abstain from metaphor? In A. Klamer, D. N. McCloskey, & R. M. Solow (Eds.), *The consequences of economic rhetoric* (pp. 100–114). Cambridge: Cambridge University Press.
Blake, D. (1993, December 12). Preemptive downsizing. *San Francisco Examiner*. Business, 4. Associated Press.

Blaug, M. (1988). *Economics through the looking glass: The distorted perspective of the New Palgrave Dictionary of Economics.* London: The Institute of Economic Affairs. [Occasional Paper 78.]

Boianovsky, M. (1993). Bohm-Bawerk, Irving Fisher, and the term "Veil of Money": A note. *History of Political Economy, 25,* 725–738.

Boulding, K. (1970). Economics as an ecological science. In K. Boulding, *Economics as a science* (pp. 23–52). New York: McGraw-Hill.

Bromley, D. W. (Ed.). (1992). *Making the commons work.* San Francisco: Institute for Contemporary Studies.

Browne, M. N., Bergeron, S., & Quinn, J. K. (1994, January). *Dominant economic metaphors and the postmodern subversion of the subject.* Paper presented at Allied Social Science Association convention, Boston, MA.

Champlin, D., & Olson, P. (1994). Post-industrial metaphors: Understanding corporate restructuring and the economic environment of the 1990's. *Journal of Economic Issues, 28,* 449–459.

Cotkin, G. (1985). William James and the cash-value metaphor. *Et cetera, 42,* 37–46.

de Marchi, N. (Ed.). (1993). *Non-natural social science: Reflecting on the enterprise of more heat than light.* Durham, NC: Duke University Press. Annual Supplement to Vol. 25, *History of Political Economy.*

Ellerman, D. P. (1991). Myth and metaphor in orthodox economics. *Journal of Post Keynesian Economics, 13,* 545–654.

Frazer, W. (1988). *Power and ideas: Milton Friedman and the big U-Turn.* Vol. II, "The U-turn." Gainsville, FA: Gulf/Atlantic Publishing Company.

Galbraith, J. K. (1994). Keynes, Einstein, and scientific revolution. *The American Prospect, 16,* 62–67.

Gelber, S. M. (1992). Free market *metaphor:* The historical dynamics of stamp collecting. *Comparative Studies in Society and History, 34,* 742–769.

Gramm, W. S. (1980). The selective interpretation of Adam Smith. *Journal of Economic Issues, 24,* 119–142.

Gudeman, S. (1986). *Economics as culture: Models and metaphors of livelihood.* London: Routledge & Kegan Paul.

Hahn, F. H. (1991). The next hundred years. *The Economic Journal, 98,* 47–50.

Hirschman, A. O. (1970). *Exit, voice and loyalty.* Cambridge: Harvard University Press.

Hobsbawm, E. (1993). The new threat to history. *New York Review of Books, 40,* 62–64.

Hodgson, G. M. (1992). The reconstruction of economics: Is there still a place for neoclassical theory? *Journal of Economic Issues, 26,* 749–767.

Ingrao, B., & Israel, G. (1990). *The invisible hand, economic equilibrium in the history of science.* Cambridge, MA: MIT Press.

Keynes, J. M. (1963). *Essays in persuasion.* New York: Norton. (Original work published 1933).

Keynes, J. M. (1936). *The general theory of employment, interest, and money.* New York: Harcourt Brace.

Klamer, A., & McCloskey, D. (1992). Accounting as the master metaphor of economics. *The European Accounting Review, 1,* 145–160.

Leamer, E. E. (1987). Econometric metaphors. In T. F. Bewley (Ed.), *Advances in econometrics fifth world congress* (Vol. 2, pp. 1–28). Cambridge: Cambridge University Press.

Leibenstein, H. (1976). *Beyond economic man: A new foundation for microeconomics.* Cambridge, MA: Harvard University Press.

Littlefield, H. M. (1964). The Wizard of Oz: Parable on populism. *American Quarterly, 16,* 47–58.

Makgetla, N. S. (1992). A note on Gary Becker's use of metaphor. *Journal of Economic Issues, 26,* 900–904.

Marshall, A. (1949). *Principles of economics.* New York: MacMillan. (Original work published 1890)

Martin, D. A. (1990). Economics as ideology: On making "the invisible hand" invisible. *Review of Social Economy, 48,* 272–287.

Mill, J. S. (1965). *Principles of political economy.* New York: A. M. Kelly. (Original work published 1848)

McCloskey, D. N. (1985). *The rhetoric of economics.* Madison, WI: University of Wisconsin Press.

Mirowski, P. (1989). How not to do things with metaphors: Paul Samuelson and the science of neoclassical economics. *Studies in History and Philosophy of Science, 20,* 175–191.

Mirowski, P. (1989). *More heat than light: Economics as social physics, physics as nature's economics.* Cambridge and New York: Cambridge University Press.

Mirowski, P. (1991). Postmodernism and the social theory of value. *Journal of Post Keynesian Economics, 13,* 565–582.

Penrose, R. (1993). Nature's biggest secret [Review of the book *Dreams of a final theory*]. *New York Review of Books, 40,* 78–82.

Polanyi, K. (1944). *The great transformation.* Boston: Beacon Press.

Reich, R. (1991). *The work of nations.* New York: Knopf.

Rogin, L. (1956). *The meaning and validity of economic theory.* New York: Harper & Brothers.

Sacks, O. (1993). The poet of chemistry [Review of the book *Humphry Davy: Science and power*]. *New York Review of Books, 40,* 50–56.

Samuels, W. J. (1993). John R. Hicks and the history of economics. In W. J. Samuels, J. Biddle, & T. W. Patchak-Schuster (Eds.), *Economic thought and discourse in the 20th century* (pp. 1–85). Hants, England: Edward Elgar.

Schumpeter, J. A. (1954). *History of economic analysis.* New York: Oxford University Press.

Shulman, S. (1992). Metaphors of discrimination: A comparison of Gunnar Myrdal and Gary Becker. *Review of Social Economy, 40,* 432–452.

Skidmore, D. (1993, December 30). The economy. *Lewiston Morning Tribune,* Lewiston, Idaho.

Smith, A. (1937). *The wealth of nations.* New York: The Modern Library. (Original work published 1776)

Stigler, G. J. (1966). *The theory of price* (3rd ed.). New York: Macmillan.

Veblen, T. (1984). Why is economics not an evolutionary science? In M. Lerner (Ed.), *The Portable Veblen* (pp. 215–240). New York: Viking. (Original work published 1898)

10

Metonymy in Political Discourse

Patricia A. Chantrill
Gonzaga University

Jeffery Scott Mio
California State Polytechnic University, Pomona

INTRODUCTION

Metaphor has taken a position within the literature as representing all forms of figurative language. Thus, although the surface differences between metaphor and other tropes may have appeared small, these differences have become overwhelmed and obscured by metaphor's preeminence.

Metonymy is a less familiar term than metaphor in our scholarship, though it is as common a persuasive device in speech and writing. Superficially, these two tropes appear to possess but a few, seemingly inconsequential, differences. Metaphor exacts an implied comparison between two primarily unlike images, whereas metonymy is often defined as a substitution of a term closely associated with the literal term. Recent scholars (Bredin, 1984; Gallop, 1987; Gibbs, 1990; Jakobson, 1971; Lacan, 1977), however, have questioned metonymy's subordinate status as a species of metaphor. It has been posited that these two tropes engage different cognitive processes and are, perhaps, generated by two opposing principles of linguistic comprehension (Jakobson, 1971).

Because metonymy, unlike metaphor, does not borrow new meaning from dissimilar planes of discourse, the meaning that is achieved in metonymic figures often involves a deletion, a condensation of related terms operating on the same discursive plane. The most familiar form of metonymy, "synecdoche," involves a literal-to-figurative association of part-to-whole, or whole-to-part. Additionally, when synecdoche is successful, the part that is made to represent the whole, or visa versa, must be particularly and significantly related to the literal meaning intended.

The old adage, *"The hand that rocks the cradle rules the world,"* contains three instances of metonymy. The first is synecdochic: the "hand" represents the mother. In fact, we might read it "The hand of the mother" to illustrate the elliptical, generative form of many metonymic structures. In this case, the hand is a contiguous part of the mother. It is significantly representative of the acts of discipline, guidance, and nurturing we often associate with idealized motherhood. Of course, the hand is also significantly involved in the literal act of rocking a cradle.

The word "cradle" demonstrates a second instance of metonymy in which the association between the literal idea and the figurative term is a "container-to-content" form (Cockcroft & Cockcroft, 1992). "Cradle" recalls the mother's infant child by uniquely and significantly highlighting that brief period in a human life when the use of cradles is appropriate. Similarly, the recent political agenda, which attempts to provide nationwide "cradle to grave" health care coverage, uses terms that relate in particular to the first and last places in which our bodies are placed. Though not synecdochic, because "cradles" and "graves" are not natural and necessary parts of birth and death, these metonymies argue for a fundamental relation between the literal and figurative ideas.

The third instance of metonymy in *"The hand that rocks the cradle rules the world"* occurs with the use of the word "world" in a somewhat more subtle "whole-to-part" representation of ideas like "society," "human relations," or even individual "personalities." The three forms of metonymy found in this single sentence mark it as exceptional, though metonymy is a subtle trope of many forms.

In *"The pen is mightier than the sword,"* we find two instances of "instrument-to-user" metonymy. Although the pen is not literally a contiguous or adjoining part of the writer it is used to represent, it certainly identifies him or her because it is the primary tool in the writer's work. The sword, also, is not part of the soldier, though it represents the battles in which it is used. Additionally, the sword stands for all battles, even those modern ones in which a sword is no longer the weapon of choice.

This last example demonstrates the curious transformation that older metonymies often undergo. In a sense, an archaic synecdoche may shift into metaphor simply because the part that used to significantly represent the whole is no longer literally relevant. Consider the colloquialism *"hit the hay"* which is commonly understood to mean "go to bed." Most people, when asked to guess whether "hay" is metaphor or metonymy, might automatically choose metaphor as their answer. The phrase, however, probably originated as a synecdoche at a time when beds used to be literally stuffed with hay. Because modern beds no longer use this substance, the figure has lost its ability to represent the bed except through metaphoric comparisons with the contents of modern mattresses.

Similarly, an apt metonymy in one area of discourse can be metaphorically applied to another area of discourse. According to Urdang (1988), our common understanding of the metaphoric phrase *"bootlegging,"* including its application to the illegal copying of computer software, began as a humble synecdoche during America's Prohibition era when "bootleggers" concealed illegal liquor in the leggy portion of their boots.

The reason that metonymy is often subordinated under metaphor may have something to do with the former's inevitable loss in the battle against linguistic evolution and semantic generalization. However, it is also true that every successful metaphor argues for a slice of similarity it its comparison between a synecdochic part of the topic to the synecdochic part of the vehicle. Thus, the relation between metaphor and metonymy, however distinct their individual properties, is a fundamental one which Lodge (1977) contended is mutually dependent: "The metaphoric work cannot totally neglect metonymic continuity if it is to be intelligible at all. Correspondingly, the metonymic text cannot eliminate all signs that it is available for metaphorical interpretation" (p. 111).

Political Implications of Metonymy

As a rhetorical device, synecdoche and other forms of metonymy serve many functions not always open to metaphor's breadth of context. When a particular rhetor chooses synecdoche, especially within key passages of a speech, we might ask how the "pragmatic" function of rhetoric, (i.e., persuasion), is best served by that choice. Brummett (1994), a professor of Rhetoric, offers one explanation:

> The challenge for the average citizen today, then, is to *personalize large and complex issues* in ways that make them understandable, without distorting those issues so much that good decisions cannot be made. We personalize issues when we translate vast and impersonal problems in smaller, more manageable images, stories, and texts. Personalization, in other words, is a *strategy of textualization or narrative.* We understand the problems of the Middle East by seeing them compressed into stories about specific hostages who have been kidnapped, or by making certain leaders the embodiment of good or evil (depending on our politics). The kind of textual strategy that is used in personalization is called *metonymy,* or *metonymization.* Metonymy occurs when something complex is reduced to a more manageable sign of that complex thing, as when the complexities of British government are reduced into the public figures of the Prime Minister, or of the reigning monarch. (p. 158)

As a rhetorical strategy, metonymy offers the public speaker an opportunity to "personalize" complicated issues for those members of an audience who suffer from either too little or too much information, or, from political disaffection. Additionally, Edelman (1977) claimed that the use of metonymy allows speakers to reduce the inherent ambiguity of complex issues by defining them according to their more simple characteristics or parts (p. 16). Metonymy, in general, makes an argument by association (Cockcroft & Cockcroft, 1992), which "represents unexpressed or implicit ideas and associations" (p. 120). One consequence of recalling only a part of the picture, especially in cases of synecdoche, is that the unmentioned parts are often ideologically "marginalized" by the speaker as trivial or unimportant. The strategy of "metonymization," then, serves to personalize issues, enhance audience understanding, and resolve ambiguity by collapsing detailed information into a more manageable, albeit simplified, form. As an argumentative structure, metonymy may be subtle, but it is a fundamental rhetorical tool with definitional power.

Political Synecdoche

In *The Modes of Modern Writing*, David Lodge (1977) claimed that all discourse shares a contextual constraint: "Since we cannot describe everything in a given context, we select certain items at the expense of not selecting others" (p. 94). The selection process, Lodge contended, differs according to the purpose of the writer and the nature of the discourse. The prose writer often shares with the poet the object of telling a story and advancing an argument, though the former selects details "based on purely logical principles: what is present implies what is absent, the whole stands for the part, the thing for its attributes . . ." (p. 94).

Lodge further stated that the writer of "pragmatic" prose writes a predominantly "metonymic text"—a synecdoche of events and ideas characterized by its "plethora of data, which [the reader] seeks to unite into one meaning" (p. 111). The predominantly metaphoric writer, by contrast, is less constrained by linear logic and may select the details for the text based not on their representativeness, but on their symbolic, analogical appeal.

Centuries ago, Quintilian (95 A.D./1976) cautioned the speaker and writer of persuasive prose against the unrestrained use of synecdoche and other kinds of metonymy, especially because the resulting condensation may be "too harsh" or "too bold for the severe style demanded in the courts" (p. 315). Although poets and other writers were free to experiment with figurative substitutions and condensations, Quintilian restricted the use of synecdoche in argumentative prose to those cases "where numbers are concerned" (p. 313). The ancient rhetor cited Levy's use of *"The Romans won the day"* for "the Romans were victorious" as an example of appropriate prose synecdoche. Note that this example contains two incidents of numerical figures in both "Romans" and "day." All "Romans" stand for those relative few who actually participated in the victory, and "day" stands for a larger, undefined increment of time. Note too, that while Quintilian's prohibition concerns argumentative prose, his interest is in the stylistic effect of metonymy and synecdoche, and not, necessarily, with their power to structure an argument.

A Synecdochic Speaker

British Prime Minister Winston Churchill provided history with one of the most memorable examples of numerical synecdoche from this century, one which has both stylistic and argumentative appeal. This figure occurred in the peroration, the concluding passages of a speech within which Bowers and Osborn (1966) analyzed only metaphor's unique power to effect attitudinal changes.

Churchill's speech to the House of Commons on June 18, 1940, compared the recent fall of France to the grim outlook for Britain against German military might. The Prime Minister cautioned and encouraged his audience with his closing words:

> ... the Battle of France is over. I expect that the battle of Britain is about to begin. Upon this battle depends the survival of Christian civilisation ... Hitler knows that he will have to break us in this island or lose the war. If we can stand up to him, all Europe may be free and the life of the world may move forward into broad, sunlit uplands. But if we fail, then the whole world ... will sink into the abyss of a new Dark Age made more sinister ... by the lights of perverted science. Let us therefore brace ourselves to our duties, and so bear ourselves that, if the British Empire and its commonwealth last for a thousand years, men will still say, "This was their finest hour." (Churchill, 1941, p. 314)

In their brief analysis of Churchill's peroration, Cockcroft and Cockcroft (1992) argued that "the last sentence derives much of its *emotive power* from the contrasted metaphors of 'broad, sunlit uplands' . . . and the looming 'abyss'" (p. 119). Curiously, however, the numerical synecdoche of "hour" in this final sentence, the sentence which has come to represent the argumentative essence of the speech, is effectively eclipsed in their analysis of the preceding metaphors.

In fact, Churchill's use of the word "hour" served several rhetorical functions well-suited to a numerical synecdoche. In addition to rallying for posterity and historic duty as Weidhorn (1972) suggested, this was an appeal to the British people to do it for their own sakes, their own honor. All the more powerful, Churchill offered a glory denied the British in their past, during the "old" Dark Ages. He extended to his audience a chance to seek a unique glory, regardless of the past or the future; it was, ultimately, a "carpe diem" appeal.

When Churchill said "hour," he did not mean the literal hour, though he relied on that association to energize the more abstract image of an indefinite and unknown period of time. The haunting question on every British mind, "When will the invasion come?" was ultimately unanswerable by the Prime Minister. He frequently spoke of this very human dilemma, though he often juxtaposed the unknown against a very hopeful vision of brevity: "The story is not yet finished, but it will not be so long" (Churchill, 1941, p. 402).

In a later speech, Churchill lamented the fall of Denmark, Holland, and Belgium while admitting, "And none can tell how long it will be before the hour of their deliverance strikes" (p. 459). This passage, in addition to the synecdochic image of a determined and powerful clock "striking" at the literal hour, allows the synecdochic "hour" to suggest a retaliatory "strike" resulting in physical freedom. It is an energized image, forcing the abstraction of unknown increments of time into an associative and concrete framework. The haunting question of "when" pales against an unknown, but assured, image of "then."

The "hour" figure permitted Churchill to infer what he dared not say explicitly: (a) that the time spent will be short, especially relative to Britain's long history, or to the hypothetical vision of a future that reaches at least "a thousand years" beyond the present; (b) that the struggle may be shortened through the vigilance and exertion Churchill advocated; and, (c) that the struggle will be bound between the proud past and the precarious future—it will be finite, with a beginning and an end. This last implication was especially important for the purpose of sustaining hope, even during the long nights of the Blitz.

A second element of audience accommodation in the word "hour" belongs to the association it provokes with Big Ben, Britain's national—and synecdochic—symbol of longevity. At regular intervals, the great bell in the famous clock tower boomed and echoed throughout the Houses of Parliament and across the left bank of the Thames. For Churchill and for the British people who had come to identify with the world famous, historic clock, every hour's peal promised the determinism of time. The "hour" represented what no other people in the world could lay claim to: a national identity intimately tied to and reinforced by the steady and predictable chimes of an ancient clock.

Finally, the "hour" recalls the homonym "our." Without jangling the audience's ears with a nearly incessant echo in "This will be our finest hour," Churchill's past tense and third person perspective suggested a world view of the united effort he promoted. The final five words are themselves a synecdoche as they represent the entire solemn text of a distant orator hypothetically engaged in reverent praise.

The rhetorical, perhaps even military, advantage to owning one's hours is best exemplified by the contrast Adolf Hitler provided as he gasped desperately on the brink of defeat:

> We have anticipated this hour. . . . In this hour, the whole German nation has its eye on you, my warriors in the East, and only hopes that—through your resolution and fanaticism, through your weapons and under your leadership the Bolshevik assault will be drowned in a bath of blood (cited in Stein, 1968, pp. 82–83).

We do not hear in Hitler's appeal the personal pronouns of "our" and "their," but rather we confront the impersonal "this hour." The effect is to discount identification with the time span, particularly reinforced by the notion that "this hour" was only anticipated and not owned by the "whole German nation."

Like Churchill's, Hitler's closure was profoundly metonymic in character. Despite the disowned hour, he invoked the "eye" of Germany and a graphic image of death to the Bolsheviks who "drown" in "blood." Within this last series of images, note that it was the synecdoche of "blood" which horrifically empowered the less malignant metaphor of "bath." The combined images in "blood bath," especially as the phrase represents those instances of multiple, violent deaths in battle, challenges the common belief that synecdoche and metonymy are necessarily more subtle than the extra-contextual power of metaphor. While these tropes may be harder to recognize as non-literal, especially when obscured by adjacent metaphors, their persuasive power is significant. In some cases, especially where bodily parts are concerned, the focus on one part or substance, like blood, generates an irresistible image made more graphic by its dismemberment from the whole.

Within Churchill's first speech to the House of Commons as the nation's Prime Minister, he declared that he had "nothing to offer but blood, toil, tears and sweat" (p. 276). In those synecdoches he summed up a very human offering, a condensed version of his promise to give to the effort all that he was. Note that Churchill's reference to "blood," in contrast to Hitler's, is benignly representative of human vigor, perhaps because it is the speaker's—and not the enemy's—blood. Later, when writing his memoirs on the historic moments of his rise to power, he would claim that "all my past life had been but a preparation for this hour and for this trial" (Irving, 1987, p. 267). This same "hour," of course, was shared by the entire nation of which Churchill was a significant, synecdochic, representative.

Thus, while it may be true that metonymy "marginalizes" what is left out of the representation, it has the capacity to condense what it represents to its fundamentals, its essence. By highlighting his human essence in "blood, toil, tears, and sweat," and by focusing on "our duties," Churchill is made essentially human, at once united with his audience. Together, they face their "hour" of glory in a very human trial. More unifying than isolating, Churchill argued that his "part"—his history, his humanity, and his destiny—was an inseparable and fundamental representative of the whole. In addition to connecting an audience to the topic, metonymy has the persuasive power to connect an audience to the speaker.

An Empirical Analysis: Metonymy
versus Metaphor

In *Reading Lacan,* Gallop (1987) argued for a gender-linked preference for
metaphor and metonymy. Metonymy, concluded Gallop, is "feminine" in
nature, while metaphor has "masculine" characteristics. This analysis borrows
heavily from feminist criticism and suggests that women may resonate more
than men to the "connectiveness" of metonymic appeals. Metaphor, Gallop
argued, received its "most-studied" status as a consequence of male-dominated
culture. Ironically, Gallop uses the metaphor of gender to describe the
distinctive essence of both tropes.

One psychological study by Graesser, Mio, and Millis (1989)
discovered that metonymic imagery in political debates was significantly more
persuasive than other figurative tropes. It must be noted, however, that this
study did not identify these persuasive examples as metonymic; instead, they
were labelled "personification metaphors." The authors offered a post-hoc
explanation for why "personification metaphors" might be more persuasive
than "other metaphors" by speculating that the former may suggest more
powerful or authoritative message sources (i.e., "The White House said . . ." as
opposed to the literal "A White House staff member said . . ."). All of the listed
examples in the research category of "personification metaphors" can be
accurately identified as whole-to-part, or synecdochic, incidents of metonymy.
These results suggest, albeit unintentionally, that metonymy may be more
persuasive than metaphor in political debates.

Gibbs (1990) proclaimed that "there are apparently no empirical
studies on comprehension of metonymy" (p. 56). In a psychological
investigation of the "sense selection" and "sense creation" processes involved
for metaphor and metonymy, Gibbs conducted a series of experiments and
found that "the interaction of these two processes may work differently for
metaphoric and metonymic statements" (p. 65). Additionally, Gibbs' findings
suggest that metaphoric references may be easier for readers to immediately
understand than metonymic ones because, in the latter condition, subjects
appeared to "momentarily" perceive a metonymic figure as a literal referent.
Metonymic figures, unlike metaphors, are contextually related to their literal
referents; they may initially invite literal interpretation simply because they do
not violate the context of the established narrative.[1] As ambitious as this study
was, however, it did not distinguish gender as a variable.

Chantrill and Mio (1994) were interested in the possible differences
metaphor and metonymy have on the persuasive strengths of speeches.
Additionally, we proposed to incorporate Gallop's suggestion of gender-linked
differences in the preference for and memory of metaphor- and metonymy-
dominant auditory speeches.

We constructed two politically opposed appeals, each derived from written materials on forest management and preservation, for a taped presentation to the subjects in our study. One appeal, labeled "The Wilderness Society" (TWS), argued for the preservation of forests. The opposing perspective, labeled the "American Forest Council" (AFC), justified the existing logging practices. These two arguments were adapted for trope-dominant imagery, including one metaphoric and one metonymic version each.

In the metaphoric version of the AFC speech, we fostered the image of a "guardian" of the forest. "Clearcutting," in this version, was promoted as "man's imitation of nature" equivalent to, for example, forest fires. The metonymic version of this same speech invoked a synecdoche: The AFC became "part of our nation's efforts to conserve natural resources." "Clearcutting," in this version, was "one of many forest management techniques."

The opposing metaphoric viewpoint invoked a *"predator in the forest"* image and compared corporate logging and clearcutting to predatory carnage. In the metonymic version of the TWS speech, the audience was asked to imagine a single, 65' tall, Lodgepole pine, "growing for nearly 100 years in Idaho's Targhee National Forest." The destruction of this single pine tree was then related to a threat to "every tree in America's National Forests." A final metonymy was then offered: "When the Corporations cut such massive quantities of trees, *they cut out a piece of us.*"

One male and one female speaker recorded each of the four versions. In an attempt to control for any preexisting topical bias, we altered the sequencing of the speeches; the first eight groups heard the AFC speech first, the TWS speech second. The second series of groups heard the TWS speech first, and the AFC speech second. The four trope-dominant versions of the speeches, combined with gender pairings of the speakers and the sequence order of the two appeals, resulted in sixteen condition pairs. Table 10.1 outlines the 16 conditions of our study.

Subjects consisted of 380 students from communication courses at Washington State University. Because of the limited sample size relative to the number of conditions of the study (including gender comparisons), we consider our results to be preliminary and our conclusions tentative. Subjects were divided first by gender, and then randomly assigned to 1 of 16 groups. Because the communication courses occurred on a two days per week schedule, subjects heard the speeches and rated them for convincingness on a Tuesday afternoon. On the Thursday two days later, we asked our subjects to recall what they could of the speeches they had heard. We then scored their responses for idea units.

We predicted an interaction effect between trope-type and gender, with women being more persuaded by metonymic speeches and recalling more of these passages. Men, conversely, were predicted to be better able to recall metaphor-dominant passages and to be more convinced by metaphoric speeches.

Our results suggest that subjects, overall, found the American Forest Council speech to be more convincing than the Wilderness Society speech, regardless of the order in which these speeches occurred. The American Forest Council speech appeared to offer a perspective that was perhaps more in line with the initial attitudes subjects brought with them into the experimental situation. This assumption would be consistent with the regional preference in favor of logging interests and suggests that participation in the study did little to fundamentally alter existing attitudes.

TABLE 10.1
Conditions Involved in Chantrill and Mio Study

Condition	Speaker Sequence	Speech Sequence	Trope Sequence
1	Female-Male	TWS-AFC*	Metaphor-Metonymy
2	Male-Female	TWS-AFC	Metaphor-Metonymy
3	Female-Male	TWS-AFC	Metaphor-Metaphor
4	Male-Female	TWS-AFC	Metaphor-Metaphor
5	Female-Male	TWS-AFC	Metonymy-Metaphor
6	Male-Female	TWS-AFC	Metonymy-Metaphor
7	Female-Male	TWS-AFC	Metonymy-Metonymy
8	Male-Female	TWS-AFC	Metonymy-Metonymy
9	Female-Male	AFC-TWS	Metaphor-Metonymy
10	Male-Female	AFC-TWS	Metaphor-Metonymy
11	Female-Male	AFC-TWS	Metaphor-Metaphor
12	Male-Female	AFC-TWS	Metaphor-Metaphor
13	Female-Male	AFC-TWS	Metonymy-Metaphor
14	Male-Female	AFC-TWS	Metonymy-Metaphor
15	Female-Male	AFC-TWS	Metonymy-Metonymy
16	Male-Female	AFC-TWS	Metonymy-Metonymy

*TWS--The Wilderness Society
AFC--American Forest Council

Our study also proposed tentative support for the gender hypothesis, especially for female subjects. Specifically, though metonymic tropes did not appear to be more persuasive and memorable for female subjects, our data suggested that women may be less convinced when a male speaker uses predominantly metaphoric speech. Additionally, female subjects tended to recall more of the opposing speech when the AFC speech was delivered by a male using metaphor.

This combination of lower convincingness ratings for the AFC speech and higher recall of the TWS speech, especially for female subjects listening to males using metaphor, leads to an interesting speculation. While female subjects may discount the TWS message upon first experiencing it, over time that message may become more convincing. Gruder, Cook, Hennigan, Flay, Alessis, and Kalamaj (1978) called this phenomenon the "sleeper effect" and based their findings on Tversky and Kahneman's (1973) "availability heuristic." Essentially, while we may forget the source of a message, upon secondary exposure to that message, our sustained memory of it suggests a heightened importance and, subsequently, a lowered resistance to the message. Because we did not collect convincingness ratings at the time of recall, this speculation was not tested directly. However, our results are certainly consistent with those found in the sleeper effect literature.

For all subjects exposed to a metaphoric version of the AFC speech first, regardless of speaker gender, followed by a metonymic version of the TWS speech, a lower recall for the AFC speech resulted. This suggests that metonymic speeches may suppress memory for their metaphoric opponents, even when those metaphors are aligned with a political perspective the audience is predisposed to agree with. Conversely, in those conditions where subjects listened first to the TWS speech and secondly to a metaphoric version of the AFC speech, a higher recall for the TWS speech resulted. This trend suggests that metaphoric speeches may actually invite increased memory for their metonymic opponents, even when those metonymies run counter to preexisting political beliefs.

A final outcome suggested that both males and females remembered more of the TWS speech in those conditions where it came first and the speaker was female, even though subjects were consistently more convinced by the second (AFC) speaker. We might surmise that a female speaker speaking first and using predominantly metonymic speech improves her chances of being memorable—at least to the female audience members.

Our study yields interesting, though cautious and inconclusive, results which serve to further indicate the need for future research into tropic influence on persuasion and memory. We did not unequivocally find that metonymic tropes would be more persuasive for female subjects, nor that metaphoric tropes would be more persuasive for male subjects. Our results merely suggest that speaker gender and trope dominance may have an indirect influence on persuasion based upon memory results, but they do not clearly demonstrate direct support of them.

In order to take this type of research any further, we may want to introduce some additional controls on the speaker's text, including a fine-tuning of the types of metonymy and metaphor we include in the speeches. For example, Gibbs (1990) identified several different types of metonymy, each exemplifying varying degrees of conventionality. It may be possible that one conventionally recognized type of metonymy (i.e., "place stands for the institution"), is less problematic for audience comprehension, memory, and persuasiveness than other types of metonymy (i.e., "object stands for the user"). Additionally, if we introduce a synecdoche, it may diversely impact audience response if we ask subjects to focus on the part, as opposed to the whole, and visa versa.

Gibbs did not mention whether certain metaphor types have greater impact on audience memory and comprehension. However, it is worth investigating the possibility that announcing the literal topic before the figurative vehicle, as we did in the *"predator"* version of The Wilderness Society speech, may influence persuasiveness differently than when we announce the vehicle first and then imply the topic, as we did in the *"guardian"* version of the American Forest Council speech. In the former condition, we retrospectively discovered that the *"predator in the forest"* metaphor (designed to suggest logging corporations) may have posed the same kind of initial literal versus figurative confusion that Gibbs said is common to "object stands for the user" metonymies (p. 65). In any event, it is clear that the *"predator"* image can be viewed as "twice true" given our adapted version of the Wilderness Society's metaphoric speech. How much these subtle differences may have influenced memory for and persuasiveness of each of the speeches can not be discerned without further examination.

CONCLUSION

Much of the literature on figurative language has focused upon metaphor as representing all of figurative language (e.g., Pollio, Hoffman, & Smith, 1986). This is because the formal definition of metaphor is the most general of the specific figurative language terms, and other terms can be considered special cases of this general definition. "Perhaps the major reason metaphor is used as the generic label for all figurative expression is that it most clearly exhibits the combinatorial nature of such usage" (Pollio, Barlow, Fine, & Pollio, 1977, p. 37).

Because of the dominance of metaphor, finer distinctions of other forms of figurative language have been lost. We contend that one of the more important forms of figurative language—at least with respect to political rhetoric—is metonymy. In Churchill's (1941) speech attempting to inspire his country during a foreboding time during World War II, we found effective use of metonymy which seemed to be a central aspect of his rhetoric.

In our own examination of the distinction between metaphor and metonymy, we found results supporting important differences between these two tropes. This was particularly true for women, who seemed to respond more to metonymic speeches, or at least respond in an unfavorable fashion to men delivering metaphorical speeches. Although our results are only preliminary, we see them as promising and encourage further examination of what we see as an important distinction.

There is an irony in our inclination to use "metaphor" as the single representative of all figurative language. When we infer that this albeit significant trope could represent metonymy and other distinct tropes, we, in fact, have "metonymized" the relation between tropes. We then blur the distinctive characteristics that metonymy and synecdoche contribute to all forms of discourse, we marginalize those tropes and collapse those distinctions. Although we may make figurative language a more "manageable" topic under the heading of "metaphor," we sacrifice a detailed understanding of the very process which made that manageability possible.

Metonymic images require audiences to make generalizations based on significant and concentrated details; we inductively reason our way from specific example to universalized conclusions. Perhaps metonymy's unique position within contemporary political discourse is strengthened most by our continuing adjustment to compact and lightning-quick sound-bite appeals; we have learned to encounter and experience our world in media-generated, metonymic bits and pieces. Perhaps, too soon, even the "hour" figure of Churchill's mid-century speech will become cumbersome and too weighty a prospect in the millennium, though a call to our "finest split-second" has a somewhat impoverished, impious ring to it. As science speedily moves to define the very essence of life in microscopic terms, we still struggle to "unite into one meaning" the profusion of detail we daily encounter. For this reason alone, and for males and females alike, metonymy may be poised to become the dominant trope in a fragmented world.

ENDNOTE

[1]Gibbs offered the metonymic example of *"the scapel"* as it was used to describe *"the surgeon."* Momentarily, it seems, Gibbs' subjects read *"the scalpel"* "as referring to the object itself rather than to some particular person. This [confusion] interferes with the search for the correct antecedents of metonymic referential descriptions" (p. 64).

REFERENCES

Bowers, J. W., & Osborn, M. M. (1966). Attidunal effects of selected types of concluding metaphors in persuasive speeches. *Speech Monographs, 33,* 147–155.

Bredin, H. (1984). Metonymy. *Poetics today, 5,* 45–48.

Brummett, B. (1994). *Rhetoric in popular culture.* New York: St. Martin's Press.

Chantrill, P. A., & Mio, J. S. (1994, April). Gender differences in the preference for metaphor vs. metonymy. In J. S. Mio (Chair), *On the politics of metaphor.* Symposium conducted at the 74th annual meeting of the Western Psychological Association, Kona, HI.

Churchill, W. S. (1941). *Blood, sweat and tears.* New York: G. P. Putnam's Sons.

Cockcroft, R., & Cockcroft, S. (1992). *Persuading people.* London: Macmillan.

Edelman, M. (1977). *Political language: Words that succeed and policies that fail.* New York: Academic Press.

Gallop, J. (1987). *Reading Lacan.* London: Cornell University Press.

Gibbs, R. W., Jr. (1990). Comprehending figurative referential descriptions. *Journal of Experimental Psychology: Learning, Memory, and Cognition, 16,* 56–66.

Graesser, A., Mio, J., & Millis, K. (1989). Metaphors in persuasive communication. In D. Meutsch & R. Viehoff (Eds.), *Comprehension of literary discourse* (pp. 131–154). New York: deGruyter.

Gruder, C. L., Cook, T. D., Hennigan, K. M., Flay, B., Alessis, C., & Kalamaj, J. (1978). Empirical tests of the absolute sleeper effect predicted from the discounting cue hypothesis. *Journal of Personality and Social Psychology, 36,* 1061–1074.

Irving, D. (1987). *Churchill's war.* New York: Avon Books.

Jakobson, R. (1971). Two aspects of language and two types of aphasic disturbances. In R. Jacobson (Ed.), *Selected writings, 2* (pp. 239–259). The Hague, Netherlands: Mouton.

Lacan, J. (1977). *Ecrits* (A. Sheridan, Trans.). New York: Norton.

Lodge, D. (1977). *The modes of modern writing.* London: Edward Arnold.

Pollio, H. R., Barlow, J. M., Fine, H. J., & Pollio, M. R. (1977). *Psychology and the poetics of growth.* Hillsdale, NJ: Lawrence Erlbaum Associates.

Pollio, H. R., Hoffman, R. R., & Smith, M. K. (1986). Editorial. *Metaphor and Symbolic Activity, 1,* 1–4.

Quintilian. (1976). *The institutio oratoria.* (H. E. Butler, Trans.). Cambridge: Harvard University Press. (Original work published 95 A.D.)

Stein, G. H. (1968). *Great lives observed: Hitler.* Englewood Cliffs, NJ: Prentice-Hall.

Tversky, A., & Kahneman, D. (1973). Availability: A heuristic for judging frequency and probability. *Cognitive Psychology, 5,* 207–232.

Urdang, L. (1988). *The whole ball of wax and other colloquial phrases: What they mean and how they started.* New York: Putnam.

Weidhorn, M. (1972). Churchill the phrase forger. *Quarterly Journal of Speech, 58,* 161–174.

11

Politics without Metaphors is Like a Fish without Water

Seth Thompson
Loyola Marymount University

INTRODUCTION

Fish need water to be fish; humans need metaphors to do and think about politics. This chapter begins with a discussion of the necessity of metaphors to political discourse, then explores the consequences of metaphorical language for political participants.

Salt water or fresh, warm water or cold—the type and quality of water affects different fish in different ways. There are significant differences in the consequences of political metaphors for those who are more actively involved in political life, as decision makers, politicians, activists or professional observers, and those who are more distant. The second section of the chapter examines the role of metaphors for elites—those with more resources, who have more interest in, and are more central to the decision-making process. A set of metaphors helps define who is inside the system and who is not and provides indispensable tools of the trade for framing issues and problems in ways that make decisions possible.

The third section explores the paradoxical role of metaphors in the political life of the mass public—the majority of people whose relation to politics ranges from casual interest and voting to alienation and apathy. Metaphors can simultaneously make politics accessible to the (metaphorical) average citizen and induce acquiescence and passivity.

THE CENTRALITY OF METAPHORS
TO POLITICAL DISCOURSE

The world of politics is complex, value-laden and both cognitively and perceptually removed from the immediacy of everyday experience (Graber,

1993). The dynamics and consequences of politics are neither tangible, self-evident, nor simple. A major function of political metaphors is to link the individual and the political by providing a way of seeing relations, reifying abstractions, and framing complexity in manageable terms.

Politics can be defined in a variety of ways, but two elements are almost invariably central: group level processes and choices among competing values and broadly defined alternative futures. (See Danziger, 1994, for a discussion of the variety of definitions in use in Political Science.) Whether the central definitional elements are structures (e.g., governmental institutions), processes (e.g., attempts to exercise power, influence or authority), or results (e.g., policy outcomes), all attempts to describe the political include some attention to groups, communities, or societies. Politics and political processes are very much about groups and group-level phenomena. Edelman (1971) pointed out, "governmental acts [are] one of the few forms of activity perceived as involving all groups and individuals in society and as reflecting the range of public interests, wants, and capabilities" (p. 9).

Metaphors are essential condensation symbols for conveying meaning, embodying values, emotions, and ideology, and leading to action (Edelman, 1964, p. 119). Politics cannot be understood as an individual level phenomenon in the way that basic physiological, cognitive, or emotive processes can be. The personal is *not* the political until a person understands that her/his life experience is a function of membership in a group or category. The modern feminist movement, for example, began with "consciousness raising" that led individual women to see that their position in society and their life chances were directly affected by the socially constructed facts of gender definitions and roles and not just their individual strengths and weaknesses.

Since group membership does not have an experiential basis in "reality" and everyday life, metaphors and metaphorical thinking are essential (Nimmo & Coombs, 1987). Although people tend to be immediately aware of their individual level experiences, it is only after reflecting on social interactions and their consequences that a person may come to attribute their own or others' behaviors to group membership. Locating oneself in a politically relevant group or attributing others' behavior to their group membership involves social psychological, political, and linguistic processes including synecdoche, which is the form of metaphorical thinking that uses a part to stand for the larger unit. Recognizing that one has been treated *as if* one were part of some larger entity rather than as completely unique and individualized is the first step in doing politics (Davies, 1977). Until and unless that metaphorical leap of understanding is made, there is no participation in politics nor in political discourse. (See Lasswell, 1960, for the classic discussion of the relation between individual level psychological processes and political life, with an emphasis on Freudian mechanisms.)

Important aspects of political life are manifest in specialized arenas and distinctive settings. National and provincial capitals are filled with governmental buildings to accommodate legislatures, ministries and departments, judicial organs, and the host of other roles and groups involved in political life, and to separate them from more quotidian pursuits. Even in smaller and simpler political systems, there is physical and psychological separation: the village or lineage elders who dominate social and political life in most peasant societies meet apart from the younger men and the women. Political roles, like all social roles, tend to be specialized. In the absence of effective bridging metaphors that bring the individual into psychic contact with political life, politics is what "they" are doing in "Washington" or a state capital or down at "City Hall."

The *existence* of metaphors describing the links between individuals and larger groups is crucial to making politics relevant. The *content* of the operative metaphors used in political life simplifies the confusingly complex and makes definition, decision, and action possible.   Even the most sophisticated or policy-obsessed participant is in constant peril of drowning in a sea of technical detail or of losing sight of the forest in the midst of trees of highly specific expertise.

"A small number of classic themes or myths serve repeatedly as explanations of what is shaping the political scene.   In contrast to the complicated network of competing influences in the empirical world, the world of the myths is simpler . . ." (Edelman, 1971, p. 72).

For example, the flow of revenue to the Federal government is determined by, among other things, macroeconomic policy, international trade and capital flows, and the perturbations of the business cycle. The pattern of expenditures is influenced by social entitlements, continuing programs, new defense or civilian programs, and the vagaries of disaster relief. Individuals have experience with budgets, but they are typically simple enough affairs— income determined by one's salary and perhaps investments, and expenditures largely determined by the necessities of survival at the level to which one has become accustomed. In several fundamental ways the federal budget is not just a personal or household budget writ large. But for the typical citizen, and even for the relatively sophisticated policy maker, thinking about the federal budget typically begins with the metaphor of a household or business budget: *"If the government were a company, it would have gone bankrupt years ago"*; *"In government, just like your own home, you can't spend money you don't have."*

The contemporary international system includes some 180 nation states, several thousand international organizations of varying size, membership, and mission, and a swarm of nongovernmental groups and individuals who, at least some of the time, make a difference. The prospective foreign policy maker or analyst would be helpless without simplifying and clarifying metaphors.

Decision makers, journalists, and casual observers all tend to rely on the metaphor of the nation state as a unitary rational actor. That is, events, intentions, and motives are attributed to the metaphoric entity *"The United States"* or *"Nigeria."* Analysis proceeds as if there were a single consciousness making an intelligible decision after weighing the costs and benefits of various alternatives. (See Allison, 1971, for a full description of *"unitary rational actors," "organizational processes,"* and *"bureaucratic politics"* as alternative theoretical metaphors for describing and explaining foreign policy outcomes.)

While, at some level, what representatives and agents of governments do can be understood as the outcome of internal political struggles; and at another level, actions are best explained as the end product of essentially mindless sets of organizational procedures, the simpler metaphor makes analysis, communication, and choice possible. The attempt to describe the variety of national, bureaucratic, personal, and political interests and motives driving a decision making process involving hundreds or even thousands of people in some capacity and analyze them in depth can go on seemingly forever and become almost hopelessly convoluted. As much as that may be grist for the historian's mill, it is a fool's errand for the person who must make some prudent choice in a finite amount of time.

It is a much more manageable task, more readily grasped by one's audience and, within limits, equally useful to use personal metaphors for national governments. Thus the *"United States"* is described as *"not trusting China,"* or *"Canada"* is said to be *"angry at the United States' insistence on curbs on wheat imports."* (The metaphorical quality of the usage is clear if one tries to imagine what concrete referent an *"angry country"* might have— perhaps millions of citizens in the streets stamping their feet, shaking their fists, and getting a bit red in the face?) Metaphors do more than simplify complexity for the analyst or decision maker. They clothe the intangible, giving life to abstractions.

The central concepts used to analyze politics—influence, authority, power, etc.—are tantalizingly intangible. The presumptive motivators of political action—interests, ideology, personal needs—projected onto public objects (Lasswell, 1960) are abstract, not concrete.[1] Political preferences and interests are intangible; they are not captured by the economist's concrete metric of tangible dollars and cents. Thus metaphors and metaphorical language become essential to political discourse.

When they do politics, whether as voters, activists or decision makers, people need some tangible metaphor or symbol in order to reify concepts and to create a sense of commonality. Metaphors need not be verbal. Perhaps because so much of the essence of political life and culture is intangible, physical metaphors are common.

The foundational basis of a political community, whether it be the tribe, the nation, the civil community, "us," is abstract. When language, religion, skin color, mythologies of descent, or shared history are used as metaphors for the group, the boundaries become manifest. At this point the content of the defining metaphor becomes crucial because it determines the rigidity of community boundaries and affects the nature of cleavages in a society.

The defining metaphor in Lebanese society, even after the recent civil war, remains religion. The metaphorical use of religion is shown by the fact that the key cleavages are not defined by differences in theological concepts or great gaps in beliefs about the ultimate meaning of life and the differences between vice and virtue. The cleavages defined by communal boundaries and religion become markers, symbols for communities that see themselves differing in politically relevant ways (Bill & Springborg, 1990). Crossing the communal boundaries becomes very difficult, in part because the divisive metaphors are so concrete and clear.

In contrast, in much of North America and Western Europe, the dominant metaphor defining political community is *"civil society"* (Seligman, 1992) based on a shared sense of citizenship and participation in a polity—far more allusive and intangible. The result is that group boundaries are less clear, national identity is more malleable, and cleavages are less unidimensional.

Totemic animals and flags are probably as old as humanity and politics. Impressive public buildings, civic ritual, and specialized clothing are used almost universally as metaphors for "the nation," "the law," or "authority." *"Candidates"* (from the Roman practice of clothing would-be office holders in white) *"run"* for a *"seat"*—even apparently prosaic political usage depends on images and comparisons.

Routine political discourse consistently uses metaphors to capture an otherwise elusive reality. A contemporary master of effective political synecdoche, Ronald Reagan routinely used the personal anecdote—the *"welfare queen buying vodka with food stamps"* (a mythical figure who condensed the generalized fear that many people on welfare were not really needy and honest but cheats who were putting one over on the taxpayers); the *"police officer wounded in a shoot out with drug lords"* (symbolizing both the humanity of law enforcement and the paramilitary nature of the *"war on drugs"*); the *"dying World War II bomber pilot"* (the apocryphal hero who refused to bail out and leave several wounded members of his ethnically diverse crew behind and instead guided the crippled craft to a crash landing, which tragically had no survivors and was meant to represent both the self-sacrifice of World War II and the long standing egalitarianism of middle America)[2]—not only to present but to essentially define a complex and multidimensional policy issue.

Political action is future oriented; politics is intimately involved with what steps are to be taken to create a desired future. But if much of the reality of the present is difficult to grasp concretely, the future is even less accessible to immediate experience and more dependent on metaphor. Martin Luther King's dream for the future was comprehensive and in his thought and writings complex and multidimensional. But the image in his 1963 speech that worked as compelling metaphor was as apparently simple and straightforward as childhood: *"little black boys and black girls will be able to join hands with little white boys and white girls as sisters and brothers"* (King, 1963/1986, p. 217.)

Since metaphor is the very stuff and substance of political discourse, which metaphor is used matters greatly. Shapiro (1990) analyzed the competing discourses, based heavily on metaphors, that are involved in the politics of foreign policy, particularly the gap between "official" and "unofficial" vocabularies. Edelman (1988) discussed the ways in which ideological diversity in constituencies leads to differing, even competing "constructions" of political life as reflected in the media. The result is that "recurring themes in political news display the curious property that each reference is typically unambiguous for an individual for the moment, while the connotations of each reference vary widely among individuals, groups and situations" (Edelman, 1988, p. 91.)

Because there are competing interests and some degree of diversity among policy makers and activists, the metaphors available to frame issues and define options are drawn from multiple sources and are not monolithic. In a particular situation there is generally more than one metaphor potentially available, although the range of potential political metaphors is more constricted than in some other kinds of discourse because the useful political metaphor must be accessible to a relatively broad spectrum of the population (Edelman, 1988). Which metaphor comes to govern a situation has consequences for both what is to be done and who is to do it. Defining the use of illegal drugs as a *"problem of addiction"* or *"symptom of social dysfunction"* directly implies strategies to deal with the situation of the individual drug abuser and to assign pride of place to counselors, therapists and social reformers. Declaring a *"war"* on drugs leads to strategies to interdict supply or punish demand, highlighting the role of law enforcement and quasi-military techniques and agencies and legitimating their involvement.

Military strategists stress the importance of controlling the high ground; political strategists stress the importance of controlling the metaphor. When the United States became involved in the effort to care for several hundred thousand Rwandan refugees in the summer of 1994, the operation was explicitly compared by both President Clinton and Chairman of the Joint Chiefs of Staff John Shalikashvili to *"Operation Provide Comfort,"* the earlier effort to take care of the Kurds in northern Iraq. The comparison, to the extent it worked for the audience, did two things through simile. First, it made the goals and intentions of the policy concrete and familiar by rooting them in a comparison to the recent past which presumptively many people would have access to. Second, it framed the effort as likely to be very successful, limited in duration, and not involve American casualties. From the President on down through the White House and Defense department, everyone explicitly denied the relevance of an ominous competing comparison—this was not, they assured the press and public, like *"Somalia."*

However, as much as they would like to, policy makers are unable to control the range of metaphors available or the uses to which they are put. Opponents and interest groups in domestic politics compete vigorously to establish the winning metaphor in policy debates and, without too much exaggeration, campaigns can be seen as struggles over metaphors. It made a great deal of difference if one saw the 1992 Democratic presidential candidate as *"Slick Willy"* or *"The Man From Hope."*

Struggles to control metaphors are not limited to internal politics. As this chapter was being written and the U.S. was stressing the irrelevance of Somalia to the operation in Rwanda, the Haitian regime was insisting that any attempt to invade Haiti would be *"just like Somalia."*

THE CONSEQUENCES OF METAPHOR FOR ELITES

The relationship between individuals and their political system spans a continuum from the object of politics who does not participate even as a spectator to the group of policy makers at the apex of the system (Hughes, 1978; Neuman, 1986). At the cost of some distortion, it is possible to pursue analysis as if there were two distinct groups: *elites* involved in making and implementing policy and *masses* who are largely spectators and only occasional participants in politics. The metaphorical vocabulary of the two groups differs and the consequences of the use of metaphor in political discourse differs.

The metaphorical vocabulary of political discourse serves two primary purposes among policy makers. Shared and reinforced metaphors help create a sense of community and solidarity among elites, and common metaphors become the vehicle for institutionalizing policy and patterns across generations.

Political systems differ in their openness and tendency to circulate elites, ranging from "governments of strangers" (Neustadt & May, 1986, p. 160) to hermetic systems of hereditary mandarins. But, to a greater or lesser extent, all systems face the problem of integrating new individuals into elite positions. Political vocabularies become important tools. In Imperial China, aspirants to elite status had to demonstrate their mastery of the Confucian texts not only because they contained the essential moral and political wisdom but also because they provided the fundamental vocabulary and stock of metaphors that served as common intellectual currency in the government. Most of the elite planters, merchants, and bankers from the disparate American states who gathered in Philadelphia in 1787 to draft the Constitution of the United States were familiar with classical Greek and Roman political history (Adair, 1974, Chapter 5). This shared pool of examples, comparisons, and admonitory lessons formed the common vocabulary of the debates, and classical allusions were common rhetorical strategies along with deduction from Locke, Hobbes, or Montesquieu. The use of references to the Romans in particular marks the Federalist Papers, the series of tracts designed to sway elite public opinion in support of the Constitution and authored under the pseudonym "Publius."

The sources of the contemporary American political vocabulary are more prosaic, drawn instead from the realm of the military, sports, or commerce. (See, for example, Nimmo & Coombs, 1987; Safire, 1993.) But they serve the same function of permitting communication among elites and the most attentive elements of the public and separating those on the inside from those more peripheral to the process. Being *"inside the Beltway"* is not a geographic fact (many people who live in Washington, D.C., are not inside; many who live elsewhere in the country are.) A sign that a person is inside the Beltway is that the person understands the metaphor.

Shared metaphors not only help create a common discourse among policy makers and other elites at any particular point in time, they also serve to maintain continuity among elites and policy-making communities over time.

For a generation of American foreign policy makers who were formed by the experience of 1930s and 1940s, *"Munich"* was the metaphor for the dire consequences of seeking to negotiate with perceived aggressors. An advocate of a *"hawkish"* policy did not have to lay out a series of theoretical propositions or if–then hypotheses. Invocation of the symbol not only captured a presumptive causal model but also added a heavy emotional valence. One element was the implicit theory that states ruled by dictators are inherently aggressive and expansionist, do not pursue self-limiting policies through reasonable compromise, and interpret attempts at conciliation or compromise as admissions of weakness. Therefore perceived threats to the status quo are to be met by threats or the actual use of force. The emotional loading of the metaphor was even more compelling—in the specific instance of the failed attempt by Britain and France to reach an accommodation with Nazi Germany at Munich, the result was the horror of World War II. The metaphor thus carried the powerful meaning that the consequences of a more moderate or softer policy can be catastrophic. For the generation that found itself in conflict with the Soviet Union immediately after the war, *"Munich"* was nearly overwhelming; it remained a dominant theme in Cold War policy discussions for the duration of the conflict and continued to work and be understood by many who were not even born at the time of the original event (Holsti & Rosenau, 1989).

A more recent generation of American policy makers was entranced with the *"domino theory"* which was used explicitly by those involved with the key decisions on the Vietnam War during the 20 years of U.S. involvement and continues to frame and define issues in other arenas (Glad & Taber, 1990; Holsti & Rosenau, 1989). The image not only allowed a large number of people with little or no exposure to Southeast Asia to believe that they had grasped a central similarity among Vietnam, Cambodia, Laos, and Thailand despite the differences that struck area specialists, but also carried an image of inevitability. As almost everyone knows from experience, once the first domino in the row tips, all the others are destined to fall.

Holsti and Rosenau (1989) argue that American foreign policy elites shared a common set of metaphors that were also widely understood by the attentive public from the end of World War II. They found empirical evidence that this consensus had splintered in the aftermath of Vietnam and a key indicator was sharp differences over the "meaning" and "lessons" of that period. (The historical event itself became a potent metaphor as in *"no more Vietnams"* and *"Vietnam syndrome."*) The fact that the metaphorical vocabulary of policy makers had become controversial helps explain the more contentious and ideologically divisive nature of debate over U.S. foreign policy in the ensuing period.

The use of metaphors is crucial in a wide range of policy domains in the United States and elsewhere. The people with executive responsibility for policy typically come from different backgrounds and career paths than the permanent staff of agencies or academic specialists in substantive issues. Policy makers have neither the time nor the inclination to master the theoretical frameworks, modes of inquiry, or research findings in a field (George, 1994). But they either come to office already knowing the dominant metaphors in use in continuing policy debates and discussions or learn them quickly.

Metaphorical thinking, particularly the use of historical analogues, is a constant in political decision making. Individuals differ in the sophistication with which they analyze the metaphors they are using and are more or less successful in finding a useful metaphor to guide action in a particular case. (Neustadt & May, 1986, provide an extended treatment of the use and abuse of historical analogies and suggestions for improving decision makers' ability to identify the most useful metaphor.)

There are three fundamental consequences that flow directly from the use of metaphors to create a policy making community. First of all, the simplifying and clarifying function of metaphors makes policy decisions possible (George, 1994; Neustadt & May, 1986). If every event or case had to be analyzed separately and apprehended in all its distinctive uniqueness, nothing would ever get done. The values at stake in a decision and the goals to be pursued are abstract and intangible; metaphor is necessary to link tangible means to intangible ends. Used effectively, metaphors can lead to actions that embody desired values; used ineffectively, metaphors can blind decision makers to the concrete impact of their choices.

The second consequence is that shared metaphors come to embody the collective memory and experience of government agencies and political actors (Neustadt & May, 1986). Use of metaphors allows decision makers, who may be very transitory in their positions, to gain access to the expertise and insights of more permanent staff of agencies or their predecessors in office. If the current problem is seen as like something that has occurred before, then the "lessons" of the past become available to guide current choice.

The third consequence is that the content and distribution of metaphors affects the ability of policy makers to communicate with a broader public to both explain what they are attempting and to generate support. When elites use metaphors that are accessible to everyone else, then political discourse and participation can be widespread and open. When they indulge in what Nimmo and Coombs (1987, p. 160) characterize as "elite fantasies," the result is isolation from the broader public. The use of "insider" metaphors can be an unanticipated and unintended consequence of the usual behavior of policy makers or it can be a relatively conscious strategy to remove policy making from public scrutiny and forestall or circumvent real or anticipated opposition.

ROLE AND CONSEQUENCES OF POLITICAL METAPHORS FOR CITIZENS

Most people most of the time are not policy makers nor directly involved in political life as activists or advocates. They are to a greater or lesser extent outside the circle of immediate participants in political discourse. Any discussion of the role of metaphors has to include two dimensions: the extent to which a common metaphorical vocabulary is shared between those elites who are most directly involved in politics and members of the mass public, and the impact of the content of politically relevant metaphors. Metaphors have implications for action because of their ability to frame issues. One of the differences between the use of metaphor in politics and other aspects of life is that the framing function is often recognized quite consciously by major actors and there are serious attempts to control the political agenda through controlling the dominant metaphors.

If metaphors are necessary for elites and policy makers as essential simplifications and clarifications and are also necessary devices to bridge the gap between general policy goals and values and the concrete means, they are even more necessary for the general observer and occasional participant in politics (Nimmo & Coombs, 1987).

The citizen may well have a reasonably clear idea of preferred outcomes in a given policy area, for example, assurances that there will be money to pay medical bills if a person gets sick. But most people are understandably at a loss if they have to go much further. It took several months of hearings with literally hundreds of experts and analysts from several academic disciplines as well as analysts and advocates from a bewildering array of groups and interests to produce the draft health reform plan introduced by the Clinton administration. How could the average person (or his or her elected representative) grasp the meaning and potential impact of key provisions?

In some cases, the answer lies in the emergence of a winning metaphor. One of the central provisions of the original Clinton plan was the creation of organizations at the state and local levels that would allow individuals and small businesses to pool their resources and bargain more effectively with insurance providers. Most people who currently have health insurance have chosen a policy from whatever options their employers have offered or selected a policy offered through an insurance agent, in much the same way that diners in a restaurant choose from a menu. There is no awareness that there is a prior decision making process in which the items on the menu and their price are negotiated among different types of diners and restaurant owners.

Proponents of the original Clinton proposal pinned great hopes on significant cost control through creation of large consumer pools. They faced an uphill battle because they had to find a simple way to explain what seemed to many an obscure and abstract idea and to convince people that it was a good idea. Most people lacked an initial basis for deciding whether they would be better or worse off under this aspect of the proposal. In contrast, those opposed to the idea tended to be insurance providers themselves who understood what was at stake and believed they would be worse off. Very early in the debate over health care reform, those opposed to mandatory consumer alliances succeeded in characterizing them as cumbersome, government-run, and bureaucratized. The metaphor of a system with *"the compassion of the IRS and the efficiency of the Post Office"* dominated—and quickly ended—consideration of the proposal.

There are relatively few *"political junkies"* in the general public, people who pay close attention to politics on a day-to-day basis, find C-SPAN more arresting than MTV, know one or more policy areas in substantial depth and, perhaps most importantly, can easily and fluently use the policy makers' repertoire of metaphors. For most people, political experience is heavily mediated by elite messages transmitted through various media. The content and implications of the metaphors in political messages is a critical factor in increasing or decreasing citizen participation and involvement.

As Murray Edelman (1988) pointed out:

> Symbols, whether language or icons, that have no relevance to every day life, frustrations and successes are meaningless and impotent. They are like the reactions of spectator in a museum to the icons of a culture with which they feel no empathy. In the measure that political advocates resort to appeals that do not touch the experiences of their audiences, indifference is to be expected. (p. 8)

There are times when political actors consciously seek to arouse mass participation, most obviously during electorial campaigns, but also when one set of players in a policy contest seeks to mobilize mass support. The National Rifle Association has used an explicitly metaphorical ad campaign to try to undo recent slippage in the organization's image and regenerate support for the organization in general. A well known person or someone with impeccable educational or professional credentials (including women and minorities) proclaims, "I am the NRA." The ads did not have to beat the reader over the head with the message, "and not the pot-bellied, red-necked 'Bubba' image that might otherwise come to mind."

The campaign was launched after a series of setbacks for the NRA in state legislatures and was very prominent during the protracted Congressional debate over the Brady Bill during which the NRA was extremely active in opposition to any limitations on hand guns. The NRA's greatest political resource has always been its ability to mobilize a significant number of voters who care deeply about candidates' positions on a specific set of issues and the inability of its opponents to counter-mobilize. If the NRA were to be seen by both politicians and the general public as just another special interest represented by lobbyists from the notorious *"Gucci gulch"* (the metaphorical hangout of high-priced wheelers and dealers) or worse, and its opponents as real or potential victims of unregulated handguns and assault rifles, much of the organization's influence would evaporate.

American political campaigns are necessarily broad exercises in the use of metaphors to convey their messages. From television ads surrounding George Bush with the symbols of the Presidency to the Clinton-Gore bus tour immediately after their nomination to Ross Perot's assertion that if *"something's broken you just get under the hood and fix it,"* the 1992 campaign season was typical. Every attempt was made to use metaphors that would simplify and highlight key features of complex issues, to invite the audience to feel a part of a larger cause and to become active participants, to persuade people that what happened in politics had a direct and immediate impact on their daily lives.

This campaign was also typical in suggesting some limits to the power of a set of political metaphors. One is that there are often competing sets being used by other actors to frame reality. In addition to commercials extolling a candidate's virtues, there are "attack ads" from opponents manipulating a very different set of images, ideas, and metaphors. A second limitation is that metaphorical and other forms of presentation of self on the part of campaigns are not the only source of information and images for prospective voters. Voters are not blank slates upon which campaigns can write what they wish; voters have both preexisting frameworks for thinking about candidates and multiple channels for gathering information. (The immense body of literature on voting behavior is obviously beyond the scope of this chapter. See Dalton and Wattenberg, 1993, for an overview.)

A final limitation is that the environment and context are often beyond the control of those who seek to create effective metaphors. Not only are campaigns and candidates surprised by developments or affected by situations and events external to the campaign, but even conscious attempts to manipulate metaphors can backfire. In 1988 Michael Dukakis sought to counter perceptions that he was weak on defense issues by posing in a tank. But the resulting picture emphasized the candidate's diminutive stature and was internally contradictory. Dukakis kept his coat on and buttoned and his tie neatly knotted and looked uncomfortably out of place amidst the military hardware (Ivie & Ritter, 1989). On the Republican side, the Bush campaign was profoundly shaped by the fact that it inherited Ronald Reagan's policies, staff, and metaphors (Ivie & Ritter 1989).

In the 1992 campaign George Bush's staff sought to counter perceptions of the president as remote from the concerns of ordinary Americans by sending him to buy socks at a J.C. Penney store. They then sent him to a trade show where he waxed enthusiastic over the latest developments in checkout scanners. The attempt to create a "regular guy" metaphor collapsed when the two events were merged in the minds of many viewers and Mr. Bush was instead perceived as being so far removed from the everyday routines of life that he had never before encountered an automated checkout stand with a scanner that read product bar codes!

While some uses of metaphor enhance democratic involvement, others isolate people from their political system and contribute to apathy and feelings of powerlessness. Much of the problem is rooted in the content of common political metaphors. In many cases the content directly or indirectly implies that politics in general, or this issue in particular, is beyond the scope or grasp of many, if not most citizens. In other cases the weight of the metaphor underlines the gap between the position and resources of elites and those of the masses and thus encourages mass acquiescence.

Media coverage of politics frequently involves metaphors that have the effect of encouraging detachment. Much media coverage of campaigns tends to focus on the *"horse race"* aspects, portraying the contest as a clash of competing organizations and stressing the tactical give and take of the day's events. This tends to reduce politics to a spectator sport and, while it is hardly the intention of the political reporters, trivializes politics.

Politics becomes one diversion among many, in critical respects indistinguishable from other entertainments (Postman, 1985). Citizens are implicitly redefined as audience, who may or may not have much of a rooting interest in one side or another. The tendency of both participants and reporters to draw metaphors from sports reinforces the tendency (Balbus, 1975; Fiddick, 1989). In fact, the crowd at a sporting event or the fans watching at home on TV may be more involved in the outcome than the spectating crowd of citizens. Sports fans usually have a significant emotional investment in the game and many have money riding on the result. The political spectator, if there are no compelling metaphors linking the campaign to her or his life, may not see how the result matters.

From the perspective of the campaign worker or political reporter, it seems obvious that the important question is who will win and information relevant to answering that question is valuable. But that is because they have already answered the prior question: Why should I care who wins? For average citizens whose attention to politics tends to begin at about the time campaigns get underway, the most relevant initial information is that which allows them to assess candidates in terms of their own interests. Only after deciding that the race makes a difference does one care about the outcome.

The extensive use of sports and military metaphors to describe politics in general and campaigns in particular tends to be exclusive in an additional sense. Whether the image is a *"horse race,"* or a candidate *"hitting a home run"* in a debate (Blankenship & Kang, 1991, provide a description of common political metaphors as used in press coverage of the 1984 campaign), or the comparison of United States military tactics in the ground phase of the Gulf War to a *"Hail Mary pass"*[3] on the football field, the language of sports tends to be more readily available to men than women. This linguistic bias reinforces the implicit message of the predominantly male faces in politics and the traditional socialization message that many women receive that politics is a man's business. (Although it is important to note that none of this has been sufficient to counter other forces making women more central to politics.)

More broadly, many of the metaphors used by elites tend to create acquiescence in the majority of citizens. Edelman (1964, 1971, 1988), Nimmo

(1974), Nimmo and Coombs (1987), and Parenti (1994) have explored a number of specific ways in which the content of American political metaphors tends to distance people from the political system. Edelman (1988) summarized this line of research:

> A set of frequently used terms also helps induce an acquiescent posture towards the acts of public officials. Words like "public," "official," "due process of law," "the public interest," and "the national interest" have no specific referent, but induce a considerable measure of acceptance of action that might otherwise be viewed with skepticism or hostility. Such terms evoke a sacred aura, as do inaugurations, flags, imposing buildings, and judicial robes. These symbols help erase the sense of guilt, humiliation or injustice that acquiescence would create if public officials were seen as ordinary people conferring valuable benefits on some and imposing severe sacrifice on others. (p. 98)

Even when the content of common political metaphors cannot be directly construed as alienating, political metaphors may have a negative effect on the citizen's relation to the realm of politics.

If the citizen does not know the content of the metaphor, then she or he cannot understand the message. The June 27, 1994, issue of Newsweek magazine captioned a picture "Marking the anniversary of Stonewall, the Bastille Day for gay Americans" (Kushner, 1994). The reader for whom *"Bastille Day"* does not evoke the beginning of the French Revolution will not be able to make any sense of the caption, let alone decode the specifically political message that when a 1969 New York City police raid on a gay bar named *"Stonewall"* was met by resistance from customers and a riot ensued, it was the symbolic beginning of the contemporary gay and lesbian movement.

Like radioactive elements, many metaphors have a half life, particularly those that refer to specific historic events. The relevance of an historical metaphor is directly related to whether it is a remembered and experienced event or whether it is something one has read or heard about. The power of *"Munich"* and its evocation of appeasement and the dire consequences of giving in to dictators like Hitler is much greater for members of the generation that lived through World War II than for their children or grandchildren.

The ambiguous nature of many metaphors, noted earlier, is also problematic. One of the reasons many citizens perceive politicians as dishonest and deceitful is that a given metaphor may have different meanings for different audiences. The United States involvement in Somalia from December, 1992, to March, 1994, has been interpreted as conveying diametrically opposed implications. *"Somalia"* as metaphor can be a cautionary tale against intervention in tribal warfare in the Third World or it can be read as an operation that was largely successful in achieving the initial goals but serves as a cautionary tale warning against trying to do too much. A pledge to not let a situation turn into *"another Somalia"* could easily be understood as a promise not to intervene when the speaker really meant that this time humanitarian intervention would not lead to political entanglements. And when action was taken, the audience would feel betrayed.

Metaphors are inevitable and are necessary to political life. When their content is broadly shared, and when that content implies room for ordinary people to become involved and effective, metaphors provide the common currency for a democratic society. When their content is obscure or specialized or when it implies the need for specialized skills or expertise, then metaphors can serve as a *"Great Wall"* keeping the masses at bay.

ENDNOTES

[1]That is true even for seemingly concrete economic interests. The perceived impact of a policy or candidate on a voter's personal financial situation is not a very useful predictor or explanation of behavior. The symbolic implications and meanings (Sears & Funk, 1990) or perceived impact on the metaphorical "nation as a whole" (Dalton & Wattenberg, 1993) are far more important to individuals' decisions.

[2]The story of the person who was seen in the checkout line (often with one or more small children in tow) at the convenience store illegally using foodstamps for liquor has been widely circulated, but always by someone who knows someone who saw the event—never by an eyewitness. The gripping drama on the faltering plane and the pilot's inspirational speech on American values and hanging together was such a good story, as the President told it, that the fact that no one survived the wreck so there were no witnesses to the events and conversations did not trouble him.

[3]The original usage refers to a very long pass thrown in desperate circumstances that needs heavenly help to succeed. The metaphor lost its air of desperation and low probability of success when used by the U.S. military commanders to refer to their Gulf War strategy.

REFERENCES

Adair, D. (1974). *Fame and the founding fathers.* New York: W.W. Norton.
Allison, G. T. (1971). *The essence of decision.* Boston: Little, Brown.
Balbus, I. (1975). Politics as sports: The political ascendency of sports metaphor in America. *Monthly Review, 26,* 26–39.
Bill, J., & Springborg, R. (1990). *Politics in the Middle East.* Glenview, IL: Scott, Foresman.
Blankenship, J., & Kang, J. G. (1991). The 1984 Presidential and Vice-Presidential debates: The printed press and the "construction" of metaphor. *Presidential Studies Quarterly, 21,* 307–318.
Dalton, R. J., & Wattenberg, M. P. (1993). The not so simple act of voting. In A. Finifter (Ed.), *The state of the discipline* (pp. 193–218). Washington, DC: The American Political Science Association.
Danziger, J. N. (1994) *The political world.* New York: Longman.
Davies, J. C. (1977). *Human nature in politics.* Westport, CT: Greenwod.

Edelman, M. (1964). *The symbolic uses of politics*. Urbana: University of Illinois Press.
Edelman, M. (1971). *Politics as symbolic action*. New York: Academic Press.
Edelman, M. (1988). *Constructing the political spectacle*. Chicago: University of Chicago Press.
Fiddick, T. (1989). Beyond the domino theory: The Vietnam War and metaphors of sport. *Journal of American Culture, 12,* 79–87.
George, A. (1994). The two cultures of academia and policymaking: Bridging the gap. *Political Psychology, 15,* 143–172.
Glad, B., & Taber, C. S. (1990). Images, learning and the decision to use force: The domino theory and the United States. In B. Glad (Ed.), *Psychological dimensions of war* (pp. 56–82). Newbury Park, CA: Sage.
Graber, D. (1993). Political communication: Scope, progress, promise. In A. Finifter (Ed.), *The state of the discipline* (pp. 305–334). Washington, DC: The American Political Science Association.
Holsti, O. R., & Rosenau, J. (1989). *American leadership in world affairs*. Boston: Allen & Unwin.
Hughes, B. (1978). *The domestic context of American foreign policy*. San Francisco: Freeman.
Ivie, R., & Ritter, K. (1989). Whither the "Evil Empire": Reagan and the presidential candidates debating foreign policy in the 1988 campaign. *American Behavioral Scientist, 32,* 436–450.
King, M. L., Jr. (1986). I Have a Dream. In J. M. Washington (Ed.), *The essential writings of Martin Luther King, Jr.* (pp. 217–220). San Francisco: Harper & Row. (Original work published 1963)
Kushner, T. (1994, June 27). Fireworks and freedom. *Newsweek, 125,* 46–48.
Lasswell, H. D. (1960). *Psychopathology and politics*. New York: Viking.
Neuman, W. R. (1986). *The paradox of mass politics: Knowledge and opinion in the American electorate*. Cambridge, MA: Harvard University Press.
Neustadt, R. E., & May, E. R. (1986). *Thinking in time*. New York: The Free Press.
Nimmo, D. R. (1974). *Popular images of politics*. Englewood Cliffs, NJ: Prentice-Hall.
Nimmo, D. R., & Coombs, J. E. (1987). *Mediated political realities*. New York: Longman.
Parenti, M. (1994). *Land of idols*. New York: St. Martin's Press.
Postman, N. (1985). *Amusing ourselves to death*. New York: Viking.
Safire, W. (1993). *Safire's new political dictionary*. New York: Random House.
Sears, D. O., & Funk, C. (1990). The limited effect of economic self-interest on the political attitudes of the mass public. *Journal of Behavioral Economics, 19,* 247–271.
Seligman, A. B. (1992). *The idea of civil society*. New York: The Free Press.
Shapiro, M. J. (1990). Strategic discourse/discursive strategy: The representation of "security policy" in the video age. *International Studies Quarterly, 34,* 327–340.

IV

The Metaphors of Everyday Life

12

Individual Differences in Metaphoric Facilitation of Comprehension

Paul Whitney
Desiree Budd
and
Jeffery Scott Mio[1]
Washington State University

Writer and reader are locked in a difficult relationship. A writer must anticipate what the intended reader knows and doesn't know. In addition, the writer must struggle to communicate what may be a very complex and essentially non-linear representation of ideas into a linear chain of sentences. The reader is trying to take this chain of sentences and recreate meaning. Often, the reader must also evaluate the meaning against experience. If the two partners are not in synchrony, the writer appears obtuse or the reader appears easily bored.

Metaphor is one instrument of communication that writers use to keep up their end of the bargain. Metaphor is often used to express ideas that are difficult to capture literally or to enliven prose that would otherwise be dull (e.g., Ortony, 1980; Pollio, Chapter 14, this volume; Searle, 1979). In fact, at least for narrative writing, the tendency to use novel metaphors increases with the experience level of the writer (Williams-Whitney, Mio, & Whitney, 1992).

Despite the prevalence of metaphoric expressions in text, we are only beginning to understand how the use of metaphor affects the writer's partner in the linguistic relationship. Is the process of understanding metaphoric expressions different from the process of understanding literal expressions? How does the use of metaphor affect comprehension and memory? These are difficult questions, so it is not surprising that researchers often have simplified the issues by investigating the comprehension of isolated metaphoric sentences (e.g., Gildea & Glucksberg, 1983; Gregory & Mergler, 1990; Keysar, 1989). Studying the comprehension of metaphor using single sentence contexts is a reasonable approach, and we will draw on some of the data from such studies in the course of this chapter.   However, our focus is on how metaphoric expressions affect the understanding of the larger discourse context in which they occur.   In particular, we examine the utility of metaphor as an aid to the understanding of expository text.

UNDERSTANDING EXPOSITORY TEXT

While narratives may sometimes be used to instruct by analogy or anecdote, we usually attempt to impart factual knowledge to a reader with an exposition. Expository text, such as the discourse used in textbooks, is usually quite different from narrative text. Unlike narratives, which tend to follow the same general plan—a setting, a problem, and a problem resolution—expositions are organized in a number of different ways (Graesser & Goodman, 1985; Meyer, 1975).   In addition, except when experts are reading a text in the domain of their expertise, readers of narratives tend to have a much richer base of background knowledge that can be used to interpret the text (Graesser, 1981).

Given their less predictable organization and their less familiar content, expositions often present a special challenge to readers, particularly if the *connections* among the ideas are to be understood.   Accordingly, researchers in psycholinguistics and educational psychology have experimented with ways of augmenting expository text in order to increase readers' understanding (e.g., Ausubel, 1968; Mayer, 1979). A number of "adjunct aids" have been developed to facilitate comprehension. These aids are presumed to facilitate comprehension by assisting in the selection of important information for further processing and by promoting the integration of information. In this chapter, we evaluate whether metaphoric statements can serve as adjunct aids to improve the comprehension of expository text. However, before turning to that research, we must consider some of the lessons learned from previous attempts to increase readers' understanding of expositions.

One important type of adjunct aid is known as signaling. Signaling does not add new content to a text. Instead, it gives emphasis to certain aspects of the content, or makes the organization of the text more clear (e.g., Meyer, 1975; Meyer, Brandt, & Bluth, 1980). Signaling thus makes explicit the nature of the relation among items in the text. Without signals, such relations have to be inferred.   For example, signals for comparison relations include the expressions *however* and *in contrast*. Expressions such as *therefore* and *as a result* are used to signal causal relations.

Several studies that have manipulated the extent of signaling have shown a facilitative effect of signals on memory for text (e.g., Meyer, 1984; Spyridakis & Standal, 1987). However, the effects of signaling are qualified by several factors. One important mediating variable is the skill of the reader.

Marshall and Glock (1979) showed that making logical connectives explicit facilitated text recall by less able readers, but such signaling had no effect on the performance of more able readers. Meyer (1975) found positive effects of signaling for poor and average readers, but no effect for good readers.

The effectiveness of specific signaling also depends on the type of criterial task used to assess comprehension and memory (Loman & Mayer, 1983; Meyer, 1975). For example, Loman and Mayer had two groups of subjects read expository passages. One group read passages with signaling and one read the same passages without signaling. The two groups did *not* differ in their ability to answer questions that assessed verbatim or factual knowledge of the texts. However, the group given signals recalled more information from the texts.

Finally, Spyridakis and Standal (1987) found that the effectiveness of signals depends on the length and difficulty of the text being read. Spyridakis and Standal manipulated the use of headings, previews, and logical connectives with texts of varying length and difficulty. They concluded that all three types of signals can enhance comprehension, but signaling appeared to be most effective with passages of moderate length and difficulty.

A similar pattern of effects can be seen in research on other types of adjunct aids. For example, adjunct questions can be inserted into a text to force rehearsal and integration of material. Whether such questions facilitate comprehension is dependent on several factors, including the skill of the reader and the difficulty of the text (e.g., Britton, Westbrook, & Holdredge, 1978).

Based on the research on adjunct aids, the simple question of "Do metaphors help people integrate text?" is the wrong question. We should expect that whatever effects metaphors have on comprehension will be qualified by other factors. The focus of the present study is on whether any facilitative effects of metaphor are qualified by individual differences in reading ability. Before presenting our data, we first consider why metaphors might aid comprehension, and then we consider who should benefit most from metaphors as adjunct aids.

WHY METAPHORS MIGHT AID TEXT INTEGRATION

Often when readers connect ideas from two literal expressions, they are able to rely on repetition of concepts or on preexisting associations in memory as a bridge to link the expressions in memory (e.g., Kintsch & van Dijk, 1978; Sanford & Garrod, 1981). For example, because of our knowledge of conceptual categories, we can easily compute the coherence of the following sentences:

> *The Peterson's dog is the bane of the neighborhood. That animal never stops digging.*

A reader can determine easily that the "animal" in the second sentence refers to the same entity as the expression "the Petersons' dog" in the first sentence. In contrast, the connections between a *metaphorical expression* in one sentence and a literal expression in another sentence depend not so much on retrieving preexisting associations in memory, but on computing similarities on-line during comprehension (cf. Camac & Glucksberg, 1984; Onishi & Murphy, 1993). For example, the reader must do more than retrieve a pre-existing association like *dog-animal* in order to understand the following:

> *The Peterson's dog is the bane of the neighborhood.   That bulldozer never stops digging.*

Viewed in this context, understanding metaphoric references in text involves a kind of elaborative processing that "goes beyond the information given." Elaborations that form memorable connections between different text elements are one of the main factors that increase recall of text (Reder, 1980). Therefore, we might expect that metaphoric expressions function as a kind of adjunct aid that improves retention of prose material.

This hypothesis was tested in a study by Reynolds and Schwartz (1983). They gave subjects brief expository passages that ended with either a metaphorical summary statement or a literal paraphrase of the metaphor. For example, one of their passages was the following:

> The people of Nazi Germany were swayed by Hitler's rhetoric.   Although he had committed his people to a course of war, he found it easy to persuade them of the virtue of his actions. Everyone in Europe at the time was aware of the consequences of war, but the Germans had a blind belief in Hitler.

For each reader, the passage ended with one of the following:

> (1) The sheep followed the leader over the cliff.
> (2) The German people blindly accepted Hitler's dangerous ideas.

Note that the metaphoric summary, sentence (1), is a context-dependent metaphor. That is, standing alone it could be literally true, but it is clearly metaphorical in the context of the passage. Using the first sentence of each passage as a retrieval cue, Reynolds and Schwartz found that passages with context-dependent metaphors were better remembered.

Reynolds and Schwartz (1983) offered two possible explanations for metaphoric facilitation. First, metaphoric summaries might lead to greater elaborative processing of the text. At first blush, this would seem to contradict previous data that suggests that there is no difference in comprehension times for metaphorical versus literal statements (e.g., Ortony, Shallert, Reynolds, & Antos, 1978). However, reading times may only indicate initial comprehension and thus not reflect subsequent additional elaborative processing. Second, Reynolds and Schwartz (1983) noted that metaphoric summaries may have led to superior performance because the metaphoric statements themselves were more memorable. At retrieval they may have been more helpful in cuing the rest of the passage.

In reality, these two explanations depend on the same basic mechanism. If a metaphorical summary is to help in the recall of the whole passage, then it must be linked strongly in memory with the other statements in the passage (Reder, 1980). Thus, the Reynolds and Schwartz (1983) study suggests that metaphoric summary statements are more elaboratively processed in the sense that a more richly interconnected representation of the passage is obtained.

A STUDY OF INDIVIDUAL DIFFERENCES IN METAPHORIC FACILITATION

As noted above, general claims for the benefit of any adjunct comprehension aid must be viewed with caution. Accordingly, we attempted to replicate and extend the findings of Reynolds and Schwartz (1983) by testing for an Aptitude x Treatment interaction in metaphoric facilitation of comprehension. Aptitude was defined in terms of performance on the reading span test (Daneman & Carpenter, 1980). This test correlates highly with standardized tests of reading ability (e.g., Masson & Miller, 1983), but it is especially sensitive to individual differences in capacity for integration of different text propositions (e.g., Daneman & Carpenter, 1983).

Our purpose in testing for reading span differences in metaphoric processing was twofold. First, there is the practical question of who might benefit from the use of metaphors in text. Second, an interaction between reading span and type of summary could tell us something about why metaphors have a facilitative effect, and about the relative difficulty of processing metaphoric versus literal text.

The key theoretical question that ties together these issues—who benefits from metaphors and why—is whether the elaborative processing induced by metaphoric summaries consumes extra processing capacity. Depending on the nature of the elaborative processing that results in metaphoric facilitation, either of two forms of an Aptitude x Treatment interaction could be obtained. If the elaboration engendered by use of metaphors takes extra processing capacity, then low span readers will be less able to make the necessary connections to support metaphoric facilitation. This follows from the finding that low span readers have less capacity for integrating information during reading (e.g., Daneman & Carpenter, 1983; Whitney, Ritchie, & Clark, 1991). In this case, the Aptitude x Treatment interaction should take the form of increased benefit of metaphors as reading span increases. In contrast, if the compact and vivid nature of metaphors (Ortony, 1975) makes it easier to hold the summary in working memory and connect it to the rest of the passage, then low spans will be more likely to integrate the material with metaphoric summaries, but high spans will integrate the material regardless of whether metaphoric or literal summaries are used. In other words, the relative benefit of metaphoric summaries should be inversely related to reading span.

Subjects and Design

The subjects were 90 undergraduates enrolled in introductory psychology classes. They were divided into high, medium, and low reading span groups based on a tertile split of reading span scores (see below). Half of the subjects at each span level were randomly assigned to each type of passage ending (metaphoric or literal).

Reading Span Test

We used a version of the Daneman and Carpenter (1980) reading span test as modified by Masson and Miller (1983) to allow for group administration. Subjects were run in groups of 5 to 20. The stimulus materials were presented on an overhead projector. The test involved reading sets of unrelated sentences (12–17 words each) and then recalling the last word of each sentence. Each subject received three trials in which they read two sentences and then tried to recall the last word of each of the two sentences. Then we moved on to three trials with three sentences in each set. This procedure continued up to a set size of six. To insure the sentences were read, at the end of each trial subjects had to fill in a missing word from two of the sentences they had just read. The subjects were paced through the task by the experimenter, who read the sentences aloud as they were shown.

Subjects were divided into groups based on the highest set size at which they recalled all the final words on at least two of the three trials. A half point was added for getting one trial correct on a given set size. Thus, if a subject was correct on all three trials of set size three, and one trial of set size four, that subject's span score was 3.5. Using this procedure, we obtained a sample of 30 subjects each at a low span (score = 2.5 or less), medium span (score = 3.0–4.0), and a high span (score = 4.5 and above) level.

Passages and Procedures

We used the example passage provided by Reynolds and Schwartz that was given above, as well as six other passages adapted from ninth grade social studies texts. The passages contained from 39 to 66 words. A metaphorical summary sentence and a literal summary sentence was written for each passage. As in the Reynolds and Schwartz study, we used context-dependent metaphors so that all the summaries could be taken literally if presented out of context.

The passages and their summary sentences were pretested on a separate group of subjects. The pretest showed that the metaphoric and literal summaries were equally memorable out of context. When presented in the context of the passages, the two types of summaries were rated as equivalent in meaning.

The experiment was conducted in two sessions. The reading span test was given in one session and the subjects returned a week later to read the passages. The experiment was presented as a test of the suitability of some materials for use in later research. Subjects were given booklets with one passage per page. They were asked to read the passages at their own pace and rate each passage for readability and interest. Each subject read seven passages, but the first and last were used as buffers to avoid primacy and recency effects, so recall of these passages was not scored.

After reading and rating the passages, the subjects were given a five-minute unrelated activity. They were then given a response booklet that provided the first sentence of each passage as a recall cue. Subjects were told to write everything they could remember for each passage. We tested incidental memory for the passages in order to get a more pure measure of the effect of the metaphors, uncontaminated by individual differences in deliberate learning strategies.

Analysis of the Experiment

The passages were divided into constituent idea units and two raters independently scored the recall protocols for the number of idea units correctly paraphrased. Interrater reliability was quite good ($r = .92$). The mean proportion of idea units recalled in each condition are shown in Fig. 12. 1.

A 3 x 2 (Span x Summary Type) ANOVA was performed on arc sine transformations of the proportion of idea units recalled by each subject. The alpha level for all tests was .05. Collapsed across span levels, there was a significant advantage for metaphoric summaries over literal summaries, $F (1,84) = 5.93$, $MSE = .01$. Thus, ignoring individual differences, our results replicated those of Reynolds and Schwartz (1983). There was no main effect of span ($F < 1$). More importantly, there was a significant Span x Summary Type interaction, $F (2,84) = 2.98$, $MSE = .01$. Tests of the simple main effects showed that there was no metaphoric advantage for the high span readers, but both medium and low span readers performed better with the metaphoric summaries. Most surprisingly, as Fig. 12.1 shows, the low span readers performed *as well as* the high span readers in the metaphoric condition.

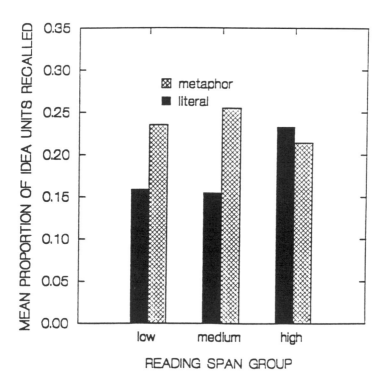

FIG. 12.1. Mean proportion of idea units recalled as a function of reading span and summary type (metaphorical or literal). The standard error for each mean is approximately .02.

HOW DO METAPHORS FACILITATE MEMORY FOR TEXT?

From a practical standpoint, these data suggest that metaphors may increase the ability of poor to average readers to learn from text, without affecting the performance of better readers. Of course, this conclusion is only tentative, given the limited scope of the present study. From a theoretical standpoint, the results are in accord with the data that suggest that metaphoric processing does not involve an extra stage of processing, or at least not one that demands working memory capacity (e.g., Keysar, 1989; Shinjo & Myers, 1987). If processing metaphors required extra capacity, then the low span readers should have shown *less* benefit, or even poorer performance, with the metaphoric summaries. Nevertheless, the metaphoric summaries were somehow processed differently, so that they improved the performance of most of the subjects. This is similar to the conclusion by Onishi and Murphy (1993) that nonliteral expressions that refer back to information presented earlier "may qualitatively change the interpretation process" (p. 770).

The advantage in recall gained with metaphoric summaries may be related to the memorability of metaphoric statements themselves (Ortony, 1975; Mio, Thompson, & Givens 1993). The metaphoric concluding statements and their literal counterparts were constructed to be equivalent summaries of the passages. For example, in the passage about Hitler leading the German people into war, both *The sheep followed the leader over the cliff* and *The German people blindly accepted Hitler's dangerous ideas* contain two ideas: (a) the German people followed Hitler, and (b) Hitler's ideas were dangerous. Four of the five other sentences in the passage were related to one of these two ideas in the concluding sentence. If the concluding sentence is connected during comprehension with the other statements (a form of elaborative processing), then recall of the concluding sentence should assist recall of the rest of the passage (Reder, 1980). If the metaphoric summaries were more memorable when in the context of the passage, then they would be expected to lead to better recall performance than their literal counterparts (cf. Reynolds & Schwartz, 1983). Marschark and Hunt (1985) showed that metaphoric statements may be well remembered for several reasons, but particularly because of their imageability.

We are still left with the question of why the benefit from metaphoric summaries was qualified by working memory span. Some clues as to why metaphors may differentially affect the discourse comprehension of high and low span readers emerge from the materials appropriate processing (MAP) framework proposed by McDaniel and his colleagues (McDaniel, Einstein, Dunay, & Cobb, 1986; Hunt & McDaniel, 1993). According to the MAP framework, there are two basic types of elaborations: *relational processing* and *proposition-specific processing*. Relational processing results from the encoding of information that defines the relations between propositions in the text. Proposition-specific processing results from the encoding of information that defines syntactic and semantic relations on an intrapropositional level.

Optimal recall for textual information results when readers perform both proposition-specific processing and relational processing.

In addition, the elaborations that result from relational and proposition-specific processing are hypothesized to influence recall of text through different mechanisms (McDaniel et al., 1986; Hunt & McDaniel, 1993). Relational elaborations are employed at retrieval to generate and access important ideas contained in the text. Proposition-specific elaborations are used to reconstruct the text from general classes of information after the idea unit has been accessed. Therefore, good text recall depends mostly on the encoding of relational information, whereas proposition-specific processing is more important for tests of recognition.

The main thrust of the MAP framework is that the effectiveness of a particular encoding manipulation depends on the type of processing invited by the materials, the type of processing induced by the encoding task, and the interaction between the two. Both the encoding task and the stimulus materials "invite" particular degrees of relational and proposition-specific processing. Some technique designed to increase text retention will facilitate performance only to the extent it encourages additional elaborative processing of the type of information (relational or proposition-specific) not encoded in the absence of the technique.

Thus, in order to be helpful to text retention, an intervention must get the readers to do elaborative processing that they would not do naturally. This aspect of the MAP framework can be used to account for data on the effectiveness of adjunct aids (cf. Loman & Mayer, 1983; Meyer et al., 1980; Spyridakis & Standal, 1987). For instance, in the Meyer et al. study, recall protocols of good and poor readers in the unsignaled condition indicated that good readers inferred the implicit (unsignaled) relations in the passage, but poor readers did not. Thus, because good readers performed relational processing whether they had relational signals or not, the addition of signals produced mostly redundant relational processing and thus had no effect on recall. However, because poor readers were not already performing the relational processing that was encouraged by the signals, the addition of signals led to increased elaborative processing and thus increased recall.

If we extend this framework to research on metaphors, then the use of metaphor should increase recall when it results in elaborative processing that would not occur as a consequence of the reader's "normal" comprehension processes. This was apparently the case with our low and medium span subjects. However, metaphors should not increase recall if subjects already performed the relational processing encouraged by the addition of the metaphor. This was apparently the case for our high span subjects.

Because recall tests tap mainly relational processing, our interpretation of the present results could be tested in future research by comparing the effects of metaphor on recognition of proposition-specific information as well as recall of whole passages. If the metaphoric summaries are encouraging more relational processing by lower span readers, then the metaphoric advantage should be attenuated when testing depends on more proposition-specific information.

ENDNOTE

[1]Jeffery Scott Mio is now at the Department of Behavioral Sciences, California State Polytechnic University, Pomona, California. Preparation of this chapter was supported in part by AFOSR Grant No. F49620-92-J-0243. We thank Bill Lee-Sammons for his help in data collection.

REFERENCES

Ausubel, D. P. (1968). *Educational psychology: A cognitive view*. New York: Holt, Rinehart & Winston.

Britton, B. K., Westbrook, R. D., & Holdredge, T. S. (1978). Reading and cognitive capacity usage: Effects of text difficulty. *Journal of Experimental Psychology: Human Learning and Memory, 4*, 582–591.

Camac, M. K., & Glucksberg, S. (1984). Metaphors do not use associations between concepts, they are used to create them. *Journal of Psycholinguistic Research, 13*, 443–455.

Daneman, M., & Carpenter, P. A. (1980). Individual differences in working memory and reading. *Journal of Verbal Learning and Verbal Behavior, 19*, 450–466.

Daneman, M., & Carpenter, P. A. (1983). Individual differences in integrating information between and within sentences. *Journal of Experimental Psychology: Learning, Memory, and Cognition, 9*, 561–584.

Gildea, P., & Glucksberg, S. (1983). On understanding metaphor: The role of context. *Journal of Verbal Learning and Verbal Behavior, 22*, 577–590.

Graesser, A. C. (1981). *Prose comprehension beyond the word*. New York: Springer-Verlag.

Graesser, A. C., & Goodman, S. M. (1985). Implicit knowledge, question answering, and the representation of expository text. In B. K. Britton and J. B. Black (Eds.), *Understanding expository text* (pp. 109–171). Hillsdale, NJ: Lawrence Erlbaum Associates.

Gregory, M. E., & Mergler, N. L. (1990). Metaphor comprehension: In search of literal truth, possible sense, and metaphoricity. *Metaphor and Symbolic Activity, 5*, 151–173.

Hunt, R. R., & McDaniel, M. A. (1993). The enigma of organization and distinctiveness. *Journal of Memory and Language, 32*, 421–445.

Keysar, B. (1989). On the functional equivalence of literal and metaphorical interpretations in discourse. *Journal of Memory and Language, 28*, 375–385.

Kintsch, W., & van Dijk, T. A. (1978). Toward a model of text comprehension and production. *Psychological Review, 85*, 363–394.

Loman, L. C. & Mayer, R. E. (1983). Signaling techniques that increase the understandability of expository text. *Journal of Educational Psychology, 75*, 402–412.

Marschark, M., & Hunt, R. R. (1985). On memory for metaphor. *Memory & Cognition, 13*, 413–424.

Marshall, N., & Glock, M. (1979). Comprehension of connected discourse: A study into the relationships between the structure of the text and information recalled. *Reading Research Quarterly, 16*, 10–56.

Masson, M. E. J., & Miller, J. A. (1983). Working memory and individual differences in comprehension and memory of text. *Journal of Educational Psychology, 75,* 314–318.

Mayer, R. E. (1979). Can advance organizers influence meaningful learning? *Review of Educational Research, 49,* 371–383.

McDaniel, M., Einstein, G., Dunay, P., & Cobb, R. (1986). Encoding difficulty and memory: Toward a unifying theory. *Journal of Memory and Language, 25,* 645–656.

Meyer, B. J. F. (1975). *The organization of prose and its effects on memory.* Amsterdam: North-Holland.

Meyer, B. J. F. (1984). Text dimensions and cognitive processing. In H. Mandl, N. L. Stein, & T. Trabasso (Eds.), *Learning and comprehension of text* (pp. 3–51). Hillsdale, NJ: Lawrence Erlbaum Associates.

Meyer, B. J. F., Brandt, D. M. & Bluth, G. J. (1980). Use of top-level structure in text: Key for reading comprehension of ninth-grade students. *Reading Research Quarterly, 16,* 72–103.

Mio, J. S., Thompson, S. C., & Givens, G. H. (1993). The commons dilemma as metaphor: Memory, influence, and implications for environmental conservation. *Metaphor and Symbolic Activity, 8,* 23–42.

Spyridakis, J. H., & Standal, T. C. (1987). Signals in expository prose: Effects on reading comprehension. *Reading Research Quarterly, 22,* 285–296.

Onishi, K. H., & Murphy, G. L. (1993). Metaphoric reference: When metaphors are not understood as easily as literal expressions. *Memory & Cognition, 21,* 763–772.

Ortony, A. (1975). Why metaphors are necessary and not just nice. *Educational Theory, 25,* 45–53.

Ortony, A. (1980). Some psycholinguistic aspects of metaphor. In R. P. Honeck & R. R. Hoffman (Eds.), *Cognition and figurative language* (pp. 69–86). Hillsdale, NJ: Lawrence Erlbaum Associates.

Ortony, A., Shallert, D. L., Reynolds, R. E., & Antos, S. J. (1978). Interpreting metaphors and idioms: Some effects of context on comprehension. *Journal of Verbal Learning and Verbal Behavior, 17,* 465–477.

Reder, L. M. (1980). The role of elaboration in the comprehension and retention of prose: A critical review. *Review of Education Research, 50,* 5–53.

Reynolds, R. E., & Schwartz, R. M. (1983). Relation of metaphoric processing to comprehension and memory. *Journal of Educational Psychology, 75,* 450–459.

Sanford, A. J., & Garrod, S. C. (1981). *Understanding written language.* New York: Wiley.

Searle, J. R. (1979). Metaphor. In A. Ortony (Ed.), *Metaphor and thought* (pp. 92–123). Cambridge: Cambridge University Press.

Shinjo, M., & Myers, J. L. (1987). The role of context in metaphor comprehension. *Journal of Memory and Language, 26,* 226–241.

Whitney, P., Ritchie, B. G., & Clark, M. B. (1991). Working memory and the use of elaborative inferences in text comprehension. *Discourse Processes, 14,* 133–145.

Williams-Whitney, D., Mio, J. S., & Whitney, P. (1992). Metaphor production in creative writing. *Journal of Psycholinguistic Research, 21,* 497–509.

13

Metaphor in Tactile Pictures for the Blind: Using Metonymy to Evoke Classification

John M. Kennedy
University of Toronto

One of the practical findings from the experimental psychology of pictures and perception in recent times is that blind people can understand raised outline drawings (Kennedy, 1993). It has been shown that blind people can draw recognizable raised-line pictures, and they can identify simple raised-line pictures. Fig. 13.1, for example, shows a dog's head (top left), an end wall of a house (top middle), and a square card overlapping an irregularly-shaped card (top right). The bottom figure shows hearts with wings—some broken by a slashed line!—a circular corral and pairs of circles representing married people inside the corral. These drawings were made by a blind woman who all lost sight before age 3. Recent research indicates many blind people can make use of pictures. As a result, it is likely that illustrations will play an increasingly important role in Braille texts for the blind. However, not only can the blind use naturalistic outline drawings, they can also appreciate when a picture shows its referent in an unrealistic way to make a point. In language, when we say *"that man is a shark,"* we misrepresent to make a point, and the result is a metaphor. Similarly, we may describe a picture as metaphoric when it shows the high-pressure sales clerk as a shark. If blind people can appreciate the proper meaning behind a distortion in a picture, they are able to understand metaphoric pictures. The scope of raised pictures is enlarged considerably if they can be metaphoric as well as simple, faithful renditions of their subject matter.

My purpose in this article is to develop a basis for understanding the blind person's facility with metaphoric pictures. One theme I develop is that pictorial input can be treated metaphorically, by the blind and the sighted alike, the blind using tactile pictures and the sighted using visible pictures. I try to

215

show the wide range of uses of tactile metaphoric pictures by summarizing several empirical studies on blind people and their interpretations of tactile forms. The theory I present to explain these lessons rests on a description of the tangible world, and the shapes within it, and hypotheses about outline representation in vision and touch. The theory will apply to vision as well as touch, because it is cognitive at heart—it involves a bridge from particular concrete objects, and images of them, to classification of the objects, including

FIG. 13.1. Copy of raised-line drawings made by a blind woman. The drawings include a dog's head shown in profile (top left), a sketch of the end-wall of a model house (top middle) and a square card overlapping a larger irregularly shaped card (top right). Also included is a sketch of "marriage," shown as a corral with married couples inside the corral, some with keys, and single people, signified by hearts with wings, outside the corral. The corral has a section that can be opened, shown by short hatch lines crossing the circular perimeter of the corral. The person who made these drawings was aged 38. As a result of retinal blastomas in the first year of life, she was diagnosed as having had normal sight in infancy for some months, which deteriorated to light perception only (no form sensitivity) for a period, and she lost all sight before age 3. In her schooling she did not use raised-line pictures, though she had raised maps and diagrams.

the metaphoric classification evident in phrases like *"Joe is a lamb"* (Glucksberg & Keysar, 1990), and pictures of, say, a giant mayor stepping on a toy-like neighborhood.

Tangible Surfaces and Pictures

To have an account of naturalistic or literal pictures, the first order of business is to establish what a literal picture is. Metaphoric pictures are defined in relation to literal pictures, because metaphoric pictures violate the rules of literal pictures. In brief, an apt violation of these rules is a metaphor.

The tangible world chiefly consists of surfaces of substances with some resistance to pressure. The surfaces can be flat or curved. Surfaces change inclination abruptly at corners, which can be concave or convex. The vantage point of the observer is defined with respect to the layout of flat and curved surfaces around the vantage point. Notably, surfaces can overlap, that is, occlude one another from the observer's vantage point. A roofline, for example, is an occluding edge provided by a convex corner acting to occlude background surfaces. Similarly, a brow of a hill is a rounded surface occluding background surfaces. At an occluding boundary of a surface, a tangent from the surface passes through the observer's vantage point.

Outline representation uses lines to stand for concave and convex corners and occluding boundaries of surfaces. There is an abrupt change in inclination at a corner. Also, there is an abrupt change in depth from foreground to background at an occluding boundary. Hence, an outline picture uses lines to stand for abrupt change in surface layout.

Both vision and touch deal with surface layout and matters of depth and inclination. Both are sensitive to abrupt change in surface layout. Vision scans a scene more rapidly than touch, and is more acute in many respects, though touch is more capable of distinguishing some texture differences, for example (Heller & Schiff, 1991). Nevertheless, touch can take its time and explore large scale environments quite adequately (Kennedy, Gabias, & Heller, 1992). The blind observer can discover the layout of a table, or a room, or a house, or a hillside or a terrain. It may take seconds to discover the rectangular shape of a table, minutes to explore a room or a house, and hours to determine the oval shape of a hill, or the basket-of-eggs shape of a drumlin-filled terrain. The observer will also discover in the course of his or her activities that there is a chair on the far side of a table, or a bookshelf occluding part of the wall of a room, or bushes covering a side of a house, or a small hill blocking the way to a larger hill when it is approached from a certain direction. That is, occlusion is evident in touch as distinctly as it is in vision. The occluding edge of a table, with a chair in the background beyond it, is a tangible notion just as it is a visual one.

        Despite much speculation to the contrary this century, sighted individuals do not have to be taught how to understand outline depiction, as evidence from children (Hochberg & Brooks, 1962) and nonpictorial cultures (Kennedy & Ross, 1975) has revealed, in empirical studies by perception researchers. The same is true for the congenitally, totally blind, it seems. Objects like people, furniture, plants, animals, vehicles, and utensils can be recognized by congenitally blind people in raised-line drawings, and can be drawn by many congenitally blind people in sketches that resemble drawings by 5- to 7-year-old sighted children. Occasionally, blind people can make drawings that resemble drawings by older children, and a rare blind person has been known to make drawings that rival the ability of a moderately talented, sighted teenager (Edman, 1992; Heller, 1989; Kennedy, 1993). The differences in levels of ability in drawing do not relate closely to the age of onset of blindness, or to the amount of sight prior to total blindness (Kennedy, 1993), when studies attempt to distinguish congenitally blind individuals from ones who had some sight for a year or two. As a result, in this article I leave in abeyance any speculation as to the possible influences of a few months or years of sight on later drawing and picture-recognition abilities. Such differences are not out of the question, but they may be minor in comparison to the basic lesson that congenitally totally blind people can use pictures with no direct training in pictorial conventions.

Metaphoric Tactile Pictures

In the midst of an experiment on drawing simple objects, I asked blind volunteers to draw objects they selected themselves. One woman drew a spinning wheel. She drew a circle, for the perimeter of the wheel, and a curved line inside the wheel to show "the motion." This took me by surprise. Lines showing motion are a latecomer in visual art. Although outline was invented in cave-art times, lines of motion are a nineteenth-century phenomenon (Carello, Rosenblum, & Grosofsky, 1986; Kennedy, Green, & Vervaeke, 1993). Indeed, they only became common currency in the latter part of the century. This volunteered drawing was the seed for a series of studies on pictorial metaphor with the blind, including the representation of motion in pictures. Consider the major lessons learned from several of the studies.

        In the first of the series, I asked blind volunteers to draw a wheel standing still, spinning, and rolling, and a man standing still, walking, and running. Blind subjects invented many devices for each referent. Some devices were fairly realistic matters of posture—for example, legs further apart to indicate someone running, and closer together to mean someone walking. At times, however, human figures were drawn with many legs or feet. Also, spinning wheels were given curved spokes while static wheels had straight spokes. The supernumerary legs and feet and the curved spokes were often accompanied by distinctive comments. For example, a woman who drew a spinning wheel with curved spokes said that she was not showing that the spokes actually curve because the wheel was spinning. Nor do the spokes feel curved, she pointed out. The curves were a way of suggesting the spin, she averred.

I followed up these comments on curved spokes in two ways. First, I asked if the curvature is in some respects an apt device for showing spin. Second, I asked the blind volunteers some explicit, pointed questions.

A colleague—Bert Forrin—queried the interpretation of the curved spokes. He said because motion cannot actually be drawn, perhaps any device that violates canons of naturalism is as good as any other. Alternatively, I replied, perhaps a particular graphic device lends itself to some referents more than others. Similarly, the metaphor *"he is a rock"* lends itself to stubbornness or reliability or strength but not to flexibility or charm or subtlety. If curved spokes are an apt device for showing spin, then they should be selected reliably from a set of alternatives. This hypothesis was tested with a group of 18 blind and 18 sighted subjects (Kennedy & Gabias, 1985). The volunteers were given five drawings with different kinds of spokes. The blind subjects were given raised-line drawings, and the sighted subjects were given normal printed-line drawings. One drawing of a wheel had curved spokes, one had V-shaped spokes (called "bent" spokes), another had sinusoidal spokes (called "wavy" spokes) another had spokes drawn by intermittent straight lines (called "dashed" spokes) and another had spokes that protruded beyond the circular perimeter of the wheel (called "extended" spokes). The volunteers were asked to assign five different kinds of motion to the wheels, one wheel to each kind of motion. The five different referents were steady spinning, a jerky motion while spinning, a wobbly motion while spinning, a spin too fast to make out, and a wheel with its brakes on.

Impressively, the options favored by the blind were the same options generally chosen by the sighted. Steady spin is best shown by curved spokes (10 blind and 12 sighted favored this pairing), jerky motion by bent spokes (12 blind, 12 sighted contend), wobbly motion by wavy spokes (11 blind, 14 sighted), too fast to make out by dashed spokes (13 blind, 13 sighted) and "brakes-on" by spokes extended beyond the wheel's perimeter (9 blind, 12 sighted). I find it astonishing that the concordance amongst the blind closely rivals the agreement amongst the sighted. The sighted have a lot of commerce with pictorial devices that goes beyond literal reenactment of the scene. The blind have little direct exposure to graphic representation, very little contact with pictures, and—so far as Gabias and I know—no acquaintance at all with the graphic devices we asked them to study.

The 18 blind volunteers included four totally blind from birth, one totally blind at 6 months, a further four totally blind before 3 years of age, two with some light sensitivity for a while (but no known pattern vision), and five with some light sensitivity. The two with the most visual experience were one who never had detailed vision but could make out shapes of large objects and one who lost sight at 7 months, could detect gross objects until 15 years of age, but only has light sensitivity now. The differences in blindness status produced no major difference in their facility with metaphoric pictures, in the Kennedy and Gabias study. (For brevity's sake, I will not describe in detail the blindness status of subjects in the other experiments I will relate. The interested reader can obtain the details in the articles cited.)

Gabias and I asked another group of 15 blind volunteers and 11 sighted recruits from New York City to rank the drawings from best at showing spin to worst. The order from both groups was curved (best), bent, wavy, dashed, and extended (worst).

There seems to be little doubt that the blind can match a motion-referent to a graphic device. But how do the blind think about the devices? Do they actually take them to be metaphoric? Maryanne Heywood and I interviewed some blind adults, questioning them about their conceptions of graphic indicators of motion and other referents and their ideas of the common ground used by pictures when one person communicates to another via a picture. We asked the following questions:

1. Do spinning wheels really have [as we indicated the device in question]?
2. Which lines in your drawing might have to be explained to other people, and which ones would they be likely to understand without any explanation?
3. Which lines would children—including blind children—find easy to understand, and which ones would they find hard?
4. Which lines are realistic, and which ones are imaginary?
5. Which ones are literal, and which ones are imaginary?

Of the three volunteers we interviewed, two drew a spinning wheel by using curved spokes, and one drew a wheel with two concentric circles, with the spokes of the inner circle extended to meet the outer circle (Kennedy, 1993). All three of the interviewees replied to our questions that their devices were unreal, might have to be explained, would be hard for children to understand, were imaginary, and were metaphoric. In contrast, the fact that the lines represented spokes or circumferences per se was more obvious—not in need of explanation, easy for children to understand, realistic, and literal.

In a related study, Ramona Domander and I asked 15 blind volunteers to make drawings of pain, wind, smell, and noise (Kennedy & Domander, 1986). We were especially interested in the spontaneous comments that accompanied the drawings, and what these spontaneous comments might indicate about the intentions governing the drawing. Did they reveal whether the devices were meant to be metaphoric in some respects? We classified a device as "meant to be metaphoric" if it was said to be anomalous, unreal, abstract, or imaginary. A comment might indicate that the line showed an edge that did not exist, or that the use of line was not in keeping with the use of lines elsewhere in the picture. For example, a drawing of a hand in pain might have lines for boundaries of the fingers and a "special" line described as an "imaginary" aura of pain around the hand. We distinguished metaphoric devices from diagrammatic devices such as writing, arrowheads, axes of graphs, and other conventional graphic symbols.

A total of 185 devices were classified. Most of the devices (132) were indirect, rather than metaphoric, for example, showing a hammer hitting a hand, with the comment that the hand would be in pain as a result of the hammerblow. Notice that this result indicates that blind people, generally, do not consider that the referents can be drawn directly, unlike, say, drawing a chair, where it would be extraordinary if someone drew a table and then said that the chair would be there as a result of the table. It seems that the referents that are beyond the scope of literal outline drawing for vision are also beyond the scope of outline drawing for touch.

When subjects drew the referent itself (53 devices), rather than its context, they most often drew a device that by their comments they indicated was meant to be metaphoric (40 devices). All but 1 of the remaining 13 devices were diagrammatic. Evidently, the blind themselves distinguish two uses of outline, one normal and one that is out-of-the-ordinary. It is this latter one that is identified as metaphoric in response to explicit questions.

Metaphor involves devices that can be graded. *"He's an angel"* is not quite as dramatic as *"He is God."* Kennedy, Gabias, and Pierantoni (1990) examined pictures in which a graded change in a graphic device was interpreted by the blind as meaning a graded change in the referent. They used pictures of balls rolling. Behind the balls the pictures showed a trail of C shapes, resembling CCCCCCO. The C-shapes could be taken to be profiles of the balls, and the location of the Cs could show the path recently taken by the balls, with the spacing of the balls showing the speed, acceleration, and deceleration of the balls. One set of C-shapes was widely spaced, one was densely packed, one increased in density of Cs close to the balls, and one increased the spacing between the Cs close to the balls.

Blind subjects were generally consistent in interpreting these devices. Fourteen blind adults were tested. Thirteen gave consistent responses, with 10 responses following the principle "speed is proportional to density of arcs" and 3 following a "stroboscopic" principle (the more widely separated the arcs, the faster the speed of the ball). (This proportion of consistent stroboscopic responses—21%—is very close to the proportion of adult sighted subjects following this principle—24% in a visual condition and 18% in a tactual condition.) The lesson is that dimensions of variation in pictorial metaphoric devices are mapped spontaneously by the blind onto dimensions of variation in the referent, in the same fashion used by the sighted.

Symbolism and Imagery

Figurative communication involves many tropes, such as exaggeration, the use of emblems, symbolism, and metonymy, as well as standard copula metaphors of the form *"A is a B."* To expand the field of enquiry, I have studied blind people attempting several kinds of figurative communication tasks. For example, one blind woman drew "marriage before and after a divorce." The image she used for marriage before a divorce (Kennedy, 1993, p. 262) included a corral with a gate in the fence, and a lock on the gate—but on the inside, she stressed. The idea was to reflect a voluntary bond, holding the couples in. In her second image (shown in Fig. 13.1), the couples she drew inside the corral at times included one of the partners in possession of a key, so she or he could get out at will, perhaps without the other member of the couple knowing. Outside the corral are individuals represented by hearts, with wings suggesting freedom, though some of the hearts are sectioned by lines to suggest being heartbroken.

I also asked a relatively young blind woman—a blind undergraduate— to draw marriage. She drew two people side-by-side, with a cross and two hearts joined by the cross (J. M. Kennedy, 1994). The images involved here— *"MARRIAGE IS A CORRAL," "MARRIAGE IS A JOINING,"* and *"WINGS ARE FREEDOM"* for example—are quite fruitful. They also provide an important theoretical lesson. As V. R. Kennedy (1994) wrote, discussion of "metaphor in literature most often has been based on a verbal description of an image with a visual referent" (p. 135). The images can be spatial, like a corral or a physical link, without being visual. Also, the significance of the image lies in its meaning rather than directly in its spatial content or its list of objects. The key, the lock, and the corral stand for abstract ideas. The abstract ideas are not fully captured by the list of objects—to claim otherwise is to commit the error of reductionism.

Spatial symbols can be highly effective for the blind while being novel and simple—far too simple and general to be specific to their symbolic referent. Liu and I tested novel uses of standard geometric forms—a circle and a square—as symbols. We were searching for pairings of these elementary forms with referents in the fashion described by Forceville (1994) discussing graphic images and their rhetorical use: The subject should attempt "to understand or experience that element in terms of another . . . without there being a pre-existing or conventional connection between these two" (p. 2).

Blind and sighted subjects were asked to determine which of two terms fits with circle and which with square (Liu & Kennedy, 1993, 1994). Clear examples are "soft" and "hard." Most sighted people pair "soft" with circle and "hard" with square. Similarly, "happy" is paired with circle and "sad" with square. Also "weak" is paired with circle and "strong" with square, "cat" with circle and "dog" with square. We provided a list of twenty such pairs to blind and sighted subjects. The sighted subjects gave us a set of pairings that ranged from 100% agreement (soft—hard) down steadily—for example to 74% agreement on spring and fall, as circle and square respectively—to chance level (deep and shallow, with only 51% agreement on deep as circle and shallow as square). We tested four adult blind subjects. Their pairings ranged from 15 to 19 of the 20 pairs being assigned in agreement with the consensus from the sighted. The highest score was obtained from a man totally blind since birth. The implication is that shape symbolism is not purely visual, even on symbols for which there is no well-established convention and for which the match must be devised trial by trial.

Generality and Specificity

Form and spatial layout are fundamental properties of perception, in touch as well as vision. But layout is not just perceptual, divorced from cognition, communication, and figurative communication. A picture only shows layout. Nevertheless it can relate to concepts, and to concepts used in metaphors in particular. Perceptible properties are the basis for classification of many kinds, though they are not the direct basis for every kind of classification (e.g., logically, they are not the direct basis of the concept of non-spatial concepts). Dent-Read and Szokolovsky (1993) noted "metaphors can be expressed and understood in action and pictures, as well as in language" (p. 230), because metaphor of any kind "involves treating one kind of thing as if it were a different kind of thing" (p. 231) based on apt commonalities between the two. Many of these apt commonalities can be perceptually evident, and evident to touch as well as vision. But the relation between perception and cognition is a tricky matter, involving metonymy and ambiguity, especially when metaphor is introduced, and the bridge from one to the other deserves careful attention.

Most emphatically, deep problems for theory of tactile pictures, tangible forms, and metaphoric images are created by the relation between perception and information. Information in perception was described as needing "inferences" in the nineteenth century by the great Helmholtz. The theory is still current in Shiffrar (1994), for example, who writes that observers give unique interpretations to underdetermined images, systematically using psychological constraints to deal with physical input that comprises inherently ambiguous representations. Her argument is that the visual system uses a hierarchy of various constraints which interact within and across levels of analysis. This proposal suffers from the problem that if the input is inherently underdetermined, it has no clear rationale for evoking one constraint rather than another. The theory itself is underdetermined, in other words. Indeed, if the results of an input are unambiguous percepts, the constraints are said to be evoked—supporting the theory. If the result is ambiguity in percepts, this is said to show that the input is ambiguous—also supporting the theory. There is no way to reject the theory, it seems. It is circular. It needs a theory of an input with a context that will evoke the constraint, which means that the total input is not ambiguous.

Gibson (1979) avoided circularity by asserting that perceptual input contains information. Information is present in perception if an input is specific to its source, in the normal environment. Specificity of input to source follows if the environment sets limits to light patterns. Only some sources are in the environment, and they only give rise to some perceptual patterns. In touch, our fingertips may only contact a flat table surface over 10% of its spots, but that should be enough in the normal environment to ensure reliable information for a continuous surface (unless for example some very odd and unrepresentative collection of freely suspended small flat surfaces just happened to be exactly what the scanning fingertips chanced to contact).

Gibson's theory needs to be expanded to deal with pictures and imagery of many kinds. All inputs—like all pictures and mental images—are representations. Physically, they are not the sources or conceptions they may be taken to indicate. An object is something that can give rise to many optic arrays or tangible arrays. Perception always samples from arrays that are themselves only samples of the infinite information for the whole object. Similarly, a picture is just one of the possible ways to depict the referent. Likewise, a mental image is just one way to indicate an object or a concept. An image or graphic representation is not specific enough on its own to be a particular representation of anything. Just as an optic array or a tangible array can only contain information if the array is constrained by the rules of the environment, a picture can only be specific if it is constrained by the rules of pictures. Outlines are constrained by the rule that outlines stand for edges of surfaces, not for anything that might have a boundary, such as pain, wind, noise, or a smell, for example. Also, a mental image can only be taken as suggesting a concept if it is understood within the procedures of cognition. An image for "meaning," such as a spade digging, has to be understood to provide some apt common features of its referent, and a host of additional features, some being relevant differences from "meaning," and some being irrelevant. A relevant commonality is that spades select from the substrate to which they apply, a relevant difference is that spades are concrete but "meaning" is abstract, and an irrelevant difference is that spades are about 1 to 5 feet in size, as Gentner and Markman (1994) might aver.

A perceptual array, a picture and an image, as individual items, are not specific enough to be representations. Indeed, when we consider any two objects, there are always an infinite number of features they share in common. The problem of ambiguity is compounded in novel metaphors and other forms of figurative communication. In these, two referents—the literal referent and the novel expression—have to be conjoined. From the infinite set of commonalities and the infinite set of differences between the referent and the figurative part of the expression, a suitable selection has to be made. Also, the form of the trope has to be understood (Kennedy, 1982). The audience must ask if the trope uses figurative class-inclusion as in the copula form *"the man is a wolf"* or adds exaggeration as in *"he's a giant"* or includes ironic reversal as in *"he's a real winner."* The same issues arise in language, in pictures, and in communicative action (such as in miming a wolf's snarl while imitating Hitler or pretending to look up to a despot in exaggerated awe as if to a self-important giant). In practice, the result is that relevant commonalities and differences are found, rapidly, and often as effortlessly as in ordinary discourse (Roberts & Kreuz, 1994). Despite the fact that items in isolation are highly ambiguous, in normal use in everyday settings representation works efficiently, even in sketchy outline pictures, metaphoric pictures, and metaphoric tactile pictures for subjects with no experience with this manner of communication. The key lesson from tactile pictures is that the principles of metaphor operate in novel media, because the principles are not part of the grammar of any particular medium of communication. Rather they are based in cognition, which can be expressed in any medium.

The facts of the case call for a general assessment of methods for ensuring that metaphoric pictures for the blind are not endlessly ambiguous. What rules and contexts delimit them?

In the first place, blind people spontaneously use outlines for the same kinds of referents as the sighted, and treat other referents as unusual or unrealistic. The principle here is that any medium's elements have a standard use, and hence variations on that use stand out as exceptional. The exceptional can be random, in which case it is unlikely to communicate anything effectively. Or it can be apt. Notably, it can reflect general knowledge, and be a suitable selection of features from an object that is to be the central target of attention. Usefully, for tactile pictures, the basic forms of objects are in common to tactile and visual observers, and to many of their simple pictures. Furthermore, in some of the experiments reported here, subjects were offered options, and constrained to make a choice between the options. This may seem artificial, but in fact it reflects the marketplace of common knowledge and rhetorical images quite fairly. A picture on the editorial page of a newspaper generally reflects events of the period. A sports figure may be given angelic wings if a scandal has been overcome, and a raptor's wings if opponents are being routed. The wings will be relevant to the issues of the day. A halo will be an accolade if a celebrity reflects the best of the good, and ironic if the Great One is known to be feigning innocence.

In some of the drawing studies on the blind, subjects were to invent devices. The task itself acts as a relevant constraint. When a literal solution is impossible, anything that is done to depart from what is natural indicates that there is something extra to be considered. However, the solutions achieved using metaphoric shape transformations are not arbitrary. Rather, in addition to features of the target object, features of other objects can be added non-realistically. Consider some cases in point. Subjects may borrow relevant common features from one location where they are physically correct and put them in a location where they are incorrect but apt. Suitable borrowings could include taking the continuous steady motion of a spinning wheel's parts, and putting this in the form of a smooth continuous curve of a spoke. Likewise, an abrupt change in direction—jerky motion—can be indicated by an abrupt bend in a spoke. Similarly, the gradual changes in location of a wobbly wheel can be shown by smoothly varying sinusoids of a spoke drawn like a wave. Just as a shark's distinctive snout, beady eyes, sharp teeth and prominent dorsal fin can be given to a sales clerk to indicate greed, a shape of a spoke can be varied distinctively to indicate its wheel's motion. The target is given transformed features. If the audience knows the task being undertaken, the solution is readily noted to be metaphoric, and its purpose is understandable.

It is not enough to know what news is being caricatured, what task has been set, or what object is the focus of attention, in order to assess a metaphoric communication. The central fact is that some vehicles are apt, and others are not. In symbolism, such as the use of a circle to symbolize SOFTNESS or MOTHER, the topic can be matched with the symbol via relevant common features. A circle is rounded and smooth while a square has sharp corners. There is something in common between smooth and soft, as there is betweeen hard and sharp. To be appreciably sharp an object must be hard to some degree, and to feel rounded is generally to feel soft. Rounded and soft are both smooth. Both yield to moving touch. These commonalities are not without exceptions, for a blade of grass can be quite soft, but still have a sharp cutting edge, a leaf can be soft but have an angular outline, and pebbles can be smoothly rounded but hard. It is a mistake to assume rhetoric's examples can readily be explained by underlying general rules that have no exceptions. They are heuristics, not algorithms. General rules that fit a case or two do not always lead straightforwardly to novel, apt examples. "To lose your temper" means quite the reverse of "to lose touch with your emotions," and it is also at variance with the "lose" in "he lost his mind." Social practice often condones specific uses of terms with quite narrow confines. Jokes often hinge on the fact that we do not immediately see the general meaning of terms and devices, and take them within narrow limits. An example is "Politicians are suffering from illness and fatigue. People are sick and tired of them." Another is "Even model parents can come unglued at times." The terms "illness" and "fatigue" are more general than the meaning normally extracted from the phrase "sick and tired." "Models" are conceived in two different narrow ways in the second example. What is true for terms and idiomatic phrases can surely be true, too, of concepts. We have narrow stereotypes of concepts that are impervious to counter-examples, for example, *"he's an animal"* does not imply that he may be an insect, even though animals are often insects, and there are many more insects than large mammals.

A theory of metaphoric pictures based on borrowing and misplacing distinctive features of objects and concepts is clearly useful, despite important cautions and disclaimers about general rules. It can apply quite widely, to political cartoons in newspapers and to advertisements (Forceville, 1994; Kennedy & Kennedy, 1994). It can also apply to movie cartoons, where creatures like Bugs Bunny grow extra arms or legs to show how busy they are, or have their feet and legs turn into spinning wheels to show how speedy they are. The cautions here are about overgeneralizing from particular concrete examples to possible general rules, and products derived from the general rules. At the moment, it is easier to describe particular examples clearly than to devise the general rules on which they may be based. In this connection, Kennedy (1982) suggested that the tenor–vehicle distinction could be applied fruitfully to the original object and the transformation, without needing to assert that the vehicle must be a general rule or a feature with an invariant meaning. THE SPOKE IS WAVY has a SPOKE as a tenor and WAVY as a vehicle. Forceville (1994) noted that Kennedy (1982) applied the tenor–vehicle distinction to all tropes, taking the term metaphor in its common-language sense as a metonymy for all forms of rhetoric. Forceville prefers to describe pictorial metaphors as having two distinct objects, identified as the primary object and a secondary one. The difference between Forceville's terms and Kennedy's is minor, since Forceville concludes like Kennedy that the primary object is used to select some of the secondary object's properties, and the two objects together have an implication or message.

Both Forceville and Kennedy stress that more than co-occurrence of two objects is involved. *"The tree as a woman"* is different than *"the woman as a tree."* In Kennedy (1990) the difference is described as "special-purpose classification." The tree is said to belong to the class of women in the first (perhaps by being fruitful), and the woman belongs to the class of trees in the second (perhaps by being well-rooted). The meaning of the vehicle (woman or tree) has to be sought by considering the tenor with which it is paired, and the fact that the vehicle is a vehicle rather than the target of the comment, as well as the general context in which the expression occurs. The result is a claim that the tenor belongs in a class known because of the vehicle. Much of the power of metaphoric communication arises from its capacity to invoke classifications. A peacemaking diplomat could be shown in a picture as a wizard if he pulled off the impossible. It is not just that he has accoutrements of a wizard that matters in interpreting the picture. It is the classification as a wizard that has to be understood. The accoutrements are a metonymy for the class. The features evident in an optic array, a picture or a verbal trope mentioning a concrete object, are a sample, in perception and cognition, that betoken the class. There is no way in perception to use physical features of an isolated object to distinctively specify "the class of" as opposed to "an item." It is impossible, therefore, in depicting an individual object to present physical features of an object in order to distinguish "wizards as a class" from "a person with some of a wizard's garb." But in context, the garb on the person indicates the level of abstraction that is meant.

To the extent that tropes use mechanisms of classification, all the types of tropes should be available in pictures, and available to the blind, for there is nothing inherent in blindness that restricts their capacity to use the principles of classification. Rather, the puzzle that needs to be addressed is how a picture can suggest, via metonymy, a class. An object is shown and a special classification is meant. That is the heart of metaphor and it is available in depiction, even in tactile pictures for the blind.

REFERENCES

Carello, C., Rosenblum, L., & Grosofsky, A. (1986). Static depiction of movement. *Perception, 15,* 41–58.

Dent-Read, C. H., & Szokolszky, A. (1993). Where do metaphors come from? *Metaphor and Symbolic Activity, 8,* 227–242.

Edman, P. K. (1992). *Tactile graphics.* New York: American Foundation for the Blind.

Forceville, C. (1994). Pictorial metaphor in advertisements. *Metaphor and Symbolic Activity, 9,* 1–30.

Gentner, D., & Markman, A. B. (1994). Structural alignment in comparison: No difference without similarity. *Psychological Science, 5,* 152–158.

Gibson, J. J. (1979). *The ecological approach to visual perception.* Boston: Houghton-Mifflin.

Glucksberg, S., & Keysar, B. (1990). Understanding metaphorical comparisons: Beyond similarity. *Psychological Review, 97,* 3–18.

Heller, M. A. (1989). Picture and pattern perception in the sighted and the blind. *Perception, 18,* 379–389.

Heller, M. A., & Schiff, W. (1991). *Touch perception.* Hillsdale, N.J.: Lawrence Erlbaum Associates.

Hochberg, J. E., & Brooks, V. (1962). Pictorial recognition as an unlearned ability. *American Journal of Psychology, 75,* 624–628.

Kennedy, J. M. (1982). Metaphor in pictures. *Perception, 11,* 589–605.

Kennedy, J. M. (1990). Metaphor—its intellectual basis. *Metaphor and Symbolic Activity, 5,* 115–123.

Kennedy, J. M. (1993). *Drawing and the blind: Pictures to touch.* New Haven, CT: Yale University Press.

Kennedy, J. M. (1994). Bilder att se och kanna [Pictures to see and touch]. In G. Jansson (Ed.), *Punkskrift och taktila bilder: Report 1* (pp. 1–11). Stockholm: Talboks-och Punktskriftbiblioteket.

Kennedy, J. M., & Domander, R. (1986). Blind people depicting states and events in metaphoric line drawings. *Metaphor and Symbolic Activity, 1,* 109–126.

Kennedy, J. M., and Gabias, P. (1985). Metaphoric devices mean the same to the blind and the sighted. *Perception, 14,* 189–195.

Kennedy, J. M., Gabias, P., & Heller, M. A. (1992). Space, haptics and the blind. *Geoforum, 23,* 175–189.

Kennedy, J. M., Gabias, P., & Pierantoni, R. (1990). Meaning, presence and absence in pictures. In K. Landwehr (Ed.), *Ecological perception research, visual communication and aesthetics* (pp. 43–56). Berlin: Springer-Verlag.

Kennedy, J. M., Green, C. D., & Vervaeke, J. (1993). Metaphoric thought and devices in pictures. *Metaphor and Symbolic Activity, 8,* 243–255.

Kennedy, J. M., & Kennedy, V. R. (1994). Realism as a basis for reinterpretation. *Canadian Journal of Rhetorical Studies, 4,* 106–120.

Kennedy, J. M., & Ross, A. S. (1975). Outline picture perception by the Songe of Papua. *Perception, 4,* 391–406.

Kennedy, V. R. (1994). Pictures as metaphors in Thackeray's illustrated novels. *Metaphor and Symbolic Activity, 9,* 135–148.

Liu, C. H., & Kennedy, J. M. (1993). Symbolic forms and cognition. *Psyke & Logos, 14,* 441–456.

Liu, C. H., & Kennedy, J. M. (1994). Symbolic forms can be mnemonics for recall. *Psychological Bulletin and Review, 1,* 494–498.

Roberts, R. M., & Kreuz, R. J. (1994) Why do people use figurative language? *Psychological Science, 5,* 159–163.

Shiffrar, M. (1994). When what meets where. *Psychological Science, 3,* 96–100.

14

Boundaries in Humor
and Metaphor

Howard R. Pollio
University of Tennessee

In an appreciative memoir of his friend the American writer James Agee, Fitzgerald (1968) remembered that he and Agee would sometimes amuse themselves by playing what they came to call the metaphor game. In this game the task was to take an inanimate object and turn it into a famous person who could then be recognized without specifically being named. Agee, not surprisingly, was good at this game; "he developed a second hand silver flute into (the actor) Leslie Howard and a Grand Rapids easy chair into Carl Sandburg." But speakers and writers less gifted than Agee also find this game easy to play and a few psychologically oriented writers (e.g., Gordon, 1961, 1968; Katz, 1989; Pitts, Smith, & Pollio, 1982) have used tasks similar to the metaphor game in teaching creative language in the elementary or high school classroom as well as in evaluating theories of metaphor and metaphor production.

Regardless of intent, one aspect of the game always seems to come along quite uninvited: the comparisons made often are extremely funny and teachers, students, research subjects, and experimenters all have been known to laugh out loud at some of those produced. So, for example, Dolly Parton has been turned into a double decker bus, Joan Rivers into a lemon, Arnold Schwarzenegger into building blocks, Dan Quayle into pots and pans, and Jesse Helms into burnt toast. When the game is played aloud, and in public, laughter follows many of the comparisons produced: it even works at faculty meetings and APA conventions (Pollio, 1992).

Although metaphor and humor may seem far apart in some abstract conceptual scheme of things, a number of years ago incidental observations made by Mawardi (1959) concerning the role of metaphor in industrial consulting groups revealed that she and other raters sometimes found it difficult to decide which remarks were intended to be funny and which were intended to deal with the present problem in a metaphorically useful way. A more detailed

231

analysis of these observations indicated that laughter occurred in one of the following three situations: (a) When either a really good or a really bad pun was made; (b) When a hopelessly muddled metaphor was used—perhaps similar to the one described by Thomas (1969) as having been produced by a high school student intent on literary immortality: "A virgin forest is one where the hand of man has never set foot"; and (c) When a really apt figure of speech summarized the group's current understanding of the problem.

All three observations suggest that laughter depends upon a novel or, at least, an improbable combination of words and that both really good and really bad puns and metaphors occur in many of the same linguistic environments. One consequence of this is that the lowly pun may be viewed both as a figure of speech and a form of joke, although in neither case does it get much in the way of respect. Despite this, puns define one among many figurative strategies useful in evoking laughter. If, along with Pepicello and Weisberg (1983), we regard the riddle as a major joke form, it is possible to see figurative usage in almost all of the various syntactic and semantic strategies used to create and understand riddles. Even though Pepicello and Weisberg were primarily concerned with such linguistically defined factors as minimal pairs, transformational structure, and irregular morphology, their text provides many examples of riddles that depend, in whole or part, on one or more of the following figures of speech: pun, metaphor, simile, hyperbole, oxymoron, irony, litote, sarcasm, parody, personification, and onomatopoeia.

Perhaps it was for reasons of this sort that Koestler (1964) assumed that a comparable intellectual process was involved in understanding or producing a joke, solving a riddle or problem, and appreciating or creating figurative language in poetry. This process was termed the bisociation of ideas and was assumed to take place whenever two initially disparate realms of thought were joined in the joke, riddle, problem-solution, or figure of speech. Differences among these events were to be found not in the cognitive act joining them but in their motivational properties: for jokes and humor, the system was a self assertive one defined by sexual and aggressive motives; for figures of speech and poetic diction, the system was a self transcending one defined by experiences of communion or rapture. To complete the theory, scientific or rational problem-solving was seen to involve a blending of both self-asserting and self-transcending emotions.

To return, once more, to the metaphor game, a series of studies by Pitts, Smith, and Pollio (1982) indicated that metaphoric comparisons produced under relaxed conditions tended to be more unique, apt, easier to produce, and more likely to yield laughter than those produced under the more formal procedures of matching attributes or solving implicit analogies. More relevant to the present context, however, it was only under relaxed conditions that subjects laughed at some of their own responses, with this laughter taking one of two forms: an Aha type of laugh suggesting excitement over the surprising match created and a more clearly humor-related laugh for comparisons experienced as funny. In the second case, subjects often looked at the experimenter to see if he or she also laughed or found the response funny.

To evaluate the relation between aptness and funniness, Pollio (1992) asked two additional groups of undergraduate students to respond to eight then-famous people such as Dan Quayle, Dolly Parton, Arnold Schwarzenegger, and Margaret Thatcher in terms of the following four categories: Animals, Vehicles, Foods, and Musical Instruments. Once participants produced the required comparisons, they were asked to select which responses were the "funnniest" and which the "most apt." Finally, they were asked to suggest new people to use as stimuli and new categories to use for matching if they wanted to help someone else produce humorous comparisons.

On the basis of suggestions made by this group of participants, one new category, household appliances, and a few new people, Roseanne, Madonna, and Jessie Helms, were added and presented to a different group of subjects; results produced by these subjects are found in Table 14.1. Although there are responses here to gladden the hearts of individuals on both the left and the right of the socio-political-sexual spectrum, the overwhelming impression is that there is little to distinguish "funny" from "apt" pairings and that both sets of comparisons easily step over the line of good manners, good taste, or both. Responses also were fairly explicit with regard to issues of sex, power, physical appearance, and intellectual ability, or lacks thereof, and this was true both for the most apt and the funniest of pairings. (For a more quantitative, and somewhat less abrasive, analysis of the relation between jokes and metaphors produced by pairing famous people with unrelated categories, see Hillson and Martin, 1994; although using Sylvester Stallone, Pope John Paul II, Woody Allen, and Manuel Noriega in the same stimulus list does not seem all that uncontentious).

We are thus led back, by a less theoretical route, to the idea that although there are differences between humor and metaphor there also are similarities. Can it be that a joke or humorous remark is nothing more than a mean-spirited metaphor or, at least, one gone bad and that a metaphor is nothing but a polite form of a more mean-spirited joke or putdown? These suggestions derive some measure of support not only from the present set of results but also from the theoretical stance taken by Koestler (1964) and to some extent by Hillson and Martin (1994). To consider these possibilities in detail, however, it is necessary to explore more fully the nature of humor and metaphor before getting to the more demanding task of determining exactly how metaphor and humor are both the same and different.

TABLE 14.1
Funniest and Most Apt Pairings Produced In the
Final Metaphor Game Experiment

Person	Funniest Pairings	Most Apt Pairings
Dan Quayle	deer staring into headlights, PEZ, ashtray, gerbil	chopped liver, second fiddle, boiled ochre
Madonna	two cherry ice cream cones, toaster, hamburger helper, tootsie roll	viper, tart, vacuum, squid
Pee Wee Herman	Water-Pik, pickle, ding dong, leaf blower	banana, pigeon, windup doll
Tammy Faye	icing on a cake, paint gun, Chihuahua	souffle, peacock, a toilet
Arnold Schwarzenegger	beef stroganoff, a hammer, beef jerky	doberman, garage door opener, beef
Dolly Parton	camel, two-eggs sunny side up, roller skates	watermelon, cream puff, horse drawn wagon
Geraldo Rivera	cheese	1/2 case Vienna Sausage, jackal, trash compactor
Joan Rivers	garbage disposal, chewing gum, a fly	rotten fish, pencil sharpener, cricket
Jessie Helms	cuckoo clock, prune	turtle, burned toast
Roseanne	buffet, radio tuned in by a 12-year-old	Shop-Vac, elephant, lasagna

HUMOR IS NOT A PRETTY THING

A number of years ago, before cable television changed the face of standup comedy, a well known comedian did a television show presenting his version of how humor and comedy worked. The title of the show was "Humor is Not a Pretty Thing," and documented a series of jokes and comic situations concerned with cruelty and sexuality as their defined content. Presumably these topics, either singly or in combination, are what he meant by the phrase "humor is not a pretty thing." Although the viewing audience might have been surprised by just how "unpretty a thing humor really was," professional comedians have long known that most of what makes people laugh depends on sex, aggression, and sex and aggression. Psychologists and philosophers also would not be surprised since theorists from Hobbes to Freud have built theories on roughly the same pair of topics.

Not all of comedy is X-rated; there are some professional comedians who take pride in the fact they do not use profanity in their act but opt instead for a nonsense of view of humor in which the paradigmatic joke is the pun and the paradigmatic principle incongruity. Basically, such humor revolves around the idea that laughter arises from a kind of trick use of words and ideas. This technique is viewed as harmless (even Freud, 1905, saw little aside from concealment in incongruity), although tricking someone about the meaning of his or her words does not seem quite that harmless. If the major contrast in sexual jokes could be described as between dirty and clean, and in aggressive ones as between being one-up and one-down, then the major contrast in incongruity may be stated as follows: "You can't trust what people say until you see what it really means."

Finally, there is an additional view as to what humor is about and the relevant principle here is spontaneity or unpredictability. Although unpredictability may be viewed as a special case of incongruity, as theorists since Kant have proposed, spontaneity does not easily coalesce into incongruity. In fact, Bergson (1911) turned things around by noting that incongruity is just one of the conditions by which spontaneity shows itself, not vice-versa. For Bergson, the contrast in humor is between being alive and being a thing, with the former concerned with ever-renewed and renewing novelty and the latter with mechanization, repetitiveness, and death. The joke, in its social husk, is a rebuke for an unthinking mechanization of human life and the mechanical nature of laughter only serves to underscore the repetitiveness (and unpredictability) of the body's appreciation of this principle.

Each theory yields a major comic form: sexual themes produce "dirty" jokes; aggressive themes, put-downs; incongruity themes, puns and riddles; and spontaneity themes, clowns, jacks-in-the-box, or both. In each case what is emphasized is a bit of content, although it is clear that the principles of competing positions also are dealt with. In addition to Bergson's use of incongruity as a subspecies of spontaneity, Freud (1905) regularly described clever incongruity as a facade serving to hide humor's more deviant content; in fact, the first half of his well-known book concerns the cognitive (or incongruity) bases of humor.

The Themes of Comedy

Not all research concerning humor has been strictly theoretical in nature. Beginning some fifty years ago, more empirical work was undertaken to determine whether or not jokes could be categorized into conceptually meaningful subgroups (Eysenck, 1942). The logical procedure for this task was factor-analysis, where each factor was assumed to define a comic style or principle; the most detailed summary of this work is presented by Eysenck and Wilson in their semi-popular book *Know Your Own Personality* (1976). In a chapter entitled "Sense of Humor," for example, they present 32 cartoons (primarily derived from *Punch* Magazine) which are said to represent four different types of humor: nonsense, social satire, aggression, and sex. Although specifics are not presented as to how these groupings were achieved, norms are provided for high and low scores. Leaving aside the implications of what it might mean to score high or low on any of these humor types, Eysenck's factors conform nicely to most of the major theories with Bergson the only one left out.

Because Bergson's theory deals primarily with clowns and theatrical performances, it is reasonable to wonder if similar factors would emerge if performers rather than jokes were used. Here a series of early studies factor-analyzed the overlap in word associations given in response to popular comedians (Pollio & Edgerly, 1976; Pollio, Edgerly, & Jordan, 1972). Results of these studies revealed that comedians were grouped on the basis of a relatively small number of associatively defined dimensions having something to do with how the comedian looked or behaved; in addition, such characteristics generally concerned negative traits such as fat, clumsy, loud, bizarre. On the basis of these results, Pollio and Edgerly (1976) concluded that the center of the comedian's world "is composed of a somewhat undesirable-looking set of people who can best be described as clownish. Although each of these performers has other attributes, their awkwardness and generally benign actions suggest that a basic form of comic art is that of the clown, and that all comedians derive their inspirations from this common center" (p. 235). If an analysis of jokes failed to support Bergson's theoretical principles, an analysis of comedians restored spontaneous performers such as the clown to his or her rightful place at the center of comedic inspiration.

In addition to studies concerning comedians, more theoretically oriented studies were undertaken by Wicker, Thorelli, Barron, and Ponder (1981) in an attempt to determine personal reactions to jokes. In this study, two different groups of students were asked a series of questions about two different sets of jokes. Included among these were questions concerning how significant the topic of the joke would be if it were not in a joke, how free or constrained the joke made the person feel, how superior the respondent felt to characters in the joke, and so on. Results of two different factor analyses yielded a three-dimensional space, with the first factor defined by the importance of the joke, the second by the originality and "good sense" of the joke, and the third by the superiority the student felt to characters in the joke. Jokes loading most strongly on the first factor concerned topics such as sickness, prejudice, and religion, whereas those loading most heavily on the third factor concerned absurd behavior by odd characters. No specific set of jokes was found to load uniquely on the second factor.

In a different study designed to capture the dimensionality of humor, Pollio and Theg-Talley (1991) asked students to rate 21 comedians on 25 different semantic differential scales defined by opposites such angel–devil, big–little, and smart–dumb. Subsets of scales were selected to define each of the major approaches to humor; thus, for psychoanalytic theory, relevant scales were clean–dirty and good–bad; for Bergsonian theory, relevant scales were awkward–graceful and spontaneous–rigid; for Hobbesian theory, superior–inferior and strong–weak; and for cognitive theory, articulate–inarticulate and wise–foolish. Semantic differential scales were used to take advantage of the fact that comedy frequently involves contrast, a reversal of perspective, or both; thus, the denouement of a joke often involves demonstrating that: (a) there is (is not) something taboo where before there was (was not) something taboo; (b) that something large (small) is really small (large); (c) that something foolish (wise) is really wise (foolish); and (d) that something human (mechanical) is really mechanical (human).

Results of two separate factor analyses yielded similar four-factor solutions involving a sacred–angel factor, a spontaneous–flexible factor, a big–slow factor, and a superior–inferior factor. Additional analysis revealed that across both studies, only a few scales were found to define a single factor with many items loading on at least three different factors. So, for example, the pair slow–fast loaded on the sacred–angel factor as a synonym for orderly, on the superior–inferior factor as a synonym for dumb, and on the big–slow factor as a description of movement. Even adjectives specifically selected to define one or another of the major theories were found to load on more than a single factor suggesting that there are no single-factor theories of humor and that each theory must implicitly consider elements of all remaining ones. To be "free" is to be spontaneous, superior, wise, and immoral; to be "slow" is to be stupid, plodding, awkward, and rigid; to be "superior" is to be flexible, bright, powerful, and moral.

Linguistic analysis thus suggests that each theory specifies only a single aspect of the comedic event that stands out when a specific instance of comedy is considered: spontaneity and mechanism are most obvious when one is concerned with theatrical performance, superiority and power are most apparent when one is concerned with either a deformed person or with someone falling down for no obvious reason, intellectual factors are most obvious when written jokes are analyzed, and sacredness, cleanliness, or both are most significant when profane, scatological, or sexual jokes are at issue. The domain of comedic art includes movement, morals, power, and intellect, and any reasonable theory must have both a single situation in which it operates best as well as a set of less criterial ones to which it may also be applied. Any principle that works in the criterial situation will work to some degree in all others, and what our theories end up with is not so much a collection of principles as a series of constantly shifting theoretical emphases mutually comprehensible to one another. The comedic event is a coherent pattern that reveals one or another of its facets in specific situations but is not reducible to any of them. In comedy, as in perception, the whole is different from the combination of its parts.

THE ANTHROPOLOGY OF HUMOR:
SACRED CLOWNS AND
PROFANE PRIESTS

Although contemporary comedians can get pretty rough—remember: humor is not a pretty thing—they often are quite tame in comparison to comic actions and ceremonies taking place outside the TV studio, Broadway theater, or night club stage. Here we may think of the behavior of ordinary middle-class mortals during Carnival, Mardi-Gras, or on New Year's Eve or, more broadly, of ritual clowns in non-technological societies around the world. What is most striking to the technological reader is that the antics of ritual clowns often take place in connection with religious ceremonies and include such actions as mock sexual attacks on people at prayer, throwing feces at other clowns and innocent bystanders, wearing absurd looking costumes (or none at all), and frequently engaging in contrary behavior.

Consider the case of contrary behavior. The anthropologist Apte (1987) has noted that such antics involve at least three different domains: gender, status, and ordinary activity. The most usual gender inversion concerns transvestism in which men dress as women, boys as girls, young men as old women, and young women as young men. The major inversions involving status concern the ridiculing of people in high status by people of low status or by people of high status behaving in a manner inconsistent with their non-festival roles. In this latter regard, the Koyemci clowns of the Zuni nation—who drink great draughts of urine and smear each other with feces (Charles, 1944)—are clowns only during the festival; at all other times they are tribal priests and anyone viewing their comedic actions is aware of their dual status as priest and clown. Finally, there are reversals in ordinary behavior: clowns walk backwards, speak strangely, and ride horses facing to the rear. In certain Native American tribes, clowns speak opposite to what is required by the situation or to what is meant; they say "Goodbye" when meeting someone and "Hello" when leaving. Arapaho clowns "pretend not to notice carrying a heavy load, but groan under the weight of a light object" (Apte, 1987, p. 157).

Ritual humor and ritual clowns make their audiences uniquely aware of issues of social control, especially in regard to sexual and scatological matters. Regardless of how sacred the locale, or how controlled sexual and eliminative behaviors ordinarily are within the group or culture, ritual clowns run riot over everyday restraint and morality. In medieval Europe, to take another example, during the Feast of Fools (a New Year's celebration), both priests and lay members of the church painted their faces with dye and made fun not only of each other but of the holy ceremonies (Cox, 1969). When the Prose of the Ass was recited, a donkey was brought into church and allowed free reign of the pulpit. If it brayed, well and good; if it eliminated, so much the better. Although this practice was severely condemned by the Church of Rome—even to the point of denying it ever existed—the practice survived until sixteenth century and died out only in the period of the Reformation (Welsford, 1935).

A different sort of comic performer is defined by the court jester. What seems most important about the jester is that despite his lowly estate, he alone is allowed to mock the King and tell unpleasant truths others cannot; see Lear's fool in this regard. Although there are many explanations for this—the jester by mocking the King keeps him from the evil eye (Willeford, 1969)—what seems clear is that the jester is the King's opposite: If the King's crown is rigid, the jester's is flaccid; if the Kings robes are whole, the jester's are a patchwork; if the King is holy, the jester is salacious; if the King is handsome, the jester is deformed; and so on.

In discussing this vast literature, Fisher and Fisher (1981) view the jester and other institutionalized comic performers as appearing to possess special power or magic. Contemporary comedians also view themselves as partaking of this dynamic and frequently characterize themselves as doctors, priests, or social reformers. In commenting on some possible reasons as to why roles such as clown or jester were not only tolerated but actively cultivated throughout much of the world, Fisher and Fisher (1981) noted: "The jester in his coarseness and apparent irrationality implied that . . . he controlled some magical supernatural stream. . . . He was a form of insurance against uncontrollable chaos . . . a form of tamed chaos" (p. 51).

Writing from an anthropological rather than from a psychological point of view, Makarius (1970) argued that ritual clowns, like court jesters, tricksters, and stand-up comics, are socially encouraged because they confront their audiences with contradictory aspects of human experience. Thus, ritual clowns regularly violate social order and ritual taboo yet, at the same time, are known to be the guardians of the very social order and ritual taboos they mock. Within the context of their performance, the clown's painted face, deformed body, and unclean gestures conceal the power of the person enacting the role, and the spectator easily senses that the clown presents an amalgam of good and evil, strength and weakness, sacredness and profanity, truth and lie. Although there is a tension here that may be broken by laughter, there also is a deeper tension involving the frightening possibility of a social life bereft of rules, truth, power, and goodness; in short, a life in which there is only the chaos of the clown.

The ritual clown, the jester, and the contrary get away with mocking social and religious order because they, in their other lives or in their own way, are the guardians of the sacred, the moral, the good, and the orderly. By going over the line from order to chaos, they demonstrate the necessity for order and civility. Because they themselves are sacred and powerful, they are capable of maintaining a balance even as they provoke chaos in their audience. It is the job of the ritual clown to demonstrate that while we may seek the exhilaration of an unconstrained existence, we must also recognize a need for the very social boundaries violated by the comic act. Only a priest could be trusted with such a demonstration, and only laughter could provide a relevant gesture recognizing what the sacred fool is, and has been, trying to teach all along: chaos and order are jointly present in every moment of social and personal existence.

METAPHOR AS THE LANGUAGE
OF IS AND IS NOT

At the simplest level, figurative language is defined by juxtaposition, either for purposes of comparison or for identifying one thing in terms of another. Such juxtaposition may take the form of metaphor, simile, personification or, in the most quixotic member of the group, oxymoron. Although there are many figures of speech, metaphor often serves as a generic term for all or most of them. Such usage seems a bit unfortunate since the term "figure of speech" suggests a more perceptual quality to the experience of poetic language than metaphor, which simply suggests a transfer of meaning from one word to another.

In his comprehensive study of metaphor, Ricoeur (1975) noted that different theories of figurative language are situated at different linguistic levels ranging from that of the word to that of a particular style of literary or philosophical discourse. In general, as he notes, earlier analyses (Aristotle) operated at the level of the word and later ones at the level of the sentence (Black) or of the poem or philosophical meditation (Ricoeur). The analysis of transfer—or substitution as this position is sometimes called—serves to make most sense at level of the word. At this level, one word takes the place of a second, with the comprehension of replacement understood as solving an implicit contradiction or analogy which then transfers the meaning of one word to another.

Because replacement or transfer theories are at least as old as Aristotle, it is important to remember that Aristotle located metaphor in two different contexts: that of argument (rhetoric) and that of poetry (poetics). In each domain, the function was different: *mimesis* in poetry and *persuasion* in argument. An additional complication is that the Aristotelian analysis deals primarily in nouns so that substitution becomes the "giving one thing the *name of another."* With this principle in place, Aristotle provides us with his usual thorough list of possibilities: from genus to species, from species to genus, from species to species, and so on. Unfortunately, such thoroughness led subsequent scholars to the tedium of taxonomy which ultimately pushed metaphor to a peripheral rather than a central location in the study of language.

Modern interest in figurative language required not only a change in perspective but also in level, and Black (1962) supplied both in his well-known interaction theory of metaphor. This theory accomplished a number of goals with respect to the theory of metaphor, including reminding us of the fact that some words in a sentence are used metaphorically and others are not, and the competent listener/hearer/reader experiences this difference directly. Consider Black's sentence *"The chairman plowed through the discussion."* In this sentence, it is clear that *"plowed"* is the metaphoric element and that each of the other words is to be understood literally. Once this distinction is sensed, the metaphoric word becomes a *focus* of metaphoric intelligence, the sentence, its *frame,* and metaphoric interpretation takes place as an interactional phenomenon of the type described by Gestalt psychology under the rubric of figure/ground.

But exactly how does this interaction work? Consider the sentence *"Man is a wolf."* The word *"wolf,"* which formally is the focus of the present sentence, is not understood solely in terms of current literal meanings but also in terms of the system of associated commonplaces (roughly, its connotations) a fluent speaker/listener brings to the interpretive situation. To call a man a wolf is to evoke both sets of meanings, such that the "wolf-metaphor supports some details (and) emphasizes others—in short (it) organizes our view of man" (Black, 1962, p. 41). In precisely this way, metaphor provides the reader with a perceptual Gestalt that not only confers a new insight but also offers an experience beyond the scope of simple linguistic paraphrase or redescription. The metaphoric assertion provides a new understanding of the term "man" (and, to be fair, of the term "wolf") that cannot be reduced to a knowledge of either of their relevant individual meanings.

The next level (beyond that of the sentence) on which to consider metaphor is discourse. At this level, the context is not set by a word or sentence but by the complete thought of the poem or philosophical work. Within these contexts, the basic question comes down to one of deciding whether an extended use of metaphor, such as in a poem or philosophical analysis, refers to anything at all and, if it does, to what? Ricoeur (1975) answers this question by noting that a poem does have reference, and that one of the major purposes of poetry—not to mention scientific models or philosophical discourse—is to redescribe or, more radically, to revise what is taken to be real. When such redescription is understood, it seems to involve what Jakobson (1960) termed "split references"; that is, where the reader is able to experience the world or the poem in terms of "the Majorcan storyteller's dictum: 'Aixo, era y no era' (it was and it was not)" (p. 371).

As should be clear, the idea of split reference yielding an experience of is-and-is-not creates a tension in the listener or reader. In the case of the figurative word, the tension is between literal and metaphorical, in the case of the figurative sentence, between *focus* and *frame,* and in the case of more extended discourse, between metaphoric and literal descriptions of what is taken to be true. In an attempt to describe the nature of the tension generated by split reference, Ricoeur notes that there is "no other way to do justice to the motive of metaphorical truth than to include the critical indecision of . . . 'is not' within the ontological vehemence of the (metaphorical) 'is.'. . . In the same way that logical distance is preserved in metaphorical proximity and (that) an impossible literal interpretation is not abolished by metaphorical interpretation but submits to it while resisting, so the ontological affirmation obeys the principle of tension and the 'law of stereoscopic vision'" (Ricoeur, 1975, pp. 255–256).

This last metaphor for metaphor is a crucial one. Even though theorists such as Black (1962) and Kohler (1947) have used visual images in presenting their views of metaphor, the reality of stereoscopic combination offers an experiential way of describing how the tension created by elements of the figure is resolved. Not only is there no clear sense of the separate perspectives presented to each eye, the resulting perception affords a new property (depth) that emerges only from their combination and, more importantly, provides a more useful and apt presentation of the world than either perspective by itself. Each eye both combines and suppresses the specifics of the picture presented to the other eye and such submission and resistance, to use Ricoeur's terms, is absolutely essential for the perception of worldly depth.

But perceptual stimuli can also mislead the eye into an illusory perception of depth. So, too, with metaphor; a particularly apt combination at the level of word, sentence, or discourse may lead the reader to a perception of the world that distorts rather than reveals or recreates it in a useful way. If used cunningly, metaphor can deceive or misdirect and only a sensitivity to the ethics of the metaphor-maker provides the listener with some hedge against accepting the reality inspired by deceptive figurative usage. Perhaps it was for this reason that early rationalist philosophers and later psychoanalytic theorists explicitly warned against being misled by clever figures of speech.

Regardless of whether or not we are concerned with metaphoric deception, what cannot be denied is that metaphor involves a fusing of separable elements at all levels of language. Although the careful scholar of metaphor will usually be sensitive to the implicit "is not" in every assertion of equivalence, the experience of metaphor is one of wholeness, automatically given, and quickly assented to. Any tension that is sensed is in figures that do not work immediately or, retrospectively, by the scholar seeking to understand why a certain figure did or did not work. Although figurative language may be construed as involving separate elements (tenor and vehicle, focus and frame), the metaphor is always experienced as a gestalt that creates what it discovers and invents what it finds; it is neither totally contrived nor totally accidental. All of this is done, as Kohler (1947) noted, with little need for any computation of points of similarity and difference. What this means is that metaphor provides linguistic figures quite as solid as the stone and metal figures of sculpture which, in both cases, are meant to present new and revealing objects to the perceiver or listener.

EXPERIMENTING WITH METAPHORS AND OTHER FIGURES OF SPEECH

The past decade or so has seen a dramatic increase in what we know about metaphors and the metaphoric process, and a number of empirical generalizations seemed warranted by our present state of knowledge. From this developing literature, the following four generalizations seem well-founded and uniquely relevant to the task of relating metaphor to humor and humor to metaphor:

1. The comprehension of metaphor is directly experienced and does not require a multi-step inferential process to take place.
2. Metaphor and other figures of speech operate in systematic and comprehensible fashion across the lexicon of a specific language community.
3. While metaphor does not have a specific set of topics it uniquely concerns, it invariably relates something known to something unknown.
4. Metaphor and other figures of speech are frequent in a wide variety of speaking and writing contexts.

The first assertion—that metaphors are understood directly—derives its empirical support from many different of sources but most especially from the continuing research reported by Glucksberg and his associates at Princeton (Glucksberg, Gildea, & Bookin, 1982; Glucksberg & Keyser, 1990, 1993). In this work, not only has it been possible to demonstrate that listeners do not wait until a literal meaning has been found to contradict an anomalous one before a metaphor is processed and understood; it also has been possible to demonstrate that under certain conditions metaphoric meanings will interfere with more literal ones. Based on these findings, Glucksberg has come to describe metaphoric comprehension as a creative attribution of properties from the vehicle to the topic of the metaphoric construction.

How this all works may be seen in Glucksberg's analysis of one of his favorite sentences, *"My job is a jail."* In this sentence, the vehicle term "jail" is used to refer both to literal jails and to the more general category named by jails; that is, situations that unduly constrain individuals and rob them of their freedom. When a listener understands this metaphor, the term "jail" functions as an attributive category that provides directly relevant properties to the topic of the metaphor "my job." Within this approach, metaphoric comprehension is seen to make use of the same principles as more literal understanding and, thereby, to pose no special problems for theories of linguistic comprehension.

The most extensive analysis of the degree to which divergent metaphors concerning the same topic exhibit systematic relations, to come now to the second empirical generalization, has been made by Lakoff and Johnson (1980; Lakoff, 1987), and their colleagues. Basically these studies have been carried out by gathering a set of standard metaphorical expressions dealing with a specific domain (e.g., argument, emotion, creativity) and of then examining this corpus to discover defining relations among metaphoric renditions of the domain in question. Not only are such relations thought to capture the core meaning of the metaphoric system, they also define the way in which the relevant speech community conducts day-to-day activities in regard to that domain. Figures of speech inevitably are figures of thought and serve not only to express an understanding but to define and make it publicly available.

This work has given rise not only to a systematic analysis of specific metaphors but also to an epistemology for human science that places "embodiment" and "ecological situatedness" at its center (Fesmire, 1994). Since the experientialist perspectives proposed by Lakoff and Johnson is not dualistic in any sense of the term, we should expect to find similar knowledge structures in us, in our language, and in our world. What this means is that metaphors are interactional systems that derive from and structure our dealings with the world:

> In just this way, metaphors are habitual (stable, but flexible) patterns of understanding and experiencing . . . [that] take an environment into themselves. With a different environment, different metaphors would emerge. . . . If we did not take journeys, then we would not have a "journey"-image schema, and so we would understand neither love nor life as a journey. If wars were not prominent in our social environment, then arguments would not be understood as war. . . . A theory of metaphor must be ecological . . . [and must] . . . always view human organisms situated in their social and physical environments. (Fesmire, 1994, pp. 152-153)

Since we know that humor depends upon a reasonably circumscribed set of topics—to come now to a consideration of our third generalization—we may wonder if there are similar content universals to metaphor. The problem here is somewhat different than in the case of humor since metaphor requires us to consider both what the metaphor is about (its topic) and the words or phrases used to render it metaphorically (its vehicle). Concern for each of these aspects of figurative language has served as a focus in the search for universal principles of metaphoric usage. If we begin on the subject or topic side, Sperber (1930) long ago formulated one such principle; namely, that topics that are problematic or, more simply, arouse intense feelings in a particular era become "centers of metaphoric attraction." Sperber's Law, as this hypothesis has come to be called, implies that the dominant concerns of an era are reflected in the topics it chooses to make metaphoric.

Although this principle is meant as a universal one, it does not specify a unique set of topics as constituting natural centers for metaphor. Considered in the light of the topics defining humor—morality, deception, death, and power—it is possible to see humor's topics as more circumscribed and universal than those of metaphor. Even if we take these four topics as enduring centers of concern, the history of metaphoric usage involves a much more variegated set of topics than those encompassed by humor. Under this reading, Sperber's Law seems to operate best at the level at which it was intended; that of historically contingent "centers of attraction" rather than of atemporal or universal concern.

If we shift from the topic to the vehicle side of figurative language, the possibility of universal principles has been considered most seriously by Ullmann (1957, 1962). On the basis of a careful reading of figures drawn from poetry, Ullmann defined four principles of metaphoric transfer: anthropomorphization, from abstract to concrete, from animals to other objects and people, and synesthesia. In terms of what is usually meant by vehicle, the first principle suggests that aspects of human life provide a continuing source of vehicles; by a similar line of analysis, concrete ideas, animals, and sensory experiences also provide universal vehicles for metaphoric transfers. Although these four categories fall at many different conceptual levels—animals, human life, and sensory experience seem a subset of the more extensive category of concrete objects and events—they do provide a starting place for any attempt at defining universal vehicles.

Considered together, there is some degree of correspondence between Sperber's Law and Ullman's principles: If, in Sperber's sense, we take as problematic the abstract or new ideas of an age, and if we take as less problematic the concrete vehicles of human, animal, and sensory experience, the two can be combined to suggest that the universal topic is "something unknown" and the universal vehicle, "something known." While this characterization is nowhere near as specific as in the case of humor, it does suggest we should seek more, rather than less, abstract principles for metaphor than for humor. In this regard, also see Katz's (1989) more empirical demonstration that in experimental tasks using a variant of the metaphor game, subjects tend to complete incomplete metaphors not only with well known vehicles but with well known vehicles that are more likely to be concrete than abstract.

In an attempt to evaluate topic and vehicle categories in a reasonably extensive corpus of naturally occurring examples, Smith, Pollio, and Pitts (1981) examined metaphoric comparisons deriving from the writings of 24 different American authors ranging from Cotton Mather and Benjamin Franklin to Ernest Hemingway and Eudora Welty. For this survey, various authors were selected so as to fall roughly into six different 50-year periods beginning in 1675 (to 1725) and ending in 1925 (to 1975). Across the complete sample, 1882 novel figures of speech were independently selected by a set of trained raters, all of whom were students in English literature. In this analysis, unlike those of Lakoff and Johnson (1980; Lakoff, 1987), the emphasis was on novel and not cliched figures of speech.

Perhaps the major conclusion to emerge from this inductive assessment was that when selecting subjects and vehicles for metaphoric expression, all facets of human experience can be, and have been, metaphoric. Considered in the light of Sperber's Law, such a pattern suggests that unknown items may be equated with Sperber's category of "problematic" on the assumption that something problematic has an unknown, unclear, or unresolved aspect to it. At the same time, if an unknown entity or idea is in need of resolution, such resolution would seem to occur most frequently in terms of a familiar or known vehicle. Sperber's Law thus represents a simple variation on the theme that metaphoric transfers are devised to render problematic topics in terms of familiar or nonproblematic vehicles.

The contrast between known and unknown, unfortunately, is difficult to define with precision. What may be construed as "known" (familiar) or "unknown" (unfamiliar) is always relative to an individual speaker, in a specific setting, in a particular culture, in a given historical period. The motivation to change the domain covered by a word or phrase depends as much on the speaker's current situation as on the structure of logical concepts embodied in the particular language spoken. Despite this relativistic interpretation, results described by Smith et al. (1981) did reveal that anthropomorphic metaphor was quite prevalent, especially in the use of the human body as a vehicle for unknown topics. Metaphoric transfers based on synaesthetic relations were generally lacking in this sample, perhaps suggesting that such transfers are limited to a specific group of writers or poets and, aside from such specific cases, do not represent an overall pattern. In general, Smith and his colleagues concluded that the major mechanism for metaphoric construction resides in an attempt to make the abstract world understandable and that this is done either by drawing the world into the person or by expanding the person into the world. In Ullmann's terms, the universal vehicle for metaphoric expansion is the concrete, living, breathing, social, human being.

Of some significance for our fourth generalization, that metaphor is a frequent aspect of language use, is the raw number of novel figures culled from this corpus: 1882. Since the total sample consisted of approximately 500,000 words, these figures indicate that the average author studied in this sample produced about 3.7 novel figures of speech in every 1,000 words. Since this value is surely an underestimate, given the exacting rating procedures and the existence of cliched usage, Pollio, Smith, and Pollio (1990), in a later article, estimated that taking both novel and cliched figurative usage into account yields a total of 6.5 figures per 1,000 words. They further calculated that if we assume 500 words per printed page, the reader of fiction will run into at least three figures of speech per page.

Because this group of researchers (Pollio, Barlow, Fine & Pollio, 1977; Pickens, Pollio, & Pollio, 1985; Pollio, Smith & Pollio, 1990) has at times been absolutely obsessed with quantifying the amount of figurative usage in any and all speech contexts, for their sanity, as well as our own, we would do well to enumerate two of their more clear-cut conclusions:

1. Speech samples deriving from a wide variety of speakers yield an average of 1.5 novel and 3.4 cliched figures per 1,000 words spoken; doing the proper arithmetic yields a total value of 15 or so million over the course of lifetime.
2. Educational texts, which are not known for an excess of imagination, reveal a 1% rate of use. This means that the average third grader "will have to deal with a figure of speech every two pages . . . [and] . . . the average eleventh grader will have to deal with approximately 5 per page" (Pollio, Smith, & Pollio, 1990, p. 143).

While these numbers may offer a sense of satisfaction to the metaphor researcher simply on the basis of their existence, what is conceptually more important is the conclusion they yield: metaphors and other figures of speech are frequent aspects of human speaking and writing. There is little that seems special about them and most language users—from children to authors of significant literature—are able to understand and create them in a wide variety of situations. If we combine this conclusion with the fact that metaphors are directly understood, that they are used to make something unknown into something known, and that they systematically intertwine not only with each other but with ongoing conceptualizations of reality, we are left with the conclusion that metaphors and other figures of speech are no more problematic to the ordinary speaker–listener than jokes or other humorous remarks, and probably no less frequent (See Pollio, 1988, continuing his obsession with frequency, for representative rates at which humorous remarks are produced in a variety of settings). Although both topics have only recently been admitted into the polite society of academic study, this should not obscure their significant role and place in everyday life outside the academy.

SPLIT-REFERENCE AND THE DYNAMICS
OF HUMOR AND METAPHOR

Both metaphor and humor seem to have something to do with split reference; that is, to refer to two different but related images or ideas that take place in proximity to one another. When we characterize humor in terms of split reference, the contrast concerns a small number of antinomies: clean/dirty, strong/weak, clear/deceptive, and alive/dead. If we characterize metaphor in terms of topic and vehicle content, the contrast is a simpler and more abstract one: known/unknown. Given these structural similarities, we are left with the problem of what makes one split-reference a joke and the other a figure of speech? The answer seems a relatively straightforward one. Split reference yields humor if the joined items (or the act joining them) emphasize the boundary or line separating them; split reference yields metaphor if the boundary between the joined items (or the act joining them) is obliterated and the two items fuse to form a single entity.

To provide some help in discussing both processes, let us introduce the following set of situations as analogies for both metaphor and humor: consider the relationship between an actor (say Dustin Hoffman, Jack Nicholson, Susan Sarandon, or Meryl Streep) and a dramatic role (say Ratso Rizzo, The Devil, Louise, or Sophie). What seems to happen in significant performances is that the actor fuses with the role: Hoffman becomes Rizzo, Streep becomes Sophie. But it is not simply that Rizzo appears and Hoffman disappears; the Rizzo that appears is Hoffman's Rizzo or the unique taking up of the role by this specific actor. As a point of contrast, consider how Nicholson might become Rizzo. It seems clear that Nicholson's Rizzo would be different from Hoffman's Rizzo; yet, if both do their work well, Rizzo appears and Hoffman and Nicholson do not. To tell the truth, Nicholson's Rizzo would probably appear more Nicholson-like and Hoffman's Rizzo would appear less Hoffman-like, suggesting Nicholson's stage presence is more apparent than Hoffman's. While there may be a moral here as to who is the better actor, this is not the place to go into such matters; suffice it, instead, to use the actor/role analogy to provide some intuition as to what split reference is like to a movie-goer and, by extension, to a reader or listener.

The explicatory metaphor of the performer/role analogy may be further expanded to the case of humor. Here, one of the prototype relationships in both technological and nontechnological societies concerns the case of a performer in drag, for example, Milton Berle, or Flip Wilson. What happens in this situation is a case not of fusion but of oscillation between the comedian and the role. The audience is always aware that Geraldine is Flip Wilson and Flip Wilson is Geraldine, that it is Milton Berle in drag and the man in drag is

Milton Berle. In short, the split reference is unresolved and two presences are simultaneously (or successively) available. Although both presences are well structured, the total event of comedian-in-drag is unstable and the audience is continuously aware of the line separating male and female or, to use the politically incorrect lexicon of comedy, separating strong from weak or rational from emotional. If we throw in the fact that nice men don't dress as women unless they have some (usually immoral) purpose in mind, it is also possible in this situation to experience an oscillation across the line defined by dirty/clean. Since a man in drag also involves deception, the line between true and false makes an appearance suggesting that a comedian in drag emphasizes not one but all of the major contrasts defining comic art.

The complexity of these issues, and their relation to humor and metaphor, may be explored further on the basis of the performer/role analogy. As a start, consider another of Dustin Hoffman's roles, that of a character called Tootsie. In the movie, Hoffman plays an out-of-work actor who, in order to demonstrate his acting prowess, impersonates a female character. The impersonation works so well that Tootsie is hired (as a woman) and the male actor finds himself in some provocative situations, for example, in a dressing room with a woman he finds sexually attractive. Although additional situations emerge that make use of our dual knowledge of both characters, the complexity of split reference here is three-fold: Hoffman, the male character, and the male character as Tootsie. There are few comic possibilities in Hoffman's fusion into his male character, whom we accept as a single character and as our metaphor for metaphor. Most of the comic possibilities derive from the clear (and confusing) dynamic in the split reference between the created male character and Tootsie. This is as it should be, since the paradigmatic experience defining comedy is a split reference that cannot be fused.

We need not only go to Tootsie to see split-reference in characters that define comedy. Much the same situation applies in those Shakespearian comedies *(Twelfth Night, As You Like It)* in which a female character dons the attire of a male character. Unfortunately, another male character, who stays male, often finds true love with the male character played by the female, and the rest of the play frequently revolves around issues of cross-gender identity. A further complexity, not currently relevant, is that women's parts were played by young boys in Shakespeare's time, thereby adding other possible comic elements to the mix. A recent, much more complicated set of cross-gender combinations characteristic of comedy takes place in the movie "Victor/Victoria." In this film, Julie Andrews plays a woman, assumed to be a man, playing a woman. A major portion of the plot concerns a contrast between a homosexual male (Robert Preston) who doesn't fall in love with Andrews and a macho man (played by James Garner) who does. Before the final denouement, a good deal of comedy results from the complex pattern of gender crossings involved in the basic setup generated by the seemingly uncrossable, yet frequently crossed, line between maleness and femaleness.

Since these boundary crossings, with their implicit emphasis on the impossibility of fusion, deal with the significant comic issues of power, morality, and deception, it is clear that tension about these issues must be created in individual audience members. Although tension has often been discussed in regard to metaphor (Foss, 1949; Wheelwright, 1959), such tension is between topic and vehicle and is resolved once the figure "makes sense." As such it is akin to the tension evoked by an incomplete problem which dissipates once the problem is solved. Like an unsolvable problem, however, the tension created by humor cannot be successfully resolved but can only be dissipated in laughter. In metaphor, the tension disappears once topic and vehicle make sense (i.e., are fused into a single comprehensible form); in humor, the boundary is emphasized by the impossibility of resolving the core contrast(s) and can be relieved only momentarily in laughter (Pollio, 1983). In metaphor, tension defines the cognitive power of the figure; in humor, it defines the irresolvability of the relevant contrast.

All of this talk about boundaries and fusion makes one wonder if additional psychological phenomena display similar properties. Although it is possible to consider the sentence ambiguity of "visiting relatives" or "shooting hunters" as transformational linguists have done, a more well worked area is provided by perceptual phenomena. Within this context, two cases would seem to parallel the discussion of humor and metaphor; ambiguous figures and the perception of stereoscopic depth. Without taking any stance on the great variety of issues raised by either or both phenomena, they do seem to provide good perceptual analogies to comedy and metaphor.

Consider the case of such well known ambiguous figures as the old woman and the young girl, the Rubin Figure or the Necker Cube. Probably the most extensive experiential analysis of these figures has been done in regard to the Necker Cube and is presented in a fine book by Ihde entitled *Experimental Phenomenology* (1986). Although Ihde's main point is to demonstrate that there are many more stable organizations of the Necker Cube than the two (or three) discussed by most experimental psychologists, his experiential demonstrations are meant to enable the reader to experience both the instability and the plausibility of the various organizations. He also enables the reader to experience these figures in sequence, thereby demonstrating that many different perceptual organizations may be seen within the literal figure provided by what others might term the stimulus picture.

Now consider the case of stereoscopic vision. Whether we are concerned with random dot patterns altered to produce two different perspectives, or with photographs of the same object taken in such a way as to mirror the disparity between the two eyes, it is clear that when the two items are fused, the separate pictures (or dots) disappear and a single three-dimensional image appears. What is significant about this phenomenon for present purposes is that the emergent perception of depth provides an experience that matches our ordinary experience of depth-in-the-world better than that provided by either perspective alone. The ability of a fused split-reference to provide a useful or illuminating metaphor for some previously unknown, or at least not clearly understood, phenomenon would seem to apply not only to the fusion achieved by figurative language but also to the depth achieved by stereoscopic vision. In both cases, the world is clarified by the fusion, and the viewer (or reader) comes to have a clearer understanding of some previously unclear facet of experience.

Both metaphor and humor, in the foregoing account, seem to focus on alternatives. A different way to frame the issue is in terms of the boundary separating items defining split-reference. As should be clear, metaphor does away with the boundary, either momentarily or more permanently, whereas humor simply emphasizes the boundary but is unable to overcome it. If we move this insight from the realm of perceptual experience to that of overt action we see that Orwell probably was not correct in characterizing jokes as "minor revolutions." Quite the contrary; although humor may point to certain needless limits, it is incapable of overcoming or altering these limits as revolutions must do. While Bergson regards laughter as a social rebuke for mechanical behavior and, therefore, may be presumed to induce change, the antics of the Koyemci clown seem a more conservative act: to demonstrate the nature of a world without order or limits. As such, these antics are designed to emphasize the need for boundaries by demonstrating what would take place if they were undone. Although humor may emphasize boundaries, it does not seek to resolve or destroy them.

Metaphor, in both its conceptual and socio-political mode, would seem the more subversive of the two phenomena. Not only do the category-crossings of figurative language serve to alter (or destroy) the boundary between the categories crossed, they also provide for a novel vision or, at least, a changed perspective. The relationship between metaphor and creative problem solving has often been noted and, on the basis of the present analysis, would seem to make good sense if metaphors resolve split references and allow for a new and more radical conceptualization or resolution of the problem situation.

A good metaphor not only makes the strange familiar, it also makes the familiar strange. Only when the familiar is made strange—which both humor and metaphor have the possibility of doing—and the resulting strangeness is used to alter or recast ordinary perceptions are we in a revolutionary setting. Although dictators often fear (and ban) both the comedian and the poet, the present analysis implies that the poet is the more dangerous since only his or her craft is meant to alter the limits of contemporary boundaries.   While humorists may be annoying, they are nowhere   near as significant as poets in shaping a new vision of the world. Even if comedy is not conceived of as a force for conservatism, it cannot be as radical as figurative language in bringing about the extraordinary changes wrought by a political declaration using figurative phrases immediately understood and acted upon by relevant political forces.   While poets sometimes are incomprehensible to nonpoets, the one thing that can be said for sure is that they do not overestimate the power of their poetic words.

REFERENCES

Apte, M. (1987). *Humor and laughter: An anthropological approach.* Ithaca: Cornell University Press.
Bergson, H. (1911). *Laughter: An essay on the meaning of the comic.* New York: Macmillan.
Black, M. (1962). *Models and metaphors.* Ithaca: Cornell University Press.
Charles, L. H. (1945). The clown's function. *Journal of American Folklore, 58,* 25–34.
Cox, H. (1969). *The feast of fools.* New York: Harper & Row.
Eysenck, H. J. (1942). The appreciation of humor: An empirical test. *British Journal of Psychology, 32,* 295–309.
Eysenck, H. & Wilson, G. (1976). *Know your own personality.* London: Penguin.
Fesmire, S. (1994). What's "cognitive" about cognitive linguistics? *Metaphor and Symbolic Activity, 9,* 149–154.
Fisher, S. & Fisher, R. (1981). *Pretend the world is funny and forever.* Hillsdale, NJ: Lawrence Erlbaum Associates.
Fitzgerald, R. (1968). *The collected short prose of James Agee.* Boston: Houghton Mifflin.
Foss, M. (1949). *Symbol and metaphor in human experience.* Princeton, NJ: Princeton University Press.
Freud, S. (1905). *Wit and its relation to the unconscious.* New York: Norton.
Glucksberg, S., Gildea, P., & Bookin, H. E. (1982). On understanding non-literal speech: Can people ignore metaphors? *Journal of Verbal Learning and Verbal Behavior, 21,* 85–98.
Glucksberg, S., & Keyser, B. (1990). Understanding metaphoric comparisons: By and similarity. *Psychological Review, 97,* 3–18.
Glucksberg, S., & Keyser, B. (1993). How metaphors work. In A. Ortony (Ed.), *Metaphor and thought* (2nd ed., pp. 401–424). London: Oxford University Press.
Gordon, W. J. J. (1961). *Synectics: The development of creative capacity.* New York: Harper & Row.
Gordon, W. J. J. (1968). *Making it strange.* New York: Harper & Row.
Hillson, R. R., & Martin, R. A. (1994) What's so funny about that? The domains-interaction approach as a model of incongruity and resolution in humor. *Motivation and Emotion, 18,* 1–29.
Ihde, D. (1986). *Experimental phenomenology.* New York: SUNY Press.
Jakobson, R. (1960). Concluding statement: Linguistics and poetics. In T. A. Sebeok (Ed.), *Style in language.* Cambridge: MIT Press.
Katz, A. (1989). On choosing the vehicles of metaphors: Referential concreteness, semantic distances, and individual differences. *Journal of Memory and Language, 28,* 486–499.
Koestler, A. (1964). *The act of creation.* London: Hutchinson.
Kohler, W. (1947). *Gestalt psychology.* New York: New American Library.
Lakoff, G. (1987). *Women, fire, and dangerous things.* Chicago: University of Chicago Press.
Lakoff, G., & Johnson, M. (1980). *Metaphors we live by.* Chicago: University of Chicago Press.
Makarius, L. (1970). Ritual clowns and symbolic behavior. *Diogenes, 69,* 44–73.
Mawardi, B. (1959). *Industrial invention: A study in group problem solving.* Unpublished doctoral dissertation, Harvard University.

Pepicello, W. J., & Weisberg, R. W. (1983). Linguistics and humor. In P. E. McGhee & H. H. Goldstein, (Eds.), *Handbook of research on humor*, (Vol. 1, pp. 59–83). New York: Springer-Verlag.

Pickens, J. D., Pollio, M. R., & Pollio, H. R. (1985). A developmental analysis of metaphoric competence and reading. In W. Paprotte & R. Dirven (Eds.), *The ubiquity of metaphor*. Philadelphia: John Benjamin Publishing Company.

Pitts, M. K., Smith, M. K., & Pollio, H. R. (1982). An evaluation of three different theories of metaphor production through the use of an intentional category mistake procedure. *Journal of Psycholinguistic Research, 11*, 347–368.

Pollio, H. R. (1983). Notes toward a field theory of humor. In P. E. McGhee & J. H. Goldstein (Eds.), *Handbook of research on humor* (Vol. 1, pp. 211–230). New York: Springer-Verlag.

Pollio, H. R. (1988). A note on some demographics of laughter-evoking situations. *Psychological Reports, 62*, 53–54.

Pollio, H. R. (1992, August). Metaphor and humor. In J. S. Mio (Chair), *Metaphor: Thought, therapy, and mirth*. Symposium presented at 100th annual convention of the American Psychological Association, Washington, DC.

Pollio, H. R., Barlow, J. M., Fine, H. J., & Pollio, M. R. (1977). *Psychology and the poetics of growth*. Hillsdale, NJ: Lawrence Erlbaum Associates.

Pollio, H. R., & Edgerly, J. (1976). Comedians and comic style. In A. J. Chapman & H. C. Foot (Eds.), *Humor and laughter: Theory, research and applications* (pp. 215–242). London: Wiley.

Pollio, H. R., Edgerly, J., & Jordan, R. (1972). The comedian's world: Some tentative mappings. *Psychological Reports, 30*, 387–391.

Pollio, H. R., Smith, M. K., & Pollio, M. R. (1990). Figurative language and cognitive psychology. *Language and Cognitive Processes, 5*, 141–167.

Pollio, H. R., & Theg-Talley, J. (1991). The concepts and language of comic art. *Journal of Humor, 4*, 1–22.

Ricoeur, P. (1975). *The rule of metaphor*. Toronto: University of Toronto Press.

Smith, M. K., Pollio, H. R., & Pitts, M. K. (1981). Metaphor as intellectual history: Conceptual categories underlying figurative usage in American English from 1675–1975. *Linguistics, 19*, 911–935.

Sperber, H. (1930). *Einfuhrung in die Bedentungslehre* [Introduction to the theory of meaning]. (2nd ed.). Leipzig: K. Schroeder Verlag.

Thomas, O. (1969). *Metaphor and related subjects*. New York: Random House.

Ullmann, S. (1957). *The principles of semantics* (2nd ed.). London: Basil Blackwell.

Ullmann, S. (1962). *Semantics: An introduction to the science of meaning*. Oxford: Basil Blackwell.

Welsford, E. (1935). *The fool: His social and literary history*. London: Faber & Faber.

Wheelwright, P. (1959). *The burning fountain: A study in the language of symbolism*. Bloomington: University of Indiana Press.

Wicker, F. W., Thorelli, I. M., Barron, W., & Ponder, M. R. (1981). Relationships among affective and cognitive factors in humor. *Journal of Research in Personality, 15*, 359–370.

Willeford, W. (1969). *The fool and his scepter*. Evanston: Northwestern University Press.

Author Index

Subject Index